spanish
christian
cabala

Catherine Swietlicki

University of Missouri Press
Columbia, 1986

spanish christian cabala

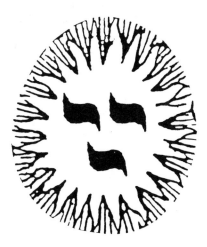

the works of luis de león, santa teresa de jesús, and san juan de la cruz

Copyright © 1986 by
The Curators of the University of Missouri
University of Missouri Press, Columbia, Missouri 65211
Printed and bound in the United States of America

Library of Congress Cataloging-in-Publication Data

Swietlicki, Catherine
  Spanish Christian Cabala.

  Bibliography: p.
  Includes index.
  1. Cabala and Christianity—Spain—History—16th
century. 2. León, Luis de, 1528?-1591. 3. Teresa, of
Avila, Saint, 1515–1582. 4. John of the Cross, Saint,
1542–1591. I. Title.
BF1595.S95 1986   230′.2′46   86–7018
ISBN 0–8262–0608–5

This book was brought to publication with the
assistance of the Program for Cultural Cooperation
Between Spain's Ministry of Culture and North
American Universities.

☞ This paper meets the minimum requirements of the
American National Standard for Permanence of Paper
for Printed Library Materials, Z39.48, 1984.

For Alain

preface

My purpose in this study is to describe and to account for evidence of the Jewish mystical tradition known as Cabala in the works of three major writers of the Spanish Renaissance. The names of Luis de León, Santa Teresa de Jesús, and San Juan de la Cruz are well known to students and scholars of Spanish literature; theologians are naturally familiar with the works of the two Spanish Carmelites, and social and cultural historians recognize the roles played by Fray Luis, Santa Teresa, and San Juan during the early-modern period in Spain. However, studies have not been undertaken to explore the relationship between the three authors and one of the major Spanish contributions to Renaissance intellectual history: the Christian Cabalistic tradition.

Historians of Renaissance thought have established that Cabala was an important component of the syncretism that characterized the revival and reinterpretation of classical antiquity during the Renaissance. The development and diffusion of Christian Cabala were facilitated by the publication of Cabalistic texts on a scale impossible to imagine during the formative years of the Christian Cabalistic tradition in Spain. The Christian Cabalism of the early-modern period varied according to the national origins and religious or philosophical concerns of the writers and artists applying its doctrines. Figures as diverse as Giovanni Pico della Mirandola, François Rabelais, and John Milton tailored Christian Cabala to the particular needs of their works. Through the contributions of the Renaissance Christian Cabalists, what had once been the domain of medieval Spanish Christian apologists and, before them, of the Spanish Jewry, was absorbed into western European culture.

Taking into consideration the testimony of Christian Cabala's influence in matters as varied as Renaissance magic, religious topoi, biblical exegesis, Church reform, and utopian political theory in other European nations, I have raised two general questions in this study. First, what aspects of popularized Judaic Cabala could have remained in the land of its flowering after the Expulsion of the Spanish Jews and the growth of the Inquisition? And second, to what extent did Christian Cabala endure in the land that had spawned its earliest development?

In addressing the two general questions, I decided to focus my research on three Spanish authors, two of whom are well known Christian mystics, Santa Teresa and San Juan de la Cruz, and one of whom is considered to be an intellectual or philosophical mystic of sorts, Fray Luis de León. I was struck by the similarities between Cabalistic traditions and various elements of the three authors' Castilian works, which are commonly held to be principal components of the Spanish Golden Age literary canon. Although each author's approach to Cabala differs according to his own particular experience and intentions, it is significant that all three are thought to be descendants of Spanish Jews. Their lives were also linked by common interests: Santa Teresa and San Juan led the Carmelite reform, Fray Luis edited Santa Teresa's works, and San Juan may have been indirectly influenced by Luis de León or his works while studying at Salamanca. By the title *Spanish Christian Cabala*, however, I do not mean to suggest that the three authors or their works constituted a cabal or that they participated in a systematic program to expose their readers to Cabalistic doctrines. As my study shows, Santa Teresa—and perhaps San Juan—may not have realized that the elements of Cabalistic symbolism they employed in their works had indeed originated with Judaic Cabala. While Fray Luis was probably aware that he was applying techniques previously used by other Christian Cabalists, his approach—like those of the Carmelite saints—was more an appeal to Spanish tradition than an attempt to introduce totally unfamiliar material to the reader.

Given the status of Santa Teresa and San Juan in Church history and theology, and considering Luis de León's reputation as a Christian humanist, it is likely that this study will not be read by Hispanists alone. And, although I do limit my discussion to the Spanish-language works of the three authors, my treatment of their use of Christian Cabala includes material that scholars of Spanish literature may find unfamiliar. I have therefore introduced this study with a survey of the contributions made by major Renaissance Christian Cabalists, and I have provided a brief overview of the traces of Christian Cabala that can be found in the works of European writers and artists roughly contemporaneous with Luis de León and the two Carmelites. In addition, I have discussed the survival of Judaic customs in the *converso* culture or the *converso*-influenced society of Golden Age Spain that nurtured Fray Luis, Santa Teresa, and San Juan. A recognition of Spain's uniquely mixed cultural predicament is essential to understanding the role that Christian Cabala played in the three authors' works and in the society in which they lived.

I believe that my research will indicate that the potential for further studies on the role of Spanish Christian Cabala is considerable. I hope that this study suggests topics for further exploration of Cabala's influence on the works of the three authors and on those of their contemporaries. In particular, studies examining the Hebrew sources of Christian Cabala and research devoted to the interrelations of Cabala and Sufism in Spain could produce valuable contributions. Similarly, the relationship of Cabala to the general study of Spain's tricultural heritage in the post-*Reconquista* era might be examined more closely.

* * *

I wish to express my gratitude to several individuals and institutions whose assistance, suggestions, or support at various times have made this book possible. I owe a particular debt of gratitude to Howard Mancing for his tenacious confidence in my project and to Charles G. Nauert, Jr., for initially encouraging me to study Renaissance Cabala. To both I am grateful for the generous contribution of their time and for their encouraging comments, especially as readers of the earliest versions of my typescript. I also appreciate the suggestions of those who read all or part of my work during the intermediate or final stages. In that regard I thank Antonio Carreño, David Hildner, and, in particular, Audrey Lumsden-Kouvel for her insightful and enthusiastic encouragement of my work on Luis de León. A special acknowledgment of appreciation also goes to Alain Swietlicki, whose cooperative commitment to my work was indispensable at every stage. My thanks too are due to the staffs of the following institutions: the University of Missouri–Columbia Library, the University of Wisconsin–Madison Library, the Biblioteca Nacional–Madrid, and the Newberry Library. I am grateful for the summer research grant from the Graduate Research Committee of the University of Wisconsin–Madison that facilitated the completion of the final revisions of my text. In addition, I appreciate the assistance provided by a publication grant from the Program for Cultural Cooperation Between Spain's Ministry of Culture and North American Universities.

C. S.
Madison, Wisconsin
July 1986

contents

1

CHRISTIAN CABALA IN THE
RENAISSANCE: AN OVERVIEW

Since the Renaissance, historians have been attempting to present a comprehensive and systematic interpretation of Renaissance thought.[1] The term *Neoplatonism* has been widely used to describe varied philosophical tendencies of the Renaissance, but it has also served to conceal elements vital to a more precise understanding of the era. Only in recent years have historians begun to uncover the relationship of Christian Cabala to Renaissance Neoplatonism and to reveal its deep and widespread influence throughout the period.[2]

The humanists' interest in Cabala was similar to their characteristic zeal for recovering the spirit of classical antiquity. Cabala, however, came to be revered by some Renaissance thinkers as the most ancient and most sacred cultural heritage. Cabala was part of the Florentine Neoplatonists' zealous attempt to synthesize the ancient religious and philosophical traditions with Christianity. Other scholars came into contact with Cabala through the enthusiastic study of original biblical sources and varied Hebrew texts in the pre-Reformation era. Hebraists such as those in the trilingual colleges discovered new exegetical allies in Cabalistic symbolism as they moved beyond literal and traditional metaphorical modes of interpretation. In their encounter with Cabala, they often exhibited techniques similar to the Christian apologists—from the earliest works of the Church Fathers to the Christian Cabalistic works of medieval Spanish apologists—whose traditions would continue

1. See Wallace Ferguson's historiographical study *The Renaissance in Historical Thought.*
2. The pioneering work of Joseph L. Blau, *The Christian Interpretation of the Cabala in the Renaissance,* has been greatly expanded by François Secret's numerous studies on Christian Cabala and his comprehensive work, *Les kabbalistes chrétiens de la Renaissance.* Several works by Frances Yates and Daniel P. Walker have dealt with the relationship of Christian Cabalism to Renaissance occult thought in general.

into the Renaissance. Christian Cabala became a very complex movement, following disparate yet intersecting paths such as those of Agrippa, Galatino, and Egidio da Viterbo, and leading to destinations as apparently contrasting as Church reform and magic. Yet all Christian Cabala was essentially religious in tone, serving not only as the tool of Christian exegetes and apologists, but also as a sacred defense to protect Renaissance magi from demonic intervention.

Jewish Cabala was not as antique as Renaissance humanists generally assumed it to be: they thought it was a secret revelation given by God to Moses (or even Adam) and passed on to initiates as a cryptic oral tradition,[3] but its roots were in the Gnostic mystical cults of the early Christian era. It later branched out to produce a rich variety of Cabalistic thought in thirteenth-century Spain.[4] Major Cabalists of the time were Abraham Abulafia (1240–1295) and Joseph Gikatila (fl. 1280–1300), but it was Moses de León (1240–1305) who synthesized the varied Gnostic, Neoplatonic, and rabbinic aspects of Spanish Cabala in his massive work *Sefer ha-Zohar* (*Book of Splendor*). By that time, two main aspects of Cabala were established: (1) the *sefirot* (i.e., the divine emanations, names, or aspects of the divinity—sometimes compared to the Platonic ideas) and their continuing relationship with the ten celestial spheres, the angels, man, and all of creation; (2) the sacred letters of the Hebrew alphabet with all the mystical properties inherent in possible permutations of Hebrew names and words through *notarikon* (an elaborate acrostic system), *gimatriyya* (numerical operations with Hebrew letters), and *temurah* (an anagrammatic system). By mystical contemplation of the *sefirot* and the Hebrew letters, Cabala sought to uncover hidden meanings of sacred Scripture and to

---

3. Doubts as to the Cabala's antiquity often centered on the dating of the *Zohar*. Secret has discussed the doubts of some sixteenth-century humanists on its age in *Les kabbalistes*, pp. 249, 251. Jewish scholars since the seventeenth century have argued the question, but not until Gershom Scholem's studies after 1935 has there been convincing evidence to date the *Zohar* in the 1280s to 1290s. See David Biale, *Gershom Scholem: Kabbalah and Counter-History*, pp. 118–20. Scholem's studies on Kabbalah have revolutionized Judaic thought and have opened a wealth of new sources of study in diverse aspects of European thought. Two particularly important Scholem works in English are *Major Trends in Jewish Mysticism*, trans. George Lichtheim, and *Kabbalah*, a collection of his extensive articles on the topic in *Encyclopedia Judaica*. Most of the Romanized orthography of Hebrew words in this study is based on the transliteration system described in Daniel C. Matt's *The Book of Mirrors*, p. xiii. The only major exception is the spelling of the word *Cabala*. This study will use *Cabala*, the preferred spelling of Renaissance Christian humanists and of *Webster's New Twentieth Century Dictionary*, 2d ed.

4. This brief historical description of the Cabala's development was taken from Scholem's *Major Trends* and *Kabbalah*.

achieve greater knowledge through union with the Deity. As always, however, the borderline between the mystico-theosophical and the magical was hard to define, and so Cabalists down to the time of the Renaissance warned against the "practical" or "black" use of the sacred names. However, "white" magic like Abulafia's self-directed mystical operations—sometimes compared to yoga—was permitted.[5]

Spanish Apologetics and Christian Cabala

During Cabala's development in Spain—just as during its primal Babylonian era in the first and second centuries A.D.—Cabalism came into contact with, and reacted with, Christianity. It flourished in the atmosphere of Judeo-Christian-Moslem cooperation in Spain, a peaceful existence symbolized by Alfonso X (1230–1284) having ordered Cabalistic works to be translated along with the Talmud and Koran.[6] The knowledge of Cabala reached Spanish Christians during the same period when Cabalistic doctrines became popularized among Spanish Jews and were no longer the exclusive domain of a secretive elite. The period of Cabala's growth at the folk level also coincided with increasing antagonism between Christians and Jews. Pressures to convert escalated with the growth of Christian political and military dominance in the Iberian peninsula. The uncertainty of the times was reinforced by the European apocalyptic movements of the era. Spanish Christians found the apocalyptic speculations of Cabala to be one of several messianic elements that could be used to persuade and to pressure Jews into becoming Christians. Through Christian apologetic arguments—many of which employed Cabala—many Jews came to see their conversion not as an adoption of a new set of moral practices, but as the fulfillment of the Mosaic law in a spiritual form.

It is not surprising that the era of Cabala's widespread dispersion among the Jewish population first witnessed the appearance of a new apologetic approach. Spanish Christians, many of whom were Jewish converts, increasingly used rabbinical texts—Cabalistic as well as Talmudic—in their efforts to persuade. Although he does not mention Cabala by name, the first Spaniard known to have

5. The self-directed magical mysticism of Abulafia could be compared to the "safe" magic practiced by Ficino and others in the Renaissance. See Daniel P. Walker, *Spiritual and Demonic Magic from Ficino to Campanella.*

6. Yitzhak Baer, *A History of the Jews in Christian Spain*, trans. Louis Schoffman, 1:111–30; Cecil Roth, *A History of the Marranos*, pp. 11–12; Karl Kottman, *Law and Apocalypse: The Moral Thought of Luis de León*, p. 10. The survey of Cabala's development in Christian Spain is based on Baer and Roth.

applied the Jewish mystical tradition to his apologetic works was
Moshe Sefardi, or Pedro Alfonso (baptized 1106).[7] His *Dialogus*
gives a Cabalistic-style proof of the Trinity based on the three
Hebrew letters used in the sacred name YHVH. That same sort of
Trinitarian proof based on the Tetragrammaton was used by
Ramón Martín,[8] a Dominican preacher who had taken part in the
Barcelona Disputation between Jews and Christians in 1263.[9] Al-
though not a *converso* (a Jewish convert to Christianity) like Pedro
Alfonso, Ramón Martín (1230?–1300?) authored what was to become the most influential work of Spanish Christian Cabala, the
Pugio fidei (c. 1280). In addition to his influential Trinitarian explanation of YHVH,[10] he argues that the plurality of sacred names
and attributes also favors the Christian concept of the Trinity (*Pugio*, pp. 402–6). It is significant to note in this regard that Ramón
Martín, like Francesco Giorgi and Luis de León, refers to the Messiah as Prince of Peace (pp. 310, 550) and associates Christ with the
letter *yod* as a sign of the future age (p. 481). In speaking of the
future, he refers to Elijah's prophecy on the end of the world—a
major Cabalistic concern. Following another tendency of Cabala,
Ramón Martín uses the numerical values of the sacred Hebrew
letters and words (pp. 544–45). Although he does not mention
specific Cabalistic texts, he does refer to Cabala by name (קבלה) (p.
294), and he mentions his Christian Cabalistic predecessor "Petrus
Alphonsi" (p. 540).

Ramón Martín's influential *Pugio* would come to be the basic
source from which most Christian applications of Cabala would
flow. Those who followed him would apply Martín's techniques,
but some surpassed him in application of additional Jewish
Cabalistic materials to their Christian apologetics. A contemporary

7. See François Secret, "Les débuts du kabbalisme chrétien en Espagne et son
histoire à la Renaissance," 37–38; and Federico Pérez Castro, *El manuscrito apologético de Alfonso de Zamora: Séfer Hokmat Elohim*, xcvii.

8. On Ramón Martín, see Baer, *History of the Jews*, passim; Secret, *Les kabbalistes*, pp. 9–10; Secret, "Notes pour une histoire du *Pugio fidei* à la Renaissance";
Secret, "Les débuts."

9. In the Barcelona Disputation, as well as in the writings of Pedro Alfonso and
Ramón Martín, Christian apologetics began to rely on rabbinical and Cabalistic
material, rather than the Old Testament alone, for proselytizing. Both sides at the
Barcelona confrontation were represented by individuals familiar with Cabala. On
Nahmanides' role in the Barcelona Disputation, see Baer, *History of the Jews*,
1:152–54; on his interest in Cabala, see Baer, 1:102. For the Barcelona and Tortosa
Disputations, see David Berger, *Judaism on Trial*.

10. See *Pugio fidei adversus mauros et judaeos cum observationibus Josephi de
Voisin, et introductione Jo. Benedicti Carpozovi* (Lipsiae et Francofurti, 1687), pp.
396–97, 540. All further references to the *Pugio* will be from this edition.

example was his disciple Arnaldo Vilanova.[11] In his *Allocution super Tetragrammaton*, Vilanova follows his mentor's example on the Trinitarian proof in YHVH and the use of *gimatriyya* with Hebrew letters, but he proceeds in a more esoteric and mystical manner. Vilanova's fascination with the sound, figure, and placement of each sacred letter is unprecedented in Christian Cabala and is reminiscent of his Jewish contemporary Abulafia's prophetic Cabala.[12]

Another contribution to Spanish Christian Cabala was produced by the confluence of the *Pugio*'s trend with new currents initiated by Spanish conversos. Abner de Burgos (1270–1348), for example, brought his erudition in Jewish and Arabic philosophy to the assistance of his Christian apologetics. Abner interpreted his own dreams in a Cabalistic manner as a sign of the truth of Christianity. He also used Cabalistic Trinitarian proofs employing YHVH and the plurality of divine names. Convinced of the need to convert other Jews, Abner wrote several apologetic works in Hebrew under the Christian name Alfonso de Valladolid. His *More Zedeq* (*Mostrador de justicia*) was translated to Spanish, perhaps in order to facilitate its use by other Christian apologists or to convert Jews who did not read Hebrew well.[13] The most influential figure to follow was Solomon Halevi (c. 1351–1435), who took the name Pablo de Santa María. Although he studied theology in Paris, his apologetic approach was not purely scholastic: he employed the Cabalistic interpretation of Elijah's prophecy on the world's end in the manner of Ramón Martín.[14] A third important converso apologist—one who also followed Martín's *Pugio* as well as the examples of Alfonso de Valladolid and Pablo de Santa María—was Joshua Halorki. As Jerónimo de la Santa Fe he was a major spokesman for the Christians at the Dispute of Tortosa (1413–1414).[15]

A contemporary Christian writer whose missionary fervor may

---

11. On Vilanova, see Joaquín Carreras y Artau, "Arnaldo de Vilanova, apologista antijudaico."

12. Ibid., pp. 60–61. In the same article Carreras y Artau indicates that not all apologists of the era followed the Cabalistic line. He notes (p. 58, n. 10) that Vilanova's cousin Bernardo Oliver was more scholastic in his approach. See Francisca Vendrell's "La obra de polémica anti-judaica de Fray Bernardo Oliver."

13. The summary on Alfonso de Valladolid is drawn from Isidore Loeb, "Polémistes chrétiens et juives en France et Espagne"; Baer, *History of the Jews*, 1:327–54, 369; Secret, *Les kabbalistes*, pp. 13–14.

14. On Pablo de Santa María, see Baer, *History of the Jews*, 2:139–42; Pérez Castro, *El manuscrito apologético*, pp. xcvii-xcix; and Secret, *Les kabbalistes*, p. 11.

15. For Jerónimo de Santa Fe, see Pérez Castro, *El manuscrito apologético*, p. xcix; Baer, *History of the Jews*, 2:139–50; and Secret, *Les kabbalistes*, p. 11.

have included Cabalistic appeals was Ramón Lull (1232–1316).[16] Frances Yates and Peter French have pointed out some salient characteristics of the Lullian art that are also Cabalistic: its basis in names or dignities, the concept of parallel worlds, and techniques of letter combination.[17] They are careful to point out that the method uses Latin rather than Hebrew letters and that it therefore lacks the linguistic mysteries the Cabalists believed were hidden in the Scripture. Lull's doctrines continued to exert influence in Spain and in northern Europe throughout the Renaissance. It is quite possible that Luis de León and San Juan de la Cruz read the Mallorcan apologist and that Santa Teresa became familiar with his work through secondary sources.[18]

Spanish Christian apologists of the fifteenth century employed Cabala in order to convince another type of disbeliever of the truth of Christianity and the importance of leaving behind the prescriptions of the Old Law. The task of writers such as Alfonso de Espina (d. 1469) was not only to convert the Jews but also to produce a Christian rhetoric capable of achieving the total conversion of the Jewish New Christians whose lapses were perceived to be heretical.[19] In his polemical approach, Espina used the works of Ramón Martín, Alfonso de Valladolid, and Jerónimo de Santa Fe.[20] Significantly, he also cited the author of the *Zohar*, Moses de León.[21]

Another effective apologist of the era was Pedro de la Caballería (c. 1450). His *Zelus Christi* quotes Joseph Gikatila's *Sha'arei-Orah*, a Spanish Cabalistic work not previously used in Christian

16. José María Millás Vallicrosa has written extensively on Lull's apologetic approach; see his *El "Liber predicationis contra judeos" de Ramón Lull*. On Lull as a Christian apologist, see also Ramon Sugranyes de Franch, *Raymond Lull, docteur des missions*.

17. Frances Yates, "The Art of Ramón Lull"; Yates, *The Art of Memory*; Yates, *The Occult Philosophy in the Elizabethan Age*, pp. 9–15; and Peter French, *John Dee*, pp. 49, 112–13. Also useful on this topic are Millás Vallicrosa, "Algunas relaciones entre la doctrina luliana y la Cábala"; and Paolo Rossi, "Le origini della pansofia e il lullismo del secolo XVII." Joaquín Carreras y Artau is hesitant to call Lull's Judaic connections Cabalistic; see his "Raimundo Lulio y la Cábala." Louis Sala-Molins, however, does remark on the possible use of Cabala by Lull. See *La philosophie de l'amour chez Raymond Lulle*, pp. 20–24.

18. Fray Luis or San Juan could have studied Lull's work, and Santa Teresa's spiritual guides could have informed her. The Mallorcan writer was studied in Alcalá, at least from the time of Cardinal Ximénez de Cisneros, and Lullist studies were taught in Salamanca in the sixteenth century. See Anthony Bonner, *Selected Works of Ramón Llull*, 1:80.

19. On the religious beliefs of the Jewish conversos see Baer, *History of the Jews*, 2:284–86; and Julio Caro Baroja, *Los judíos en la España moderna y contemporánea*, 1:283–84.

20. For Alfonso de Espina see Caro Baroja, *Los judíos en la España*, 1:284; Loeb, "Polémistes chrétiens," p. 60; and Secret, *Les kabbalistes*, p. 14.

21. Loeb, "Polémistes chrétiens," p. 62.

apologetic literature.[22] Caballería's personal situation is symptomatic of his era: he painstakingly covered the evidence of his own conversion, yet he showed his thorough knowledge of Hebrew in citing Judaic sources for his polemical work. The *Zelus* was not published until 1592. At that time the editor, Martín Alfonso Vivaldo de Toledo, fortified it with glosses taken from Italian Christian Cabalistic works such as those of Pietro Galatino, which had in turn been influenced by earlier Spanish Christian Cabalists—most notably Ramón Martín.[23]

An account of Martín's followers has brought our discussion of Spanish Christian apologetics into the Renaissance. Elements of Martín's *Pugio fidei* would resound in sixteenth-century works ranging from those of the Christian Cabalists Johannes Reuchlin and Girolamo Seripando to the Spaniards Alfonso de Zamora, Juan Luis Vives, and Luis de León. Alfonso's knowledge of varied Hebrew and rabbinical works served him well as an editor of the Complutense Bible and as author of *Sefer Hokhmah Elohim* (1532).[24] Although he did not read Hebrew, Vives used Christian Cabalistic proofs in *De veritate fidei christanae* (1544), his last and most extensive treatise.[25] The work cites Pablo de Santa María on the abrogation of the Old Law and uses Pedro Alfonso and Galatino on the Trinitarian indications found in the numerous sacred Hebrew names for God. For Luis de León, as an Hebraist, the possibilities of using Christian Cabala were greater than for Vives, as we will show when the Augustinian friar's work is more closely examined in Chapters 4 and 5.

Our attention must now be focused on the expansion of Spanish Cabala beyond the Peninsula. The Spanish apologetic tradition was carried across the frontiers by scholars such as Peter Schwartz, the German Dominican who studied in Salamanca and published his Cabalistic *Stella Messiae* (1475) in Cologne. Spanish Christian Cabala would take on new dimensions in Italy and then elsewhere on the continent as it merged with the new enthusiasm for humanistic and Evangelical studies. As the political and social crises of the era intensified, Christian interest in the more apocalyptic aspects of Cabala deepened. This development was paralleled and, perhaps, influenced by developments in Jewish Cabala. After the Expulsion,

22. See Baer, *History of the Jews*, 2:276; and Secret, *Les kabbalistes*, p. 16.
23. Secret, *Les kabbalistes*, p. 17.
24. See Pérez Castro's edition with its numerous references to rabbinical texts used in the *Sefer Hokmat Elohim* and the *Pugio fidei*.
25. On Vives's use of Cabalistic elements, see Pablo Graf's *Luis Vives como apologeta*, trans. José María Millás Vallicrosa, pp. 93–97.

and partially in reaction to the traumatic exile from Spain, Judaic
Cabala began to take on more messianic and apocalyptic tones.[26]
The ideas of Moses Cordovero and especially of Isaac Luria and his
disciples created a Cabala emphasizing redemption and restoration
that would come to dominate Jewish philosophy until the Enlightenment. Their work may have been known to Christian Cabalists who were concerned with restoration of the Church and
establishment of a peaceful world order and spiritual values for all
mankind. Those same concerns are reflected in the writings of
Christian Cabalists outside Spain who built on the traditions of
Spanish Christian Cabala. The Italian and northern European
Christian Cabalists eventually produced works that would later
reinforce Spanish Christian apologetics in the Golden Age.

Pico della Mirandola

Giovanni Pico della Mirandola (1463–1494) was apparently un-
aware of the Christian Cabala in Spanish apologetic literature since
he referred to himself as the first to expand Christian exegesis to
include Cabala.[27] Pico was, rather, the first to bring Cabala into the
humanistic realm in which he and Marsilio Ficino had established
the so-called Neoplatonic movement. In search of further confirmation of the Florentine Neoplatonic synthesis, Pico studied
Hebrew and Cabala. His masters were the Cretan Jew Elijah del
Medigo and the converts Pablo de Heredia of Aragón and Flavius
Mithridates (Guglielmo Raimondo da Moncada) of Sicily.[28] Pico's
Cabalistic sources were meager compared to the vast reservoir of
works from which later Christian Cabalists could draw.[29] It seems
that he knew only the *Sha'arei-Orah* and a few sections of the
Zohar until 1492, when he may have acquired other Cabalistic
works from Clemente Abraham, a Spanish Dominican converso.

For Pico, Cabala was a source of great antiquity and sanctity that
would confirm the truth of Christianity upheld by other *prisca
theologia* of his Neoplatonic synthesis. In his syncretic view, Plato-

26. Scholem, *Major Trends*, pp. 244–86.
27. Kottman, *Law and Apocalypse*, p. 32; Secret, *Les kabbalistes*, p. 8.
28. Pablo de Heredia will be discussed later in this chapter. On Elijah del Medigo,
see Cecil Roth, *The Jews in the Renaissance*, pp. 112–14, et passim; on Flavius
Mithridates, see Roth, *The Jews*, pp. 117–18, 145–46; Secret, *Les kabbalistes*, pp.
25–26; Kottman, *Law and Apocalypse*, p. 30; and Chaim Wirszubski, "Giovanni
Pico's Companion to Kabbalistic Symbolism." Flavius was a curious character who
enjoyed the patronage of popes and princes. Wirszubski has shown that he seems to
have encouraged Pico's Christian interpretations of Cabala by inserting his own
interpolations into Pico's Latin texts.
29. Secret, *Les kabbalistes*, pp. 31–38.

nism and Neoplatonism were the two major elements that mingled with Hermeticism, Orphism, Pythagoreanism, Zoroastrianism, and other branches of antique occult thought. He held that Pythagoras, Plato, Aristotle, Jesus, Saint Paul, and Dionysius the Areopagite were all privy to the secret, unwritten Cabalistic doctrine of Moses. In Pico's view, Cabala was the sacred key that bound the more occult aspects of the *prisca theologia* to Christianity, safeguarding the magical aspects of the Neoplatonic synthesis from demonic interference or ecclesiastical objection.

Of Pico's famous nine hundred theses (the *Conclusiones*), forty-seven were drawn from Cabalistic sources and twenty-five were his own Cabalistic deductions on those sources.[30] The *Conclusiones* (1486) introduced to the humanistic world some of the main themes later employed by Christian Cabalists. Pico described the ten *sefirot* and correlated them with the ten celestial spheres. He expounded on the powers of the Hebrew alphabet, the influence of divine names, and the interpretation of YHVH to signify *Jesus*. These elements were to become more clearly defined in his disciple Reuchlin's *De Verbo Mirifico*. Pico also combined Platonic, Christian (i.e., of the Areopagite), and Cabalistic cosmologies to produce a four-world view. He mentioned Elijah's prophecy, but he avoided speculations on the end of the world—a theme that would become increasingly important to reform-minded Christian Cabalists such as Egidio da Viterbo, Guillaume Postel, and Luis de León.

Perhaps the most shocking aspects of Pico's *Conclusiones* were his beliefs that magic and Cabala confirmed the truths of Christianity and his intimation that Christ's miracles involved Cabala.[31] Statements like these caused such a stir in Rome that Pope Innocent VIII appointed an investigative commission to examine Pico's theses more closely. The Spanish bishop Pedro García, a commission member, condemned the *Conclusiones* and summarized ecclesiastical arguments against magic.[32] Pico was forced to retract three hundred suspect theses, but with the election of Cardinal Borja as Alexander VI in 1492, Pico's fortune turned. The Aragonese pope disavowed his predecessor's accusation of heresy and encouraged readers to accept the young humanist's orthodoxy. The

30. The following summary of Pico's Cabalistic themes was drawn from Secret, *Les kabbalistes*, pp. 24–43, et passim; Frances Yates, *Giordano Bruno and the Hermetic Tradition*, pp. 84–116; Blau, *The Christian Interpretation*, pp. 17–30; Yates, *The Occult Philosophy*, pp. 17–22.

31. On Pico's magic, in addition to Yates's *Giordano Bruno*, see Walker, *Spiritual and Demonic Magic*, pp. 54–59.

32. For a more extensive account of the proceedings and the fate of the theses, see Lynn Thorndike, *The History of Magic and Experimental Science*, 4:485–511.

Borgia pope himself was apparently as enthusiastic about the occult[33] as his countryman García was antagonistic. In effect, Alexander VI's approval of Pico's work encouraged the magico-religious ties of Cabala and Renaissance magic in general.

Giovanni Pico's use of Cabala fell into two patterns, just as the old Jewish Cabala had done: the magical Cabala and the mystical-exegetical. In his concern for scriptural exegesis, Pico had tried to show that the three Jewish (and Cabalistic) methods of interpretation were subclasses of Augustine's four types.[34] This exegetical aspect of Cabala—as a confirmation of Christian truths—and not its magical or its *prisca theologia* aspects is what interested Pico's nearest contemporaries Pablo de Heredia, Agostino Giustiniani, and Pietro Galatino.

Neo-Apologetics and Humanistic Christian Cabala

Italy, in Pico's time, experienced a renewed use of Cabala to confirm the truths of Christianity to the Jews. Traditional apologetics came to be affected by the humanistic dimension brought by Pico to Christian Cabala. The new Christian apologetics were characterized by greater concern for humanistic moral values as well as by stylistics and the use of original sources.

Pablo de Heredia, mentioned above as having been acquainted with Pico, was probably more concerned with apologetics and less with humanistic values than were the other Christian Cabalists discussed in this section. Although he was one of the least well known, his works had the widest diffusion, for they were included in Galatino's *De arcanis catholicae veritatis*, the most widely known Christian Cabalistic opus of the Renaissance.[35] It is known that Heredia, a Spanish converso, traveled extensively in the Mediterranean countries and that he dedicated his *Epistola secretorum* to Don Íñigo López de Mendoza, Spanish ambassador to Rome from 1486 to 1488. Further evidence of Heredia's Spanish heritage is found in his *Ensis Pauli*; his position against the marranos in that work has been termed "an apotheosis of the Spanish princes."[36]

Pablo de Heredia's major contributions to Christian Cabalism were his translation from Hebrew of the *Gali Razaya* and the inter-

33. Yates, *Giordano Bruno*, pp. 115–16, describes Alexander's taste for the occult as revealed by Fritz Saxl's study, "The Appartamento Borgia," in his *Lectures* (London: The Warburg Institute, n.d. given), 1:174–88, 2:115–24.

34. Kottman, *Law and Apocalypse*, p. 32.

35. Secret, *Les kabbalistes*, p. 102.

36. Secret, "L'*Ensis Pauli* de Paulus de Heredia," p. 89.

pretations of the *Zohar* in his *Epistola secretorum*.[37] Heredia focused on the Trinity, redemption, Christ's essence, the Virgin, and Old Testament prophecies. In treating these themes, his Cabalistic exegesis was limited to numerical applications of the Hebrew alphabet; yet Heredia's Cabalistic writings would influence other Christian Cabalists in Italy, Spain, and northern Europe whose works represented a much wider range of Cabalistic methodologies.

Agostino Giustiniani (1470–1536) is an example of a humanist applying Christian Cabala to biblical studies in the pre-Reformation era. Born in Genoa, he studied in Valencia and then returned home to join the Dominican Order. As Secret has pointed out, Giustiniani's sincerely religious interest in Cabala is one of several examples disproving Blau's generalization that the Franciscans—predisposed to name symbolism in the manner of Joachim da Fiore—were the order involved in Cabalism while the Dominicans—heirs of Thomistic rationalism—became the Inquisitors and censors of Hebrew books.[38] Giustiniani was acquainted with Pico, but it is important to consider their different approaches to Cabala. Giustiniani did not use Cabalism in the syncretic spirit of Pico, hoping to discover evidence of Platonism or to find indications of Pythagoras in the manner of Pico's disciple Reuchlin. Instead, the Dominican held that it was "better to spend time in treating Scripture than writing speculative sacred questions full of useless arguments, or on any human things condescending to my age and profession."[39] Indeed, Giustiniani is remembered for his use of Cabala in the scholia to his polyglot *Psalterium* (1516)—the first Christian Cabalistic work in the tradition of the trilingual colleges, printed the same year as the Complutensian Bible.[40] He also published a Hebrew grammar, a prayer book of the seventy-two divine names in Latin and Hebrew, and a translation of *Guide of the Perplexed* by Maimonides.

Giustiniani's contemporary, Pietro Galatino (1460–1520), demonstrates the combined tendencies of neo-apologetics and human-

37. Information on Heredia was drawn from Secret, *Les kabbalistes*, pp. 24–29, et passim; and Secret, "L'*Ensis Pauli* de Paulus de Heredia," pp. 79–102, 253–71.

38. Secret, "Les dominicains et la kabbale chrétienne à la Renaissance," p. 319; Blau, *The Christian Interpretation*, p. 61.

39. From the *Annali . . . Genova* as cited by Secret, "Les dominicains," p. 324: "meglio spender il tempo in trattare queste litere che scrivere questioni sacre e speculative piene di inutili argomenti, ne anchor cose di humanita poco condecenti all eta e alla professione mia."

40. Secret, "Les dominicains," pp. 321–23, and *Les kabbalistes*, pp. 99–101. Although the six volumes of the Complutensian Polyglot were printed by 1517, the Bible was not approved for release until 1520.

ism. His *De arcanis catholicae veritatis* (1518) was not only the most widely circulated Christian Cabalistic work in the Renaissance, but it was also one of the most used sources of anti-Jewish material. His announced dual purpose for *De arcanis* was to attack the obstinacy of the Jews through their own works[41] and to defend the German humanist Reuchlin's *De Verbo Mirifico*,[42] a Christian Cabalistic work. Galatino's Cabalistic material was not highly original; he was indebted to Martín's *Pugio fidei*, Giustiniani's edition of the *Victoria Porcheti*, and Heredia's interpolations of the *Zohar*. In fact, Galatino has frequently been accused of plagiarism.[43]

A more interesting area in Galatino's Cabalism is the apocalyptic-prophetic concern in his *Commentaria in Apocalypsim*, a work dedicated to Carlos V in hope that the monarch would aid an angelic pope in uniting all mankind under one pastor. The message of this treatise would be echoed in Postel. Galatino also influenced Luis de León's acceptance of Elijah's prophecy and his treatment of the name *Pimpollo* in *De los nombres de Cristo*.[44] In general, there is also some resemblance between Galatino's application of Cabalistic material in *De arcanis* and that of Fray Luis in the *Nombres*. Both use Trinitarian proofs based on the Tetragrammaton, and both emphasize the Judaic names for Christ in a similar apologetic manner. We find in *De arcanis*, for example, references to the names *Germen*,[45] *Mons* (3.19.86v–87v), *Pax* (3.24.92r–94r), and *Salus* (6.16.195r–196r and 6.1–2.171r–174r). Similarly, Luis de León's *Nombres* treats *Pimpollo*, *Monte*, *Paz*, and *Salud* as characteristic names for Christ. The Augustinian friar, however, uses fewer Hebrew words and less specific references to Cabalistic texts than Galatino. Moreover, the tone of Galatino's work is more polemical and less concerned with the Christological message of peace and harmony than is Luis de León's magnum opus.[46]

41. Blau, *The Christian Interpretation*, p. 61.

42. Kottman, *Law and Apocalypse*, p. 22, n. 5.

43. On Galatino, see Secret, *Les kabbalistes*, pp. 102–4, and *Le "Zohar" chez les kabbalistes chrétiens de la Renaissance*, pp. 30–31.

44. Kottman, *Law and Apocalypse*, pp. 72–75.

45. Pietro Galatino, *Opus toti christianae, reipublicae maxime utile, de arcanis catholicae veritatis, contra obstinatissimam iudaeorum nostrae tempestatis perfidiam: ex Talmud, aliisque hebraicis libris nuper excerptum: & quadruplici linguarum genere eleganter congestum* (Ortona: H. Suncinum, 1518), 3.14.80r–81r. All further citations are from this edition.

46. Galatino also refers to Cabalistic texts with a freedom not apparent in Fray Luis. For example, the Italian Cabalist mentions the *Gali Razaya* (2.9.47r, and 3.64.64r), an anonymous Cabalistic text from Safed.

The Ricci Brothers

A major Christian Cabalist in the era after Pico's death was German-born Paolo Ricci or Paulus Israelita (d. 1541).[47] His varied personal acquaintances included Emperor Maximilian, whom he served as physician; Erasmus; Pomponazzi, his professor; Dürer; Moncetto, the Augustinian prophetic hermit; and Gometius, the Portuguese vicar-general of the Franciscans. Ricci's *De coelesti agricultura* (1540) was a widely known Cabalistic work whose influence on Reuchlin and Guy Le Fèvre de la Boderie was especially notable. In the four-part work, Ricci treated the correspondence of the ten *sefirot* to the ten spheres and to the orders of angels, and he discussed the divine names—including the Tetragrammaton. Book 4 was especially significant for containing a Latin translation (*Portae lucis*) of Gikatilla's *Sha'arei-Orah*. Although Ricci's *De coelesti agricultura* was much praised by Catholic theological faculties when it appeared, the work was included on the *Index* of 1570.

Ricci's Cabala was relatively free of dangerous magical and unorthodox elements. He did not emphasize letter permutations like Reuchlin or an interest in numbers like Agrippa. Instead, Ricci developed a view of mankind's progress since the Fall that stressed the rule of law and the role of prayer.[48] He held that Jews and Christians alike were subject to eternal laws and that Christ's teachings were the proper continuation of the Old Law—a line of argument found in the Spanish Christian apologists and later in Luis de León.[49] And, as Fray Luis would do, he attempted to link Aquinas and Cabala on the subject of law. Through Thomism and Cabala, Ricci felt the conversion of the Jews and the reform of the Church would be realized, since, in his view, Cabala presented close ties to Christian morality and mysticism. Prayer or mystical contemplation seemed to be the path for man to regain the divine union lost to him since Adam's sin. In prayer, correspondence with the angels in charge of mystic life was a necessity—a view Ricci and Agrippa held in common with the Pseudo-Dionysius. Since prayer depended on angelic contacts, knowing their names in the Cabalistic sense was essential. Although Ricci held that Cabala was syn-

47. On Ricci, see Secret, "Notes sur Paulus Ricius et la kabbale chrétienne en Italie"; Secret, *Les kabbalistes*, pp. 87–99; Blau, *The Christian Interpretation*, pp. 65–74.

48. On law and prayer, see Kottman, *Law and Apocalypse*, pp. 34–38; Secret, *Les kabbalistes*, pp. 92–93; Blau, *The Christian Interpretation*, pp. 74–75.

49. Kottman, *Law and Apocalypse*, p. 35, et passim.

onymous with mysticism, the Christianized scheme he described was more concerned with individual mystical union and salvation than Jewish Cabala's emphasis on salvation for all Israel. Ultimately, Ricci's treatment of *Salus* and *Salvador* resembles that of Fray Luis. Both authors used Cabala to emphasize that Christ is the promised solution and prosperity of Israel (i.e., all mankind) and that salvation is spiritual—not material. As Luis de León would do in *Nombres*, Ricci—in his *Compendium*—traces the argument through its Judaic sources before concluding that "Christ was therefore the true Savior."[50]

More is known of Paolo than of Agostino Ricci, reported to be the brother of the famous Cabalist.[51] Agostino, an astronomer and astrologer, claimed that he studied in Salamanca with Abraham Zacuto, astrologer for the Spanish and Portuguese courts. Agostino's opus *De motu octavae spherae* (1513) is an amalgam of astronomy, mathematics, Platonism, and Cabala (therein referred to as "ancient Hebrew magic"). Agostino Ricci speculated Cabalistically on the prophesied end of the world and perhaps influenced an Augustinian hermit with millenarian concerns, Pedro Valderama. Agostino used León Hebreo's theme on the ages of the world according to Cabalistic considerations. Particularly notable in Ricci's *De motu* is his identification of the *sefirot* with the Trinity and the divine attributes. Clearly, for him the three uppermost *sefirot* are the Trinity, whose light is reflected throughout the lower seven *sefirot* or seven divine ideas, as he calls them.[52] (The similarities between Ricci's Cabalistic conception of the Trinity above the seven lower *sefirot* and Santa Teresa's description of the divine Trinity of light as viewed from the seventh *morada* will be examined in Chapter 3.) Agostino Ricci's connections with Spain provide examples of how Spanish Cabala was introduced to other Europeans during the Renaissance. In addition, Ricci's contact with Spaniards illustrates how European Christian Cabalism could become available in Spain and could, in turn, reinforce native Christian Cabalistic traditions.

50. See *Compendium quo mirifico acumine . . . apostolicam veritatem: Ratione: Prophetice: Talmudistice: Cabalistice: plane confirmat.* The citation "Christus igitur verus Salvator est" is used as the conclusion to the arguments on *Salus*, folios 15r–50r.

51. On Agostino Ricci, see Secret, *Les kabbalistes*, pp. 81–83, and "L'astrologie et les kabbalistes chrétiens à la Renaissance."

52. See *De motu octavae sphaere, opus mathematica atque philosophia plenum . . . .*, f. 45v. On folios 46v to 47v Agostino Ricci continues to describe the lower seven *sefirot* as divine attributes or emanations.

Johannes Reuchlin

Pico's major disciple and another leading figure in the development of Christian Cabala was Johannes Reuchlin (1455–1522).
Reuchlin has been recognized as one of the founders of German
humanism,[53] a bearer of Florentine Neoplatonism beyond the
Alps. His acquaintance with Ficino, Pico, and their circle introduced him to the *prisca theologia*. His interest in those ancient
writings, along with his Cabalistic and Hebraic studies (his chief
motivation for going to Italy), opened to him a new world of
thought. Reuchlin became aware of the philosophical, religious,
and magical aspects of the new learning, and he perceived them as a
means of attaining new spiritual strength to replace the worn-out
philosophical directives of scholasticism in which he had initially
been trained. Upon his return to the North, he penned *De Verbo
Mirifico* (1494) and began to indoctrinate his countrymen into the
ways of the Italian humanists, albeit with less emphasis on magic
and more on Christianity than he had learned from his mentor
Pico.[54]

Reuchlin's *De Verbo* was the first of a line of sixteenth-century
works on the divine name that would conclude with Luis de León's
De los nombres de Cristo. *De Verbo*, like Reuchlin's later Cabalistic masterpiece *De arte cabalistica*, took the form of a dialogue
between representatives of three different philosophical and theological viewpoints.[55] Their conversations reveal the author's intent
"to examine the occult property of names and the secret power of
words used by men in ancient times in the performance of sacred
rites; to correct erroneous conceptions concerning the marvellous
effects of mysteries; and in this way, to choose that name which is
supreme and most powerful in the performance of wonders."[56]
Central to Reuchlin's intent is the relationship of Cabala to Christianity and the *prisca theologia*. In the religious hymns, invoca-

---

53. For an account of Reuchlin's contribution to northern humanism, see Lewis
W. Spitz, *The Religious Renaissance of the German Humanists*; and Charles Zika,
"Reuchlin's *De Verbo Mirifico* and the Magic Debate of the Late Fifteenth
Century."

54. Zika, "Reuchlin's *De Verbo Mirifico*," p. 138.

55. It is appropriate that Reuchlin employed three interlocutors for the three
books of his dialogues. Fray Luis de León would follow the same pattern for the final
edition of *Nombres* published before his death. Three is a highly significant number,
not only in Christianity, but also in Cabala and the *prisca theologia*. On the significance of numbers see V. F. Hopper, *Medieval Number Symbolism*, and Christopher
Butler, *Number Symbolism*.

56. Zika, "Reuchlin's *De Verbo Mirifico*," p. 106.

tions, and ceremonies of the ancient theology he saw elements of
Hebrew doctrine and prophetic signs of Christian truth. Reuchlin
assumed that the ancient cultures learned of the power of words
from the Hebrews who had introduced them to language. In this
view—a common one among Christian Cabalists—Hebrew had to
have been the first language since it was the original, divine one
God created for communicating with mankind.[57] Therefore
Hebrew and, to a lesser extent, the other ancient languages (Phoe-
nician and Egyptian) that were influenced by the sacred tongue
were endowed with pristine powers that Greek, with its excessive
emphasis on philosophical novelty and the cult of rhetorical arts,
had lost. Thus the original Hebrew, with complementary aspects of
other *barbara verba*, in the simple search for truth would provide
the most pure and powerful means of restoring power to sacred
words.[58]

In *De Verbo*,[59] Reuchlin's Cabalistic persona Capnion describes
the names by which the divinity has been revealed to man. The
interlocutor Capnion also details the relationship of the divine
names to the Tetragrammaton, and he demonstrates how hidden
meanings of the sacred names can be revealed through *gimatriyya*
and *notarikon*. The Cabalist can, he explains, reach union with the
divine through use of the proper name, sacred characters, signs, or
seals, and with appeals to the seventy-two angels, in order to pass
through the seventy-two regions and three worlds or levels of consciousness. Reuchlin called this technique *soliloquia* and likened it
to the divine pact between God and his priest, who pronounces the
sacred words and participates in the wondrous act of transubstantiation of the Eucharist.[60] Of course the most powerful name on
which the *soliloquia* depended was the Pentagrammaton (YHSVH
for *Yehoshuah* or *Jesus*). Capnion explained at length the rich symbolism of the letter *S* (*shin*), the one additional character that dif-
ferentiates YHSVH from YHVH. The addition of the *S* to the
Tetragrammaton is, in effect, the new covenant of God with man
and man's new power for sharing in the Divinity through Christ. In

57. Spitz, *The Religious Renaissance*, p. 63.

58. Zika, "Reuchlin's *De Verbo Mirifico*," pp. 122–25, 136–37, et passim.

59. This summary is based on Secret, *Les kabbalistes*; Zika, "Reuchlin's *De
Verbo Mirifico*"; and Blau, *The Christian Interpretation*. It is best to read Blau's
summary with Secret's emendations.

60. Zika notes that the Scotists had explained transubstantiation as a pact or
promise made by God to produce effects when certain words were pronounced in
the Mass and Eucharist ("Reuchlin's *De Verbo Mirifico*," p. 121).

turn, the Pentagrammaton becomes the instrument by which man performs external miraculous activities in the world.[61]

After *De Verbo*, Reuchlin composed a Hebrew grammar—one of the few adequate ones by a Christian—and continued his Hebrew studies.[62] Several years later he produced a new Cabalistic treatise that reflected the recent availability of works formerly unknown to him. The *De arte cabalistica* (1517) revealed a Reuchlin better-informed on Cabala through the works of Paolo Ricci, Agostino Giustiniani, and editions of the *Zohar*, *Sefer ha-Bahir*, *Sefer Yezirah*, and other Cabalistic treatises that had become available to him since the *De Verbo*. The Reuchlin of *De arte* styled himself as "Pythagoras redivivus," referring to the work's emphasis on the ancient philosopher's numerical theories and their coincidence with Cabalistic methodology and beliefs.[63] The "second Pythagoras" believed that Pythagorean ideas bound together philosophy and religion better than any pre-Socratic group and that their antique origin in the East qualified them as a sort of *prisca theologia* that in essence was the same as Cabala. In other words, the *De arte* was an elaboration on the themes Reuchlin had established in the *De Verbo*. All aspects of his Christian Cabala ultimately focused on the Messiah and his relationships with man, the united Deity, and the whole cosmos. For Reuchlin, therefore, the Messiah was not the conquering liberator of the Talmud but a Cabalistic Messiah, a herald of a peaceful golden age and a divine link in the cosmic ladder.

As a whole, Reuchlin's works are concerned with the interdependence of philosophy, religion, and magic. He had condemned magic that was aided by evil demons, reduced the elements of natural magic inherited from Pico and Ficino to the magical power of words, and presented a system he believed to be orthodox while disguising potentially controversial elements. Nevertheless, Reuchlin's ties to magic contributed to Erasmus's fading support for the humanist whose Hebraic studies for biblical exegesis he had admired[64] and whose position he had subscribed to during the

61. Ibid., pp. 106–7.

62. Secret, *Les kabbalistes*, p. 51; Spitz, *The Religious Renaissance*, p. 62.

63. This information and the subsequent references to the *De arte cabalistica* were drawn from Secret, *Les kabbalistes*, pp. 52–70; and Spitz, *The Religious Renaissance*, pp. 69–74. See also the facsimile of *De arte* in Johannes Pistorius, ed., *Ars cabalistica*, pp. 609–730; and the French translation by Secret in *La kabbale*.

64. Werner L. Gundersheimer, "Erasmus, Humanism, and the Christian Cabala"; Zika, "Reuchlin and Erasmus," pp. 226–27.

Pfefferkorn affair.[65] Erasmus cooled toward Reuchlin's Hebrew studies in what Zika characterized as a fundamental ideological split in the Christian humanist camp in the North: "The esoteric and elitist character of Reuchlin's knowledge, the permeation of mystery, the emphasis on ceremony and ritual, . . . the validation of philosophy and religion by wonders and miracles, the analogy between Christian prayer and ancient magic—all these ran counter to the style and content of the Erasmian reform program."[66] These tendencies are what Erasmus feared in the revival of Hebrew studies. Yet, the Hebrew-Cabalistic contribution Reuchlin made to Renaissance thought was a sincere effort to revitalize Christianity in a manner he deemed more viable than scholasticism or the Erasmian-style humanistic program; he sought a "mystical synthesis" of the religious program rather than a clear-cut reformation in the manner of Luther.[67]

Agrippa

Reuchlin's religious-magical orientation was perhaps his greatest legacy to his countryman Heinrich Cornelius Agrippa von Nettesheim (1486–1535). Agrippa "brought magic wholly into the sphere of religion through the modification of religious ceremonies and rites, and thereby endeavored to endow those ceremonies and rites with new energy and power."[68] Yet it was the magical aspect of the Nettesheimer's work that created his reputation as a master of black magic. He is, in fact, reputed to be the sorcerer on whom Christopher Marlowe modeled his Dr. Faustus and thus inspired a literary tradition.[69] In recent years, scholars have shown that Agrippa's complex thought included a Neoplatonic structure, a magical Hermetic-Cabalistic core, Erasmian-style reform sympathies, and a certain skepticism.[70]

65. Pfefferkorn was a converted Jew whose bitter anti-Semitism set off a rash of confiscation and burning of Jewish books—primarily Hebrew prayer books and Talmudic treatises. Reuchlin was also a target of Pfefferkorn's attack—presumably for his Hebrew and Cabalistic interests. Humanist support rallied to his cause, and Pfefferkorn was made to appear ridiculous. See Gundersheimer, "Erasmus, Humanism, and the Christian Cabala," pp. 42–45; Zika, "Reuchlin and Erasmus," pp. 223–27; and Roth, The Jews, pp. 128, 161.

66. "Reuchlin and Erasmus," p. 240.

67. Yates, The Occult Philosophy, pp. 26–27.

68. Zika, "Reuchlin's De Verbo," p. 138.

69. Charles G. Nauert, Agrippa and the Crisis of Renaissance Thought, p. 1, et passim; Yates, The Occult Philosophy, p. 116.

70. Nauert, Agrippa; Paola Zambelli, "Umanesimo magico-astrologico e reggrupamenti segreti nei platonici della preriforma"; Zambelli, "Cornelio Agrippa, Erasmo e la teologia umanistica"; Yates, The Occult Philosophy, pp. 37–47.

Agrippa's philosophy was a result of his intensive studies and wide range of personal contacts established through travel and maintained by correspondence.[71] His student days in Cologne and Paris introduced him to scholastic and humanistic studies and, it is speculated, to secret societies interested in the occult. He traveled in England, where he had contact with John Colet and was exposed to early Erasmian ideas of reform. During a trip to Spain, he is thought to have been associated with conversos and become acquainted with the *Zohar*. Agrippa's visits to Italy provided an opportunity to reinforce and expand his humanistic interests—including his more occult concerns. He had contact with Ludovico Lazzarelli, a less orthodox heir to the Neoplatonic-Hermetic tradition of Ficino and Pico, and with the Christian Cabalists Agostino and Paolo Ricci. He also knew the major work of the Cabalists Friar Francesco Giorgi and Cardinal Egidio da Viterbo. Later, ultramontane travels brought him into contact with the German Protestants and with early French humanistic and Evangelical circles.

The varied voyages of the Nettesheimer have a parallel in what Nauert has termed "the odyssey of Agrippa's mind" in referring to his wide range of ideas and the complex character of his apparently contradictory thought.[72] His *De occulta philosophia*[73] (1533) is a three-part treatment of his Neoplatonic, Hermetic, and Cabalistic beliefs. Book 1 deals with Ficinian-style magic of the elemental world, which uses natural objects according to their occult sympathies. The second book covers magic of the celestial world and how one might use astrological influences. Book 3 treats the magic of the angelic world, the one closest to God. It is a Cabalistic world dependent on Hebrew letters, their numerical values, and wider connections with the *sefirot* as well as all of the divine and angelic names. It is religious magic which Agrippa, like Pico, felt would sanctify all his magical practices and make them safe from demonic intervention.

The Nettesheimer's second major opus, *De incertitudine et vanitate scientiarum* (1526), appears to be a rejection of all human learning as uncertain. All is considered vain except the name of Christ—the essence of all divine revelation. It is curious that *De occulta* existed in manuscript from 1510 and that it was followed by *De vanitate* and the more elaborate published form of *De occulta*

71. This summary of Agrippa's background was mainly drawn from Nauert, *Agrippa*.

72. Ibid., pp. 194–221.

73. In English, see *Three Books of Occult Philosophy Translated Out of the Latin into the English Tongue by J[ohn] F[rench]* (London: 1651).

(1533). The apparent contrast between Agrippa's two great treatises is solved by a close examination of his writings. Nauert has shown that Agrippa's magic, which was basically fideist in its reliance on the revealed truths of the esoteric and religious traditions, was not incompatible with the fideist-skeptical point of view.[74]

Agrippa had long doubted the powers of unaided human reason. His *Encomium Asini* recalls Erasmus's *Encomium Moriae* and the fideistic skepticism the two hold in common.[75] Agrippa's criticism of ecclesiastical abuses and his Evangelical sympathies are further evidence of his Erasmian outlook. Although Agrippa never abandoned his interest in the occult, he did come to doubt the validity of the "revealed truth" of some ancient wisdom. He moved closer to a more Erasmian appeal to pure Gospel as the only source of truth. Still, it is important to recognize that—like most Christian Cabalists—he always considered the "true" or Christian Cabala as the valid continuation of God's secret revelation to Moses for divine interpretation of the Old Testament and its associated teachings.[76]

Giorgi

Francesco Giorgi of Venice (1466–1540) represents a type of Christian Cabalism resembling Agrippa's but demonstrating more clearly Sefirotic connections softened, as Yates has described it, "by a gentler Italian coloring."[77] That subdued approach stems from the religious influence of Giorgi's Franciscan training and Hebraic studies in his native city. Venice was a "new Jerusalem" in the era after the Expulsion when editors and printers of Hebrew literature such as Daniel Bomberg made it the center for the diffusion of Christian Cabalism.[78] Indeed, so great was the city's reputation as a center for Hebrew learning that the representatives of Spain and England (both having expelled Judaism from their shores) had to seek counsel among Venetian Hebrew scholars in the disputed divorce of Henry VIII from Catherine of Aragón.[79] Francesco Giorgi was one of the consulted erudites who gave his interpretation of Old Testament divorce laws in favor of King Henry.

74. *Agrippa*, pp. 200–220. Nauert also relies on the groundwork done by Eugenio Garin on the significance of magic in Renaissance culture in his *Medioevo e Rinascimento*.

75. Yates, *The Occult Philosophy*, pp. 43–44. On the origins of modern skepticism, see Richard Popkin, *The History of Scepticism from Erasmus to Descartes*.

76. Nauert, *Agrippa*, p. 212.

77. *The Occult Philosophy*, p. 39.

78. Secret, *Les kabbalistes*, p. 126; Roth, *The Jews*, pp. 162–64.

79. Roth, *The Jews*, pp. 158–61; Secret, *Les kabbalistes*, p. 127; and Yates, *The Occult Philosophy*, p. 31.

Giorgi, then, was not considered an eccentric magician, but was a respected scholar of patrician stock whose works were among the most influential of Christian Cabalists. His *De harmonia mundi* (1525) maintains the major themes of Christian Cabalism: the importance of the sacred language, the secret and divine significance of letters and numbers, and the power of divine words and names. Giorgi does exhibit a rather more independent interpretation of the names of the Virgin Mary and of Christ (as ISU),[80] but his most interesting variation of the Cabalistic tradition is his view of universal harmony. Giorgi's vision is a reservoir of Platonic, Pythogorean, Hermetic, and Christian Cabalistic confluences.[81] He sees a cosmos in which divine influences filter down through the angelic hierarchies (equated with the planets). All relationships between the components of the universe interact according to divinely ordained mathematical harmonies. Christ's power as a unifying force is emphasized, as is man's role as a microcosm—a medieval theme to which Giorgi adds Hermetic-Cabalistic complexities in a Renaissance manner. Giorgi's *Problemata* (1536) continues theories of his *De harmonia* with stronger magical and esoteric implications, treating three thousand questions posed by the Old and New Testaments, Cabala, and various *prisci theologi*.[82]

Although the *Problemata* and *De harmonia* were placed on the *Index* before their emendation, neither can be considered a guide to practical Renaissance magic. As D. P. Walker points out, Giorgi's "astrology is too Christian, his musical theory too metaphorical, his conception of spirit too comprehensive and hence fluid."[83] In effect, Giorgi is too poetic and too arbitrary for his mathematical harmonies to be scientifically operative. Yet, it was the metaphorical-Cabalistic quality of the Franciscan friar's work that made it attractive in Renaissance culture. Giorgi was consulted in the construction of San Francesco della Vigna in Venice, a convent whose design illustrates his harmonic theories.[84] *De harmonia mundi* was

---

80. For an explanation of Giorgi's theories on both names, see Secret, *Les kabalistes*, pp. 133–35.

81. Information for the summary was drawn from *De harmonia mundi*; Yates, *The Occult Philosophy*, pp. 29–35; Yates, *Giordano Bruno*, p. 151; and Secret, *Les kabbalistes*, pp. 127–35.

82. For information on *In Scripturam Sacram et philosophiam tria millia problemata*, see Secret, *Le "Zohar,"* pp. 43–49; Secret, *Les kabbalistes*, pp. 128, 138; and Yates, *The Occult*, p. 35.

83. Walker, *Spiritual and Demonic Magic*, p. 112.

84. Rudolf Wittkower, "Architectural Principles in the Age of Humanism," pp. 90–100, 136–37. Wittkower's study does not reflect more recent scholarship on the Hermetic-Cabalistic core of the term *Neoplatonism*, which he uses to describe Giorgi's theories.

warmly received and enthusiastically praised by the Parisian circle
of Guy Le Fèvre de la Boderie, who translated the work to French
(1578). As with Ronsard and Baïf's Academy, La Boderie and Pontus de Tyard hoped to create a poetic revolution based on the
philosophical musico-mathematical analogies Giorgi provided.[85]
The influence of Francesco Giorgi has even been observed in
Robert Fludd and the Rosicrucian view of the world and of human
harmony.[86] Giorgi's preoccupation with world peace and order
was shared by Cardinal Egidio da Viterbo: both foresaw an end to
their present age of discord and anticipated a reform of societal ills
in a prophesied era of unity and universal accord.

Egidio da Viterbo

The reputation of Cardinal Egidio da Viterbo (1465–1532) as a
Christian Cabalist has greatly increased in stature since his name[87]
was simply listed among other Italians with similar interests.[88] As
Francis Martin has shown, Renaissance historians' esteem for the
cardinal as an orator, scholar, and pious reform-minded general of
the Augustinians long concealed the role he played in contemporary Cabalistic studies.[89] Secret has concluded that Egidio da Viterbo's work is the most remarkable effort of assimilation of Cabala
among the Christian humanists as witnessed by his Christian interpretation of Cabala.[90] The cardinal had benefited from his contact
with the major Italian Christian Cabalists: Pico, the Ricci brothers,
Giustiniani, Galatino, and Giorgi. He also knew well and greatly
admired Reuchlin. He employed numerous Jewish and converso
scholars of Hebrew—the foremost among them being Elias Levita.[91] Of the humanists interested in the *prisca theologia* and its
magical connections, Ficino, Pico, and Giorgi had contact with
Egidio, and the cardinal may have had some connection with
Agrippa.[92]

An overview of Egidio's readings reveals a range of interests

85. Walker, *Spiritual and Demonic Magic*, pp. 119–26.
86. See Yates, *The Occult Philosophy*, pp. 36, 169–75, and also her *The Rosicrucian Enlightenment*. See also on Fludd's theories William Huffman, "Robert Fludd:
The End of an Era," Ph.D. diss., University of Missouri-Columbia, 1977.
87. In the village of Viterbo, he was born Egidio Antonini, not Canisio. See John
W. O'Malley, *Giles of Viterbo on Church and Reform*, p. 4.
88. Blau, *The Christian Interpretation*, p. 13.
89. "The Problem of Giles of Viterbo: A Historiographical Survey," pp. 366–67,
et passim.
90. *Les kabbalistes*, p. 120.
91. On Elias Levita (Elijah Bahur) see Roth, *The Jews*, pp. 156–57.
92. Nauert, *Agrippa*, pp. 227–28.

coinciding with his varied personal contacts.[93] Through his Paduan studies he knew the Aristotelians, and his Florentine contacts provided ample resources for his knowledge of Plato (whom he also knew through Augustine) and the Neoplatonists. His interests also included Greek and Roman literature. Of special note are Orpheus, whom he regarded as a poet and theologian, and Virgil, whom he saw as a source of deep and genuine spiritual enlightenment when the poet's Platonic, Sibylline, and Etruscan messages were understood. Less orthodox sources included Origen, whom Egidio respected for his Platonism and exegesis, and Dionysius the Areopagite, whom the cardinal regarded for his transmission of "secret theology" from Saint Paul and of the theology of divine names. Some of Egidio's ideas are compatible with the Joachimite apocalyptic tradition; he did not discourage Silverio Meucci and his group of Venetian Augustinians from publishing a number of Joachimite works.[94]

Naturally the influence of St. Augustine on the cardinal, the general of his order, is quite powerful. However, it is highly significant that Egidio stressed those elements of his founder's thought that he believed would agree with his Cabalistic interests: e.g., the importance of learning Hebrew and the key significance of Trinitarian theology. None of the cardinal's readings discussed above was as prominent in his work as Scripture. He was thoroughly familiar with the Old and New Testaments, but his knowledge of the former was enlightened by his study of Hebrew after 1494. To him, St. John was the greatest of the Evangelists, the one most imbued with divine wisdom and the one whose doctrines were found in Plato's works. John O'Malley notes that Egidio, "unlike his contemporaries, Erasmus and Luther, gives no indication that he felt any particular reserve was required in using John's Apocalypse."[95]

Scripture—from both the Old and New Testaments—was the chief influence in the cardinal's major works: the *Sententiae ad mentem Platonis*, the *Historia XX saeculorum*, and the most Cabalistic opus, *Scechina et libellus de litteris ebraicis* (1530). However, his readings in Hebrew were not limited to Scripture. He knew and used the Talmud and the Midrashim, but the predomi-

93. This general survey was drawn largely from O'Malley, *Giles of Viterbo*, pp. 29–66.

94. Ibid., pp. 61–62. For information on Joachim di Fiore and his role in eschatalogical movements, see Marjorie Reeves, *The Influence of Prophecy in the Later Middle Ages: A Study of Joachimism*.

95. O'Malley, *Giles of Viterbo*, p. 71.

nant Hebrew sources for him were Cabalistic: the *Zohar*, the *Bahir*, the *Sha'arei-Orah*, and numerous others.[96] Indeed, it is his knowledge and his translation of some of the Cabalistic *opera* that has significantly contributed to his reputation as a foremost Christian Cabalist. The cardinal's works were chiefly known in manuscript and through other Cabalists' publications.[97] His original treatises on Cabala remained unpublished in his own day; O'Malley speculates that Egidio's inaction was due to fear of criticism in some ecclesiastical circles.[98]

Scripture may have been the predominant force in the cardinal's thought, but that influence was entirely colored by Cabalistic exegesis. It was for Egidio the only method "non peregrina, sed domestica" and the only "divina dialectica"[99] for understanding the revealed word of God and the whole course of human history—in both sacred and profane texts. In his view, the discovery of Cabala by Christians in his own day marked a major turning point in biblical exegesis. The Old Law had not been abolished by the New. Revelation continued with the Apostles; yet their Gospels alone did not reveal the complete meaning of Christ's teaching.[100] Egidio held that Christian doctrine was too rich and too concise to be grasped in any one age. Cabala would be the great culmination of the age-old process of revelation since it alone could provide the inexhaustible abundance of divinely created metaphors and the sacred methodology reflecting the unfathomable richness of the Godhead.[101] Cabalism saw Scripture as a symbolic representation of the process by which divine life expands through the *sefirot* to all aspects of earthly existence. This belief, along with the Cabalistic techniques of *gimatriyya* and *notarikon* and the associated credence in the power of names, was central to Egidio's method.

Egidio's vast studies, assisted by Cabala's allegorical interpretation of Scripture and certain aspects of Cabala's complementary view of terrestrial history, led him to interpret contemporary events rather apocalyptically. He was saddened by the need for ecclesiastical reform, the disunity of Christendom, and the Turkish threat to

96. Secret, "Le symbolisme de la kabbale chrétienne dans la *Scechina* de Egidio da Viterbo," p. 135.

97. For examples of Egidio's other Hebrew sources, see Secret, "Aegidiana Hebraica."

98. *Giles of Viterbo*, p. 98. Secret has published a modern edition of the *Scechina*. Egidio's two other major works remain unpublished.

99. Cited in Secret, "Le symbolisme," pp. 136–37.

100. See O'Malley, *Giles of Viterbo*, pp. 97–98; and Secret, "Le symbolisme," pp. 138–39.

101. O'Malley, *Giles of Viterbo*, pp. 35–37, 90–94.

world unity. Yet, for him, the signs of the times also indicated that
an age of renewal for mankind was at hand. The imperial reign of
Carlos V, the sack of Rome, the discovery of the New World, and
the adoption of Cabala by Christians were all seen as indications of
a new order that would restore the ancient customs and beliefs.[102]
The basic message of Egidio's *Scechina* is his appeal to Carlos V,
who is seen as the new Solomon, new Cyrus, and new David who
can purge evil from the Church, send missions to pagan lands, and
promote scriptural studies with the new methods.[103]

We have dwelt on the role of Egidio da Viterbo in this brief
survey of the major Renaissance Christian Cabalists because he
exemplifies the kind of cautious and concerned application of
Cabala that is found in Fray Luis. The cardinal was deeply admired
by Carlos V for his "excellenti doctrina et integritate vitae."[104]
Contemporary churchmen were more inclined to support Egidio's
emphasis on exegetical Cabala than the more speculative and dangerous sort of Cabala that Pico personified.[105] Fray Luis was nurtured among the Salamancan Augustinians in the wake of Egidio's
reform measures for the order and of the visits of the cardinal and
his successor Seripando to Salamanca. The Augustinian general
had long emphasized the importance of *hebraica veritas*—i.e., the
most clearly understood reading of the divinely created tongue—
for all potential Augustinian biblical scholars. Egidio was cautious,
only recommending the study of *litterae sacrae* in his letters to
fellow Augustinians and making no formal effort to institute
Cabalistic studies as part of the brothers' regular training.
However, "there were certainly individual instances of his encouraging friars in the study of the Cabala and 'Caldaeas litteras.' "[106]

Cabalistic Restoration at the Dawn of the Counter-Reformation

The Neapolitan Augustinian Girolamo Seripando (1493–1561)
was not only Egidio's successor as general of the order and as a
cardinal, but he also remained in close contact with his mentor
throughout his life and was strongly influenced by his views on

102. Ibid., pp. 114–15, et passim.
103. Secret, "Le symbolisme," pp. 141–42, 149; and O'Malley, *Giles of Viterbo*,
pp. 116, 175–77, et passim.
104. O'Malley, *Giles of Viterbo*, pp. 6–7, n. 2.
105. See Secret, "Le symbolisme," p. 137, on Bishop Aloysius Lippomanus of
Verona's preference for Egidio.
106. O'Malley, *Giles of Viterbo*, p. 173, cites the cardinal's personal letters.

moral reform and world order.[107] However, the religious tensions and the reform issues Seripando encountered were more complicated than when Egidio had had to deal with the rebellious Augustinian Luther. Seripando would have to perform on a wider stage at the Council of Trent, to which he was a highly respected and influential delegate. The skills he brought to the task were similar to his mentor's: humanistic studies, admirable oratorical ability, respected Ciceronian style, and a knowledge of Christian Cabala.

Seripando's knowledge of Cabala—influenced by Egidio—was wide, but perhaps less deep than Egidio's since he lacked his predecessor's strength in Oriental languages.[108] The Neapolitan was quite familiar with Reuchlin's work, from which he adopted his emphasis on the name *Jesus*, descriptions of the *sefirot*, references to angelic messengers, and some Cabalistic uses of numbers in scriptural exegesis. Seripando also used the Zoharic texts for references to the Trinity and Elijah's prophecy, and he probably had contact with Galatino, Giustiniani, Agrippa, and perhaps Giorgi—with whom he shared concerns for world order and apocalyptic speculation.

Apocalyptic prophecies in Scripture and elsewhere had been used by both Egidio and Seripando in promoting moral reform within the order and in mankind as a whole. Yet, with his mentor, Seripando came to rely more on Cabalistic methods of exegesis and appeals for personal moral reformation in his writings. In particular, as Kottman has shown, the role of Cabalistic interpretation of Canticles was central to theories of Church history and Christian spirituality used by Egidio, Seripando, and Postel in promoting moral reform.[109]

As with Egidio and Seripando, the intellectual training of Guillaume Postel (1510–1581) was both scholastic and humanistic, but he surpassed them in his knowledge of Oriental languages and his less-than-orthodox use of Cabala.[110] In the tradition of Pico, Reuchlin, Giorgi, and other Christian Cabalists, his approach was highly syncretic. However, he included the Druids among his ad-

107. For information on Seripando's life, his relationship to Egidio, and his participation in the Council of Trent, see Hubert Jedin, *Papal Legate at the Council of Trent: Cardinal Seripando*, trans. Frederic Eckhoff.

108. Secret has expanded Jedin's list of Cabalistic sources used by Seripando. See his *Les kabbalistes*, p. 123.

109. *Law and Apocalypse*, pp. 98–101.

110. This summary on Postel was drawn largely from William Bouwsma's work on Postel, *Concordia Mundi: The Career and Thought of Guillaume Postel*, with material updated by Secret, "Notes sur Guillaume Postel," and Secret, *Les kabbalistes*, pp. 171–86.

mired *prisci theologi*, revealing the highly Gallican character of his views. Postel's syncretic technique even advocated the unity of revelation and natural reason since, like Ramón Lull, he believed that intellectual appeals would convert the infidels and quickly contribute to the restoration of world harmony. Like Lull, he felt that the problem of unifying mankind was an epistemological one in which language was the key. For Postel, Cabala would provide the linguistic key and the basis for world reform and the restoration of mankind to God in the final age of the world. These broad philosophic and social goals, in Postel's view, would become a political reality through the leadership of the French Bourbon kings—whom he saw as the true heirs of Noah. Such an extreme view, along with his belief in the prophecies of the "Virgin of Venice" and the conception of himself as a sort of messianic assistant, explain why Postel was expelled from the Jesuits, tried by the Inquisition, and acquitted by reason of insanity.

Postel was an eccentric, but aspects of his thought were quite influential in France,[111] and, as Kottman points out, Fray Luis de León does follow the reasoning of Postel, Egidio, and Seripando in the belief that the Apocalypse was near and in their Cabalistic interpretation of the Canticles for ideas on Church history and moral reform.[112] The influence of the two Augustinian generals on the friar is quite likely, but his use of other Christian Cabalistic sources—both inside and outside Spain—is probable, as succeeding chapters will show. Fray Luis could have been aware of the varieties of Cabala manifested in the works of Pico, Agrippa, Giorgi, and Postel, but his Cabalism did not delve into practical magic and fantastic speculation. The Augustinian of Salamanca supported a more cautious Cabalism at the service of sincere concerns for moral reform and a personal longing for mystical contact with the Divinity. That is the same spirit that could have motivated San Juan de la Cruz's and Santa Teresa's uses of Cabalistic symbolism. However, San Juan was not a humanist nor a Hebrew scholar of Luis de León's caliber. His reading of Christian Cabalistic works in Latin would have been more limited. Santa Teresa's knowledge of Christian Cabala had to be through secondary sources. Through the diffusion of Christian Cabalism in Renaissance culture, Cabala reached a wider public that appreciated its symbolic value. In Spain, Renaissance Cabalistic symbolism could renew surviving native traditions and inspire new Christian modes of Cabalistic expression.

111. For Postel's more far-reaching influences, see Secret, *Les kabbalistes*, pp. 187–202, and "Notes sur Guillaume Postel."
112. *Law and Apocalypse*, pp. 100–102.

2

the diffusion of
christian cabala in renaissance culture

s the sixteenth century pro-
gressed, the enthusiasm of
humanists for Cabala
spread throughout Renais-
sance culture. The over-
flow of Cabalistic influences into the arts was most often expressed
as an attitude or a tendency that mingled with the general pansophic currents of the late Renaissance.[1] In some literary figures,
musicians, and artists, there is evidence of varied degrees of familiarity or fascination with the Cabalistic tendency. In others—such
as Fray Luis de León, Guy Le Fèvre de la Boderie, and John Dee—
the influence of Christian Cabala is an integral part of a more
profound philosophical point of view.

The dispersion of Christian Cabalistic tenets was stimulated by
the great Christian Cabalists and their works, of course, but other
influential tools were bibliographies such as Gesner's *Bibliothèque
universelle* (1545) and Henri Mauroy's *Apologie pour les juifs con-
vertis* (1553).[2] Perhaps more influential in the general culture were
iconographic works such as the *Hieroglyphica* of Horapollo, Piero
Valeriano's work of the same title, and Andrea Alciati's emblem
books. Renaissance humanists saw hieroglyphs as cryptic sources
of syncretic wisdom handed down by ancient Cabalists along with
Egyptian Hermeticists and a whole host of Chaldean, Zoroastrian,
Orphic, Sibylline, Platonic, and Christian influences.[3] There is contemporary evidence that Renaissance humanists merged Renaissance allegory and symbolism with hieroglyphics, seeing the latter
also as symbols whose deep meanings were to be enlightening to
and appreciated by the few.[4] Thus it is that emblem books by

1. Robert James Weston Evans, *Rudolf II and His World*, pp. 236–42, et passim.
2. Secret, *Les kabbalistes*, pp. 307–8.
3. Rudolf Wittkower, *Allegory and the Migration of Symbols*, pp. 115–16; Secret,
Les kabbalistes, pp. 308–9; Aquilino Sánchez Pérez, *La literatura emblemática
española*, pp. 31, 38.
4. Wittkower, *Allegory and the Migration of Symbols*, p. 127.

Alciati and others, great sources of iconographic-literary symbolism in the diffusion of Renaissance culture, need to be understood as an expression of humanistic pansophy and humanism's fascination with the esoteric—of which Cabala is an integral part.[5] Cabala remains, along with other aspects of occult Renaissance thought, beneath the surface of Renaissance culture as observed by the spectator from the twentieth century. But critical investigations have begun to scratch the surface and to reveal the influence of Cabala in Renaissance belles lettres as well as in the plastic and performing arts.

Italy

Many Italian contributions to Christian Cabala were theoretical and abstract, as exemplified by the works of Pico, Giorgi, Egidio, and others. However, their influence overflowed into the broader aspects of Renaissance culture, as witnessed by Giorgi's influence on the architectural design of San Francesco della Vigna and Pico's possible influence on Alexander VI or on the artist Pinturicchio's frescoes for the Borgia apartments.[6] D. P. Walker even speculates that Pico may have influenced Savonarola since the Dominican prophet was judged by his friends to be like a Cabalist in his knowledge of Scriptures and in his ability "to extract from them all science and knowledge, even of future things."[7]

Egidio da Viterbo associated closely with the literary circles of late Renaissance Italy. He sparked the enthusiasm of Angelo Poliziano (1454–1494) for *hebraica veritas*[8] and possible accompanying interests in Cabala. The cardinal also influenced Jacopo Sannazzaro (1456–1530), whose *De Partu Virginis*[9] was embellished by *prisca theologia* prophecies on the Redeemer. Egidio's name is also mentioned in connection with Giulio Camillo (c. 1485–1544),[10] the Venetian humanist who created a great Theater of the World. This mnemonic device used the *sefirot*, Cabalistic angels, and Cabala's three-soul concept. Camillo is also said to have had contact with Pico, Giorgi, Bembo, and Francis I.[11]

5. Secret, *Les kabbalistes*, pp. 308–9, and Sánchez Pérez, *La literatura emblemática española*, pp. 32–36, in particular, mention Cabala's possible involvement.

6. See Chapter 1, note 33.

7. *The Ancient Theology*, pp. 57–58.

8. O'Malley, *Giles of Viterbo*, pp. 75–77.

9. Martin, "The Problem of Egidio da Viterbo," p. 360.

10. Secret, *Le "Zohar,"* p. 49.

11. Secret, *Les kabbalistes*, pp. 309–11. On Camillo's memory theater see Frances Yates's *The Art of Memory*.

Further evidence of Cabala in Italian Renaissance culture is demonstrated by the author of *Lives of the Painters*, Giorgio Vasari
(1511–1574).[12] His "Ragionamenti" describes the ten Sefirotic
powers of God, which he depicted in his painting for the Palais-
Vieux. A more magical fascination with Cabala is seen in the work
of Francesco Piccolomini (1520–1604), a former Paduan classmate
of Pope Sixtus V, and in Teófilo Folengo's *L'historia macarónica*.

Of particular interest to the study of Christian Cabala in Fray
Luis and the Spanish mystics are two Italian monks. Ambrogio
Fiandino, an Augustinian bishop and hermit of Platonic and
Cabalistic interests in the manner of Cardinal Egidio, referred to
various Cabalistic doctrines, including *gilgul* (the transmigration of
souls). He also alluded to the symbol of the nut[13]—an image used
by Joseph Gikatilla and the *Zohar* and somewhat similar to one
found in Santa Teresa. The work of the Dominican monk Sixtus of
Siena illustrated a more cautious approach to Cabala in the era of
the Inquisition.[14] Sixtus distinguished between good Cabala (pious
and Christian) and bad (antiquated, powerless Jewish Cabala). He
also attempted to adapt the radical Christian Cabala of Agrippa to
his own more spiritualist point of view. Sixtus's use of Cabala in
Scriptural exegesis showed that it was possible to follow both post-
Tridentine Catholic exegesis and Jewish authorities simultaneously. He used Cabalistic and rabbinical exegetical principles
in his *Bibliotheca sancta*, a major source for Luis de León's use of
Cabala in exegesis.[15]

France

Lefèvre d'Etaples (1455–1537) was probably the first Christian
Cabalistic writer in France.[16] As with later French authors, his
main fascination with Cabala concerned the power of words, holy
names, and the secret names of God, in particular. Like Luis de
León, he shared his era's interest in linguistic theories centered
about hieroglyphic symbolism and on the Cabalistic notion that a

12. Secret, *Les kabbalistes*, pp. 313–14.

13. Secret, "Notes sur Paulus Ricius," p. 186; *Les kabbalistes*, pp. 266–67. Some
Christian Cabalistic applications of the nut image were based on Gikatilla's comparison of the nut and the golden apple in *Ginat Egoz (The Nut Garden)*. See *De arte
cabalistica*, 1:631.

14. On Sixtus, see Secret, "Les dominicains," pp. 328–29; Paola Zambelli,
"Magic and Radical Reformation in Agrippa of Nettesheim," pp. 88–89; and Yosef
Hayim Yerushalmi, *From Spanish Court to Italian Ghetto*, pp. 283, 287.

15. Kottman, *Law and Apocalypse*, pp. 70–72.

16. Brian Copenhaver, "LeFèvre d'Etaples, Symphorien Champier, and the Secret
Names of God."

simple Hebrew sentence can provide many profound meanings.[17] Lefèvre spoke of the addition of *shin* to the Tetragrammaton—somewhat in the manner of Pico and Reuchlin[18]—but, as a whole, he was cautious about magical names. His *Psalterium* (1509) follows Pico's notion that the songs of David are suited to Cabala just as those of Orpheus are to natural magic. Lefèvre's Cabalistic sources for the *Psalterium* were probably the Spaniards Pedro Alfonso, Pablo de Santa María, and Leonard Pomar, along with Reuchlin's *De Verbo*.[19] Lefèvre's work strongly influenced Symphorien Champier (c. 1471–1539), the earliest and most active transmitter of Ficinian Platonism in France. However, Champier was even more careful than Lefèvre on the magical aspects of Cabala.[20]

The poet Maurice Scève (1510–1564) shared the Platonic and Cabalistic interests of his fellow Lyonnais, Champier. Some critics have seen Cabalistic elements in Scève's interest in numerical symbolism and hidden meanings and in his vision of man as a microcosm.[21] *Les prisons* of Scève's contemporary Marguerite de Navarre (1492–1549) has also been judged to illustrate Cabalistic elements in combination with the Platonic.[22]

The work of François Rabelais (1490–1553) demonstrates a more extensive use of Cabala. His first three books satirize the abuses of practical Cabala, while his *Quart Livre* and *Cinquiesme Livre* use Cabalistic and other elements of Hebraic symbolism in a rather mystical treatment of wine and sex.[23]

The French name most prominently associated with the diffusion of Christian Cabalism in Renaissance culture is, perhaps, that of

17. Edward Schuster, in "Fray Luis de León and the Linguistic Approach to Epistemology," notes the sense of parallelism between the worlds of creation and the world of language in Fray Luis. He does not, however, note that this is a Cabalistic treatment.

18. Secret, *Les kabbalistes*, pp. 136–37; and Walker, *Spiritual and Demonic Magic*, pp. 167–70.

19. Copenhaver, "LeFèvre d'Etaples," pp. 197–206.

20. Walker, *The Ancient Theology*, pp. 100–101, and *Spiritual and Demonic Magic*, pp. 167–70; Copenhaver, "LeFèvre d'Etaples," pp. 209–11.

21. V. L. Saulnier, *Maurice Scève*, notes that Brunetiere, Parturier, and others saw Cabalistic elements in *Delie* and other works, but Saulnier sees Scève as using Cabala only as a metaphor for tradition and knowledge (1:133–42; 2:71–73).

22. Dudley Wilson, *French Renaissance Scientific Poetry*, p. 156, n. 3, suggests that vague Cabalistic notions about Canticles may have influenced *Les prisons*. Henry Hornik in "More on the Hermetica and French Renaissance Literature," pp. 4–5, denies the evidence of Cabalistic doctrines that Eugene Parturier had seen in Marguerite de Navarre.

23. See G. Mallory Masters, *The Rabelasian Dialectic*, p. 105, et passim. Masters (pp. 105–6) concludes that the continued use of Cabala and other elements of the occult tradition by Rabelais points to the authenticity of the last book.

Guy Le Fèvre de la Boderie (1541–1598).[24] Like his friend Pontus de Tyard, young Ronsard, and members of Baïf's Academy, La Boderie sought to unite powerful effect-producing music with poetry of profound religious or philosophical meaning. To this end, he blended his knowledge of Cabala with Platonic and other sources from the *prisca theologia*, and he relied heavily on Postel and Giorgi, whose *De harmonia mundi* he translated to French. La Boderie applied Cabalistic elements in his imagery as well as in his harmonic theories. His *L'encyclie* and *Le tabernacle* were constructed on the names of God. In *Hymnes ecclesiastiques*, La Boderie employed the Zoharic interpretation of Canticles—an approach also found in Fray Luis—and Zoharic references to silkworms—a symbol found in Santa Teresa's *Moradas*.[25]

With his brother Nicolas Lefèvre de la Boderie, Guy shared an interest in symbolic numbers and their Cabalistic connections. His friend Pontus de Tyard (1521–1605) used Cabala's *Sefer Yezirah* (*Book of Creation*) and several Christian Cabalistic works, as well as Cabalistic elements in León Hebreo's *Dialoghi d'amore*, which Tyard translated. Even in the mid-seventeenth century, these two works continued to serve as Christian Cabalistic sources in France. Marin Mersenne (d. 1648) used them, along with Giorgi's works, in his Christian apologetic treatise, *Quaestiones*.[26]

England

The Christian Cabala came late to England, but there is evidence that it endured until the Restoration.[27] And, although the Elizabethan era saw rapid growth in Cabalistic interests, the roots of the English fascination with Cabala were visible in the early sixteenth century. A notable example is the humanist John Colet, who, despite the hesitation of his friend Erasmus, was quite interested in Reuchlin's work. By Elizabethan times, works of Christian Cabala were available to interested circles such as that of the math-

24. On La Boderie, see Walker, *Ancient Theology*, pp. 93–96, 103–4, and *Spiritual and Demonic Magic*, pp. 119–26; Wilson, *French Renaissance Scientific Poetry*, pp. 161–62, 165, 169–77; Secret, *Les kabbalistes*, pp. 192–98 et passim; and Jean Dagens, "Hermétisme et cabale en France de Lefèvre d'Etaples à Bossuet," p. 6.
    25. Discussed below, Chapter 3.
    26. On the Cabala in sixteenth- and seventeenth-century France, see Walker, *Ancient Theology*, pp. 63–131, 174–190. Other references to Cabala in seventeenth-century France are found in Secret, *Les kabbalistes*, and Dagens, "Hermétisme et cabale en France."
    27. Joseph Blau, "The Diffusion of the Christian Interpretation of the Cabala in English Literature," p. 158.

ematician-philosopher John Dee (1527–1608).[28] Through his contacts, Dee was instrumental in spreading Christian Cabalistic ideas in England—and, perhaps, in Spain and the Empire, as we shall see. Dee was a theoretical Christian Cabalist whose enthusiasm for mathematics was easily related to the numerological bases of angel summoning. It was through his acquaintance with Dee that Edmund Spenser (1552–1599) learned to anglicize Christian Cabalistic ideas on reform and millennial change.[29] As portrayed in Spenser's *The Faerie Queene*, Elizabeth I the Virgin Queen—not the Emperor Carlos V—would be the instrument of divine restoration of peace and order. The major Cabalistic influence on *The Faerie Queene*, however, was Giorgi. Spenser followed the Venetian friar in his use of angels, the *sefirot*, and the design of Solomon's Temple.[30] Although Cabala explains many aspects of Spenser's work not clarified by the strictly Neoplatonic interpretations of earlier critics, not all scholars agree that Spenser was a full-fledged Cabalist.[31]

The evidence of Cabala in the works of William Shakespeare (1564–1616) is perhaps less clear than in Spenser, but it adds an interesting dimension to Shakespearean scholarship. Frances Yates sees the fairies in *The Merry Wives of Windsor* and especially in *A Midsummer Night's Dream* as literary (Arthurian) and religious (Cabalistic) in origin.[32] Like Prospero in *The Tempest*, they cultivate white Cabalistic magic—the safe sort that Agrippa tried to develop.

In the case of John Milton (1608–1674), there is general critical agreement that Milton used Cabala. The chief Cabalistic influence on Milton was probably Robert Fludd, a disciple of Dee and Giorgi.[33] Fludd's mark is visible in the world of angels and demons Milton created. Milton also portrayed England Cabalistically as the chosen leader of Protestant peoples—somewhat as Egidio da Viterbo had hoped Cabala would be used in a program for Catholic reform.

28. See Peter French, *John Dee*, pp. 28, 32, et passim; and Yates, *The Occult Philosophy*, pp. 82–89.

29. On the philosophy of Elizabethan imperialism, see Yates, *Astrea*.

30. Yates, *The Occult Philosophy*, pp. 97–100.

31. Denis Saurat associates Spenser's Sapience in the *Faerie Queene* and minor poems with the *Shekhinah* in *Literature and Occult Tradition*, trans. Dorothy Bolton, pp. 222–37. Blau disagrees with Saurat in "The Diffusion," p. 157. Yates is inclined to see a Cabalistic influence in the *Faerie Queene*, although she does not defend Saurat's point on Sapience; see *The Occult Philosophy*, pp. 107–8, 148, 179.

32. *The Occult Philosophy*, pp. 148–49, 160.

33. Ibid., pp. 177–79.

In addition to Milton, other English seventeenth-century literary figures can be seen to have been influenced by Christian Cabala. The works of Cambridge Platonists Ralph Cudworth, John Smith, and Henry More, in particular, display favorable views of Cabala.[34] In the verses of the metaphysical poets, however, the Cabalistic influence is said to have been reduced to an "attitude"— one impossible to separate from similar philosophical ideas of the poets.

Spain

Christian Cabalism—as well as Renaissance occult thought in general—was subject to more restraints in sixteenth-century Spain than elsewhere in Europe. Nevertheless, Inquisitional pressures did not eradicate Spanish preoccupations with the same pansophic interests that had attracted other European intellectuals and artists. Perhaps nowhere is the evidence of Spanish interests stronger than in the royal house itself. Carlos V and his courtiers were associated with reform-minded Italians such as Cardinal Egidio da Viterbo who saw the emperor as the prophesied unifier and pacifier of the world—a view frequently dependent on Cabalistic interpretations. The great esteem in which Carlos V held Egidio[35] and the promotion of spiritual and political reforms under the emperor's direction are evidence of possible Cabalistic influences at court. The reform measures defended by courtiers such as Alfonso de Valdés in his *Diàlogo de las cosas occuridas en Roma* might be more fully understood in their ties to Christian Cabalist Egidio and not solely in their relationship to Erasmian irenism as described by Bataillon.[36] Further evidence of a Spanish elite interested in Cabala and reform was Cardinal Bernardino Carvajal, a courtier of Jewish descent.[37] With the emperor's support, he promoted conciliar reform and even requested that Agrippa—as a Cabalistic authority of the time—visit the Council of Pisa (1511–1512).

Hapsburg associations with Agrippa offer further evidence of

34. Blau, "The Diffusion," pp. 159–60; Ernst Cassirer, *The Platonic Renaissance in England*, trans. James Pettegrove, pp. 131–32; John Smith, "The Excellency and Nobleness of True Religion," in *The Cambridge Platonists*, ed. C. A. Patrides, pp. xxix, 146, 186.

35. O'Malley, *Giles of Viterbo*, pp. 6–7, quotes a letter from Carlos V's associate Girolamo Aleander (1480–1542) to the cardinal in March 1521.

36. Marcel Bataillon, *Erasmo y España*, trans. Antonio Alatorre, pp. 226–36, 494–509. Bataillon refers to the courtiers of the emperor supporting militant religious and political reforms.

37. On Carvajal, see Secret, *Les kabbalistes*, p. 79, and Kottman, *Law and Apocalypse*, p. 32, n. 18.

Carlos V's interest in Renaissance occult thought. Agrippa, whom the Spanish humanist Juan Luis Vives called "the wonder of letters and literary men," is thought to have served the Hapsburgs between 1502 and 1507.[38] In 1529 he was made imperial archivist and historiographer, and a year later he wrote a history of Carlos V's coronation.[39] The young emperor is said to have protected Agrippa from his creditors and to have commuted a death sentence passed on him.[40] It was reported that Carlos's aunt, Catherine of Aragón, had wanted Agrippa to defend her in the royal divorce case. The Nettesheimer could have provided the appropriate Old Testament interpretations to counterbalance those of Giorgi in Henry VIII's favor.[41]

When we recall that Agrippa might have been exposed to Cabala while in Spain,[42] it is not difficult to realize that Renaissance occult materials were available to interested parties in sixteenth-century Spain. None less than royal family members cultivated their occult fascination. Carlos V kept certain "philosopher stones" in his possession, but Felipe II has been called the greatest protector of the occult arts in the Spanish royal house.[43] Among the volumes he acquired for the Escorial's San Lorenzo Library are some of the major Renaissance occult works that use Cabala.[44] Of particular interest is Camillo's *Theater of the World*, a work dedicated to Diego Hurtado de Mendoza, Spanish governor of Naples. King Felipe also had a copy of John Dee's *Monas hieroglyphica*. Dee had served as an astrologer to Felipe's wife, Mary Tudor, and had been closely associated with the Hapsburg court of Felipe's nephew, the Emperor Rudolf II. San Clemente, the king's ambassador to the imperial court, was a close associate of Dee and of Rudolf's whole circle of artists and writers, who were interested in Cabala as an aspect of late Renaissance pansophy.[45]

Felipe II's constant companion, with whom he shared ideas on the occult as well as on architecture, was Juan de Herrera, the architect of the Escorial. In addition to the vast resources of the king's library, Herrera also had at his disposal numerous Pythagorean, Neoplatonic, Lullist, Hermetic, and Cabalistic

---

38. Nauert, *Agrippa and the Crisis of Renaissance Thought*, p. 14, n. 14; p. 323.

39. Ibid., p. 105.

40. Paola Zambelli, "Magic and Radical Reformation in Agrippa of Nettesheim," p. 87.

41. Yates, *The Occult Philosophy*, p. 40.

42. See above, Chapter 1, "Agrippa" section.

43. Javier Ruiz, "Los alquimistas de Felipe II," p. 49.

44. René Taylor, "Architecture and Magic," p. 96.

45. Evans, *Rudolf II and His World*, pp. 222–23, et passim.

works—in effect, a library of the *prisca theologia*. René Taylor has
described the influence of such occult Renaissance sources on the
design of the Escorial.[46] Cabalistic elements are particularly evident in the frescoes of the San Lorenzo Library.

A collaborator on the subject matter of the frescoes was Benito
Arias Montano, whom Felipe II had appointed librarian of the
Escorial after the completion of his work on the Antwerp *Biblia
regia*.[47] Rekers has characterized the years Arias Montano spent in
the Escorial as the "most heretical of his life."[48] Since his Antwerp
days, Arias Montano had been involved in the secret society known
as the Family of Love. The Familists have been compared to Eras-
mists, Spanish mystics, and *alumbrados* for their interest in interiorized religion and their less-than-orthodox inclinations. Arias's
Familist associations also included ties to Christian Cabalists Guy
Le Fèvre de la Boderie and Guillaume Postel.[49] The Familists and
Cabalists shared an enthusiasm for irenism and Hebrew methods
of scriptural exegesis. It is in this light that one must consider the
relationship between Arias Montano and Luis de León. Friends
since their early days at Alcalá and Salamanca, the two Hebraists
had similar ideas on biblical interpretation and a special interest in
Canticles. In addition, Fray Luis's *De los nombres de Cristo* is
thought to show the influence of Arias's *De arcano sermone*.[50]

Benito Arias Montano, among others, was instrumental in making occult Renaissance texts available in Spain. He helped his Familist friend, the Antwerp printer Christophe Plantin, to open a
branch office in Salamanca. Through Plantin's bookshop, Fray
Luis de León and other humanist friends could acquire a wide range
of foreign books.[51] Arias himself had been one of the many sources
outside Spain who had purchased works for Felipe II. Juan de
Herrera also imported occult books, relying mainly on Venetian
dealers, and it is speculated that he was simultaneously in touch
with Venetian occultist academies.[52] François Secret concludes

46. See his "Architecture and Magic." For a more moderate view of Herrera's and
Felipe II's interest in the occult, see George Kubler, *Building the Escorial*, pp. 128–
30.
47. Information on Arias Montano was drawn from B. Rekers, *Benito Arias
Montano*.
48. Ibid., p. 109. Also on the question of Arias Montano's heterodoxy see J. A.
Jones, "Arias Montano and Pedro de Valencia."
49. Yates, *Astrea*, p. 192.
50. Rekers, *Benito Arias Montano*, pp. 123–26.
51. Ibid., p. 121.
52. Taylor, "Architecture and Magic," p. 84. Paul Grendler discusses the large
volume of books purchased from Venetian dealers in Spain in *The Roman Inquisition and the Venetian Press, 1540–1605*, p. 16. He also establishes that Jewish and

that the major works of Christian Cabalists were available in Spain and that Galatino's and Reuchlin's works were especially well known.[53] The fact that Pedro Ciruelo in a 1538 work condemned the use of Cabala by Christians in Spain, Italy, and Germany testifies to Spanish awareness of developments in post-1492 Christian Cabala.[54] Perhaps Ciruelo was not aware that his close associate on the Complutensian Bible, Alfonso de Zamora (d. 1531), had written a Christian apologetic work that relied heavily on Ramón Martín's *Pugio fidei*, the magnum opus of early Spanish Christian Cabala.[55] Secret notes that Ciruelo condemned Egidio da Viterbo's use of Cabala even before Egidio's Cabalistic works were published.[56] This fact supports the theory that the Augustinian general's views on Cabala were known through his relationship with Carlos V and/or through personal contacts in Spain such as those Egidio had with Augustinian houses. It also provides further evidence that Fray Luis may have gained some knowledge of Christian Cabala from his brothers within the Augustinian order.

Apparently another Spanish order, the Company of Jesus, was involved with Christian Cabala.[57] Felipe II's companion Juan Bautista de Villalpando (1552–1608) was a Jesuit familiar with Cabalistic chariot mysticism, exegesis of the name *Jesus*, and comments on Ezekiel's prophecy. Martín del Río (1551–1608) distinguished between good Cabala (of the philosophers and Church Fathers) and the bad (Jewish and magical). The Jesuits must have given the impression that they were well informed on Cabala since a 1602 work published in Leiden condemns them for being agents of Cabala and Felipe II.

There are numerous other references to Spaniards having been involved with Cabala. Bartolomeo de Valverde y Gandía is seen as perhaps one of the most important Cabalists of the century.[58] His *Ignis purgatoris* (1581) relies on the *Zohar* to prove the existence of Purgatory. Lodovico Istella, a Valencian Dominican, speaks of

---

Cabalistic books were printed and that a clandestine book trade existed despite the efforts of censors and Italian customs inspectors (pp. 142, 193–99).

53. "Les débuts du kabbalisme chrétien en Espagne et son histoire à la Renaissance," pp. 44–45.

54. See Secret's comments in his modern edition of Ciruelo's *De cabala Judeorum* in "Pedro Ciruelo: critique de la kabbale et son usage par les chrétiens." See also Pedro Ciruelo, *A Treatise Reproving All Superstition and Forms of Witchcraft*, ed. and trans. Eugene Maio and D'Orsay Pearson, pp. 203n, 209n.

55. See Federico Pérez Castro's Spanish edition of Alfonso de Zamora's *Sefer Hokmat Elohim* in *El manuscrito apologético de Alfonso de Zamora*.

56. "Pedro Ciruelo," pp. 52–53.

57. Secret, "Les jésuites et le kabbalisme chrétien à la Renaissance."

58. Secret, "Les débuts," pp. 45–47.

Reuchlin's *De Verbo* and of Galatino in his *Comentarios sobre Génesis y el Exodus* (1609).[59] Also citing Galatino, San Juan de los Ángeles presents an exegesis of the name *Jesus* based on the symbolic significance of the original Hebrew letters. In a Lyonnaise publication, Ludovico Alcázar (1554–1613) recalls Christian Cabalistic references to angels and to exegesis of the Tetragrammaton. Luis de Carvajal, in a 1545 work dedicated to Carlos V, approves of some aspects of Cabala and rejects others. Even writers who disapprove of Christian Cabala, such as Miguel de Medina, a delegate to Trent, and Francisco Valles, Felipe II's physician, demonstrate some knowledge of Cabala.

Some of the more interesting references to Cabala may be found among sixteenth-century belles lettres authors. León Hebreo, the eldest son of Jewish scholar-statesman Isaac Abravanel, was an exiled Spanish Jew who studied with members of Ficino's Platonic Academy.[60] His *Dialoghi d'amore* became one of the most influential Renaissance treatises on Neoplatonic love—especially in Spain.[61] In the dialogues, Hebreo includes Cabalistic references to the secret oral tradition of Adam, Moses, and their successors and to the Judaic Jubilee as signifying 50,000—a type of apocalyptic speculation that also interested Fray Luis. León Hebreo's syncretic treatment of Plato, seeing him and other ancient philosophers as Cabalists, explains why Johannes Pistorius includes the *Dialoghi* in his *Ars cabalistica* (Basel, 1587) along with the works of Reuchlin and Paolo Ricci.[62]

It is likely that neighboring Portugal shared many of the same Cabalistic legacies as Spain. A study by Helder Macedo reveals the Cabalistic significance of the work *Menina e Moça* (1554–1559) and the probable influence of Spanish Cabala on Portuguese Jews and conversos. Macedo also points out the continued use of Cabala in sixteenth- and seventeenth-century Portuguese writers.[63] In a 1586 work, Luiz de Sao Francisco employed Hebrew letters and the numerical equivalents of holy names.[64] Blas Viegas de Evora followed Giorgi in a 1614 commentary on Apocalypse.[65] In *Diálogo*

59. These varied references are from Secret, *Les kabbalistes*, pp. 220–25.

60. Roth, *The Jews*, pp. 128–36.

61. Hebreo's influence on Aldana, Cervantes, Montemayor, Lope, Tirso, Quevedo, and others is discussed in Otis H. Green's *Spain and the Western Tradition*, vols. 1–3.

62. Facsimile edition (Frankfurt: Minerva GMBH, 1970).

63. *Do significado oculto da "Menina e Moça."*

64. Secret, *Les kabbalistes*, p. 223.

65. Ibid., p. 224.

entre discipulo e mestre catequizante (1621), Joan Baptista de Este used Cabala to explain the mysteries of Christianity to converts.[66]

Spanish emblem books of the period show the possible influence of Cabalistic symbolism, as did other emblematic works of the period. Juan de Borja, son of the Jesuit San Francisco de Borja, dedicated his *Empresas morales* (1581) to Felipe II.[67] It is significant that the work was published in Prague while Borja was ambassador to Rudolf II. That emperor's court was most infatuated with Renaissance occult thought—including Cabala. The work of a later contemporary Spanish emblemist, Juan de Horozco y Covarubias, was quite similar to Borja's although Horozco more straightforwardly recognized the occult Hebrew connections of his emblems. In *Emblemas morales* (Segovia, 1591), he stated that the origins of the hieroglyphic-emblema art were not Egyptian but Hebrew. Horozco all but used the word *Cabala* as he noted that the Jews, "enseñados de Dios y de los Prophetas, supieron maravillosamente aprovecharse de las figuras y semejanças de que vemos estar llena la Sagrada Escritura" (instructed by God and the prophets, marvelously knew how to apply the images and similes with which the Holy Scripture is filled).[68]

It is possible that other literary works of the Spanish Golden Age contain attitudinal evidence of Cabala similar to the characteristic inclinations Blau found in English literature of the same period. One indication of Cabala's lasting influence may be seen in what Lynn Thorndike called "a somewhat more favorable attitude towards occult science than elsewhere in Western Europe, and less of an inclination to account for all magic as diabolical."[69] Since Cabala had been used by many Renaissance magicians to avoid diabolical influences in their occult activities, it is possible that the same attitude was applied to the magical arts in Spain. Nondiabolic or white magicians, such as those described by Yates in the work of Spenser and Shakespeare, are present in Spanish literature also. A prime example is Severo, the magician-seer who cures the madness of Albanio in Garcilaso de la Vega's second eclogue (11. 1059–85). As Audrey Lumsden-Kouvel has pointed out, Severo is a curiously dignified and transformed classical magician.[70] However, this

66. Helder, *Do significado oculto da "Menina e Moça,"* p. 129.

67. Sánchez Pérez, *La literatura emblemática española*, pp. 88–89; Evans, *Rudolf II and His World*, pp. 134, 171.

68. Sánchez Pérez, *La literatura emblemática española*, pp. 101–2. The translation is my own.

69. *A History of Magic and Experimental Science*, 7:323.

70. "Problems in Garcilaso's *Egloga II*." Georgina Sabat de Rivers also hints at

character is not so puzzling in light of contemporary interest in Cabala-blessed magic and Cabalistic exegesis, of which Garcilaso could have been aware. We should recall that the poet associated closely with the court of Carlos V,[71] a circle whose interest in Cabala has been discussed above.

White magic, such as that found in Garcilaso's eclogue, seems to be the sort found in the works of his Golden Age successors. Nondiabolic magic appears in varied Spanish works of the era,[72] but its presence has been most observed in *comedias*.[73] References to acceptable magic are found in the plays of Juan Ruiz de Alarcón,[74] and they are abundant in Lope de Vega's *comedias*.[75] In the novels of María de Zayas, the numerous signs of magic could be the sort protected by Cabala because they are said to occur "only temporarily and seemingly with divine dispensation."[76]

A curious case of magic in Golden Age writing is the mention in several fictional works of Don Enrique de Villena (1384–1434), a Castilian nobleman reputedly interested in varied occult sciences. He was renowned for his Latin scholarship, his impressive library with its large collection of occult works, and his amicable relationships with Jews and Muslims, from whom he supposedly learned the magical arts.[77] Of special interest was his apparent knowledge

Severo's special "scientific" character without mentioning its importance to Renaissance occult thought. See her "Sor Juana y su *Sueño*."

71. See Garcilaso's major biography by Hayward Keniston, *Life and Works of Garcilaso*.

72. The following studies discuss white magic in varied Spanish literary works that should be reexamined for evidence of Cabalistic influences: José Amador de los Ríos, "De las artes mágicas"; Marcelino Menéndez y Pelayo, *Historia de los heterodoxos*, in *Edición nacional de las obras completas*, vols. 37–38; Samuel Waxman, "Chapters on Magic in Spanish Literature"; Julio Caro Baroja, "La magia en Castilla durante los siglos XVI y XVII"; and Antonio Hurtado Torres, *La astrología en la literatura del Siglo de Oro, Índice bibliográfico*.

73. A general work revealing the variety of plays involved is by Mario Pavia, *Drama of the "Siglo de Oro."*

74. David Darst, "El discurso sobre la magia en *La cueva de Salamanca* de Ruiz de Alarcón"; Darst, "Teorías de la magia en Ruiz de Alarcón"; and A. Espantoso-Foley, *The Occult Art and Doctrines in the Theater of Alarcón*.

75. See two studies by Frederick de Armas: "The Hunter and the Twins: Astrological Imagery in *La estrella de Sevilla*," and "The Saturn Factor: Examples of Astrological Imagery in Lope de Vega's Works." A closer look at the use of angels in Lope's works might yield evidence of Christian Cabala. For some works involved, see Delfín Leocadio Garasa, "Ángeles y demonios en el teatro de Lope de Vega." The possible use of astrological magic in Calderón's *La vida es sueño* continues to stir critical interest. See De Armas, "El planeta más impío: Basilio's Role in *La vida es sueño*."

76. Kenneth Stackhouse, "Verisimilitude, Magic and the Supernatural in the *Novelas* of María de Zayas y Sotomayor," p. 68.

77. Emilio Cotarelo y Mori, *Don Enrique de Villena*, pp. 125–30, 151–75.

of Cabalistic prayers for healing.[78] Don Enrique's reputation for speculation and magical interests endured into the nineteenth century, but mention of him was most frequent in the Siglo de Oro. *Comedia* writers refer to him: Lope de Vega in *Porfiar hasta morir*, Ruiz de Alarcón in *La cueva de Salamanca*, and Francisco de Rojas Zorrilla in *Lo que quería ver el Marqués de Villena*.[79] Francisco de Quevedo seems rather sympathetic toward the Marqués de Villena in his satirical work *El sueño de la muerte* (1622).[80]

Cervantes possibly knew of the Cabalistic pursuits of Pico and the Florentine Academy. Secret points out that Cervantes was familiar with the heretical Doctor Eugenio Torralba (*Don Quixote*, 2.41), who claimed that he had been transported to Rome during the sack of 1527 by a benign spirit called Zequiel.[81] Torralba was also said to have known Maestro Alfonso, a renegade Jew in whom Secret finds similarities with Flavius Mithridates, Pico's famous master of Hebrew and Cabala.[82]

Further evidence of possible Cabalistic magic in *Don Quijote* is discussed by Dominique Aubier, who looks rather imaginatively at the relationship between the *Zohar* and Cervantes' *Quijote*. However, more positive evidence of Cabala in the *Quijote* is to be found in her discussion of the visions and fantasies of the old knight errant.[83] His experiences reflect the concerns of Cervantes' contemporaries for white magic in opposition to black magic.

In general, therefore, a favorable attitude toward white magic—of the sort protected by Cabala—appears to have persisted in Spain despite the threatening force of the Inquisition and despite the condemnations of Cabala and magic that were evident in some works of Spanish literature. There is strong evidence that interested parties were well-informed of the major Cabalistic works whether they concentrated on magical forces, on theosophic speculation, or on biblical exegesis. Garcilaso, Lope, Quevedo, and Cervantes seem to have been interested mainly in the magical side of Cabala, while León Hebreo preferred its more philosophical aspects. As we

78. Yitzhak Baer, *A History of the Jews in Christian Spain*, trans. Louis Schoffman, 2:476–77, n. 49.

79. Cotarelo y Mori, *Don Enrique de Villena*, pp. 134–36.

80. Francisco de Quevedo y Villegas, *Sueños y discursos*, ed. Felipe Maldonado, pp. 207–15. Waxman ("Chapters on Magic in Spanish Literature," p. 408) feels that the apparent sympathy Quevedo showed for the marqués in the "Sueño de la muerte" was abrogated by a letter he wrote seven years later to the Conde-Duque de Olivares.

81. *Les kabbalistes*, p. 27, and "Pedro Ciruelo," p. 75.

82. Amador de los Ríos, "De las artes mágicas," p. 334; Waxman, "Chapters on Magic in Spanish Literature"; and Secret, "Pedro Ciruelo," p. 75.

83. *Don Quichotte, prophète d'Israël*, especially pp. 200–201, 212.

examine closely the use of Christian Cabala by three important writers, we will see that Fray Luis de León used it in a philosophical and theological context, while for the Carmelite mystics, Santa Teresa and San Juan, Cabala was most valuable as a way to express symbolically the mystical experience.

sаnta tеrеsа dе jеsús:
chrіstіаn cаbаlіsm аnd mystіcаl symbоlіsm

I n 1589, Luis de León prepared for publication the manuscripts of the late Teresa Sánchez de Cepeda y Ahumada at the request of her confreres of the Discalced Carmelites.[1] Like her editor, the future Santa Teresa de Jesús was of converso stock and, like him, she revealed a knowledge of Cabala in her writings. But unlike the scholarly Augustinian, her use of Cabala cannot be attributed directly to Hebrew sources or the works of the great Renaissance Christian Cabalists. She was not schooled in the language of her Jewish forefathers, and her knowledge of Latin was quite superficial. It is possible that Santa Teresa learned something of Cabalistic imagery through her reading of earlier Spanish mystics such as Francisco de Osuna and Bernardino de Laredo, for whom Latin sources were more accessible. In addition, the saint's confessors and spiritual guides were able to read Cabalistic sources—Christian or Hebrew—and could have transmitted to her their understanding of Cabala's sacred links to Christian spirituality. It is not difficult to imagine the Jesuits Francisco de Borja and Baltasar Álvarez, the Dominicans Vicente Barrón and Pedro Ibáñez, or the often-mentioned Franciscan Pedro de Alcántara trying to help the saint further her spiritual development or understand and describe her mystical experiences with the assistance of Christian Cabala.

Another spiritual leader who may have been a source of Santa Teresa's Cabalistic imagery is San Juan de la Cruz. The two saints were in daily contact for five years (1572–1577), providing numerous occasions for their discussions of spiritual goals and experiences. Although Carmelite scholars do not agree entirely on the degree to which the two mystics shared their knowledge or to what extent their works are interdependent, some interrelationship of

1. Enrique Llamas Martínez, *Santa Teresa de Jesús y la Inquisición española*, pp. 287–89.

their mystical writing is recognized.[2] Some of the elements of Santa Teresa's Cabalistic imagery could be attributed to the friar since, as this study will show, his work displays Cabalistic imagery related to hers. That neither saint directly mentions Cabala by name is not surprising, given the climate of suspicion and Inquisitorial pressure surrounding any mystical writings after the heresy of the *alumbrados* was uncovered.[3] However, the Cabalistic elements found in the writings of the two Carmelites were never cited by the Inquisition for having heretical content.[4] Such apparent acceptability of the imagery could indicate that Cabalistic symbolism was considered orthodox—due, perhaps, to the use of Cabala in Spanish Christian apologetics from the twelfth century onward. It is also possible that Cabala—particularly by means of its vivid and captivating images—had been absorbed into the dominant culture through contact with Jews and conversos in Spanish communities.

Folk Traditions and Cabala

The converso heritage shared by Santa Teresa, San Juan, and Fray Luis was a popular tradition rich in varied folk elements—including Cabala. Beyond the substantial historical development of Cabala among Spain's philosophers and rabbis (as discussed in Chapter 1), Cabala was widely influential in the Sephardic population as a whole. In the thirteenth century, Cabalists for the first time sought to bring their ideas to a larger public.[5] Abulafia's more mystical approach to Judaism had great appeal among middle- and lower-class Jews. Moses of León's interpretations of the books of Ruth, Canticles, and Lamentations set off arguments while spreading knowledge of Cabala and assuring its acceptance. The popularity of the *Zohar* is evident from the vast amount of exegetical literature and the large number of manuals that were composed for it. In addition to the proliferation of exclusively Cabalistic texts, allusions to Cabalistic ideas were found in works not basically Cabalistic. Popular customs and faith were also affected by the spread of Cabala. Cabalistic doctrines such as those concerning the

    2. E. W. Trueman Dicken, "The Imagery of the Interior Castle and Its Implications," pp. 190–91, and *The Crucible of Love*, pp. 7, 19, 28.
    3. Llamas Martínez, *Santa Teresa*, pp. 14–24.
    4. See ibid., pp. 71–77 et passim; Enrique del Sagrado Corazón, "Santa Teresa de Jesús ante la Inquisición española" and "Santa Teresa de Jesús ante la Inquisición española: estudio introductivo."
    5. This summary of the popularization of Cabala in Spain was drawn from Gershom Scholem's *Kabbalah*, pp. 48, 58, 194–95, et passim; and José Millás Vallicrosa, "Algunas relaciones entre la doctrina luliana y la Cábala," pp. 251–52.

Messiah, the transmigration of souls, and demonology were absorbed at the level of folk beliefs. Most of the concepts were taken directly from the *Zohar*, but other Cabalistic sources were also influential. Sephardic Jews were accustomed to reciting the *Zohar* aloud, sometimes paying no attention to its content, simply repeating it for the wholesome effects on the soul.

In thirteenth-century Spain, the popularization of Cabala found practical expression in the struggle between rationalist philosophy and mysticism.[6] The conflict within Judaism was ancient, but Cabala instilled a new vigor in the defense of traditional piety. Cabalism was used to raise the level of religious and moral life of the Sephardim against threatening secularization and modernization. It was largely a popular struggle against the dominant courtier class and Maimonidean-influenced intellectuals. Roving Cabalistic scholars spread the pietistic trend to the Jewish masses, somewhat as the Franciscan preachers did among the Christian common folk of the same era.[7] The message of piety that the wandering Cabalists brought to the simple tradesmen, craftsmen, and poorer classes in the villages of Spain was enthusiastically accepted.[8] They captured the hearts of the common man in a way that the intellectuals had not been able to do. Vivid Cabalistic imagery may have been a key to the rapid assimilation of Cabala's message among the Jewish common folk, for the symbols associated with Cabalistic piety could be easily absorbed into the oral traditions—not only the popular oral traditions of the Jews but also those of their Christian and Moslem neighbors. It is quite feasible that Jewish Cabala interacted with elements of Christian and Sufi religious imagery at the popular level in the era.

The Cabalistic, pietistic revival extended its influence into the upper classes as well. By the mid-fifteenth century, many powerful Castilian Jews were among the chief proponents of Cabala.[9] One such figure was Hasdai Crescas, a Jewish civic leader sympathetic to popular religious customs. Crescas is also an example of an educated and prominent Jew with significant contacts in Christian society; he knew Don Enrique de Villena, the Christian nobleman discussed in Chapter 2 who studied humanistic and occult topics,

6. On the social aspects of this struggle, see Yitzhak Baer, *A History of the Jews in Christian Spain*, 1:188–89, 243–62; and Federico Pérez Castro, "España y los judíos españoles," pp. 292–94.

7. Baer has compared the Franciscans and Cabalists in greater detail; see *History of the Jews*, 1:267–71.

8. Ibid., 1:243–45.

9. Scholem, *Kabbalah*, p. 67; Georges Vajda, "La philosophie juive en Espagne," pp. 100–105; Baer, *History of the Jews*, 2:162, et passim.

which could easily include Cabalistic material. Through contacts with literate Christians or through interaction at the popular level, Jewish enthusiasm for Cabala could spread beyond the *aljamas*. Ultimately, within the Jewish communities, Cabalistic pietism touched all social classes and came to dominate the more rationalistic elements of Judaic theology. Even by conservative estimates, Cabala was widely considered to be the true Jewish theology in the general period from 1500 to 1800.[10]

It is clear that Cabala was a powerful force among Spanish Jews through the fifteenth century, and it is probable that elements of Cabala's imagery and pietistic message had been absorbed into the dominant culture. A study of the continuity of Cabalistic tradition among Jewish converts may help to indicate one of the ways in which Cabala became more accessible to Christian society. To what extent did the conversos maintain Cabalistic folk wisdom and even more esoteric knowledge of Cabala after the pogroms and conversions of 1391 and the subsequent establishment of the Inquisition? There is evidence that some converso poets of the *Cancionero de Baena* used Cabalistic terms referring to the *sefirot*.[11] The cases of two seventeenth-century conversos illustrate the persistence of Cabalistic tendencies nearly two centuries after the period of the Baena poets. Antonio Enríquez Gómez's *El siglo pitagórico y vida de Don Gregorio Guadañaa* (1644) describes the Cabala-like transmigrations of the main character's soul. There are indications that *La política angélica* (1647) by Enríquez Gómez also shows the influence of Cabala.[12] Another converso, Abraham Miguel Cardoso, was schooled in medicine and theology at Salamanca along with his brother Isaac Cardoso, the distinguished courtier-physician.[13] Both later reverted to Judaism in Italy, and Abraham became a radical Cabalist and promoter of the Cabalistic messiah Shabbatai Zev.

Evidence of continuing Cabalistic concerns among Portugal's converted Jews further supports the probability of persisting

10. Scholem, *Kabbalah*, p. 190.

11. On the *sefirot* as *grados* in the *Baena*, see Charles F. Fraker, *Studies on the "Cancionero de Baena,"* pp. 24–30. On the use of Hebrew names for God by Jewish converts, see Francisco Cantera Burgos, "El Cancionero de Baena: judíos y conversos en él."

12. See the comments of Constance Rose and Timothy Oelman in their forthcoming edition of Enríquez Gómez's *Loa sacramental de los siete planetas*. They find the Cabalistic aspect of the *Loa* (1659) to be a vestigial version of the 1647 work, *La política angélica*.

13. On Isaac, see Yosef Hayim Yerushalmi, *From Spanish Court to Italian Ghetto*. On Abraham, see Scholem, *Kaballah*, pp. 396–400.

Cabalistic elements being used by Spanish conversos.[14] The Portuguese convert Joan Baptista de Este used several Cabalistic sources in his seventeenth-century Christian apologetic work. The Inquisition awarded him with a pension for attempting to bring his former coreligionists to the Church. Another seventeenth-century treatise, *Tratado de çiençia cabala* by Francisco Manuel de Melo, has similar apologetic tones.

How were Cabalistic concepts maintained in converso households? Several studies have revealed documentary evidence of the preservation of Judaic religious and folk customs well past the seventeenth century.[15] Secrecy, the essential factor, was carefully guarded and even strengthened as the Inquisition became more powerful. Intermarriage of converso families was a common practice. Women became the chief guardians of the faith: they were the ones to initiate the children into their heritage, and they became the customary leaders of prayer groups and of the spiritual community in general. Prayers were taught by word of mouth, but many Jewish prayerbooks written in Romance were used.

Scholars disagree as to the precise character of the converso religious beliefs. For Nicolás López Martínez, "el converso . . . del fin del siglo quince . . . . ante todo y por encima de todo era judío."[16] Even Benzion Netanyahu, the harshest critic of studies on the Marranos, agrees that in all probability the conversos were neither all Jewish nor all Christian.[17] Julio Caro Baroja has classified the varied types of converso religious convictions, ranging from Jewish martyrs and apologists to totally orthodox Christians and radical persecutors of heterodox conversos.[18] He notes that although there is evidence of continued contact with practicing Jews inside and outside of Spain, many Sephardic converts developed a kind of syncretic religious belief and worship combining elements of both Christianity and Judaism.[19] They were known to possess prayer

14. Helder Macedo, *Do significado oculto da "Menina e Moça,"* pp. 129–30.

15. This summary was drawn from the following studies: Julio Caro Baroja, *Los judíos en la España moderna y contemporánea,* vol. 1, and *Inquisición, brujería, y criptojudaísmo*; Melquíades Andrés Martín, "Tradición conversa y alumbramiento"; Nicolás López Martínez, *Los judaizantes castellanos y la Inquisición en tiempo de Isabel la Católica*; Haim Beinart, "The Converso Community in Sixteenth and Seventeenth-Century Spain"; Antonio Domínguez Ortiz, *Los conversos de origen judío después de la Expulsión*; and Cecil Roth, *A History of the Marranos.*

16. *Los judaizantes castellanos,* p. 145.

17. *The Marranos of Spain,* pp. 206–7.

18. *Los judíos,* 1:274–98.

19. Ibid., 1:387–88. Further support for his view is found in Baer, *History of the Jews,* 2:424–26; in Domínguez Ortiz, *Los conversos,* p. 184; in Andrés Martín,

books that mixed Christian and Jewish terms so that, for example, *Adonai* and the Tetragrammaton were sometimes equated with Christ.[20] Other conversos sought spiritual asylum in Cabala, some aspects of which could be conveniently reconciled with their Catholicism.[21] Mysticism, including such Cabalistic elements as the *sefirot*, numerology, and the transmigration and preexistence of souls, were possible religious alternatives that could be clandestinely maintained.[22] Other Cabalistic interests, such as messianic beliefs, were known to produce notorious reports of conversos having been visited by the prophet Elijah or the Messiah himself.[23]

From the time of the late-fourteenth-century conversions through the establishment of the Inquisition and on into the post-Expulsion era, intense religious and familial pressures produced varying degrees of compliance with Christianity and Judaism. It is not difficult to understand that religious ties differed between individuals of the same family and even between the outward expression and inward religious convictions of the same individual.[24] The cases of four of Santa Teresa's famous contemporaries illustrate the problems and pressures of religious and general acculturation of the converso. Evidence shows that Fernando de Rojas (1476?–1541) was reared in a converso community that suffered the difficulties of assimilation into Christian culture.[25] His father must have found the pressures particularly trying, for he is thought to have been executed for Judaizing. Rojas's father-in-law was twice arrested by the Inquisition for adhering to Judaic customs in his diet and prayer. The humanist Juan Luis Vives (1492–1540) was said to have witnessed as a child Judaizing rituals of the sort that eventually brought his own father to the Inquisition's stake.[26] A statement by Benito Arias Montano points out the persistent Judaic religious and folk customs in otherwise totally orthodox conversos.

"Tradición conversa y alumbramiento," p. 283; and in Roth, *History of the Marranos*, p. 169.

20. López Martínez, *Los judaizantes castellanos*, pp. 154–55; Roth, *History of the Marranos*, pp. 155–56.

21. Caro Baroja, *Los judíos*, 1:503.

22. López Martínez, *Los judaizantes castellanos*, p. 149; Caro Baroja, *Los judíos*, 1:503.

23. López Martínez, *Los judaizantes castellanos*, pp. 157–59; Baer, *History of the Jews*, 2:308, 350, 356–58, et passim.

24. Beinart, "The Converso Community," pp. 464–71.

25. See Stephen Gilman, *The Spain of Fernando de Rojas*, especially pp. 45, 72–79, 113–58, and 207–12.

26. Caro Baroja, *Los judíos*, 1:394, n. 43, relies on José Amador de los Ríos, Américo Castro, and Armando Cotarelo Valledor.

He wrote that he could not eat pork without feeling physically ill.[27] A similar cleaving to dietary customs also kept the mystic Juan de Ávila from becoming a Jesuit despite his long observance of the society's rules.[28] The Society of Jesus had followed other religious orders in establishing purity of blood standards to restrict converso membership. The late-fifteenth-century cases of widespread Judaizing and unorthodox Christianity in Hieronymite monasteries were probably not unique, and they served as catalysts for the extension of racial purity codes in other orders.[29] A curious case of Jewish customs of identity persisting into the nineteenth century is that of the Chuetas—the Catholic-Jews of Mallorca.[30] Although, admittedly, the conditions on the island may have differed from those on the peninsula, the tenacious Jewish identity of the Chuetas supports the view that Judaic traditions could have persisted among the conversos in Golden Age Spain.

We must now consider to what extent another famous religious of the Renaissance, Santa Teresa de Jesús, was cognizant of her Judaic heritage. That she was of converso descent on her paternal side is now generally recognized.[31] Her parents were from two communities that were formerly very Jewish and, after the Expulsion, converso strongholds: Toledo and Ávila.[32] In communities so densely populated by conversos, their full assimilation into the Christian mainstream was sluggish. Converso families continued to intermarry and to live in the formerly Jewish neighborhoods. They remained in professions previously dominated by Jews: artisan, tradesman, merchant, and physician. After conversion, the fields of tax-collecting and the clergy opened new vocational opportunities to many. Santa Teresa's progenitors were mainly artisans. Her paternal grandfather, Juan Sánchez de Toledo, was a

27. Albert Sicroff, "Clandestine Judaism in the Hieronymite Monastery of Nuestra Señora de Guadalupe."

28. Sicroff, *Les controverses des statuts de "Pureté de sang" en Espagne du XVe au XVIIe siècle*, p. 276, n. 48, and "Clandestine Judaism," p. 91, n. 8.

29. Beinart, "The Judaizing Movement in the Order of San Jerónimo in Castile"; Sicroff, *Les controverses* and "Clandestine Judaism."

30. On the persistence of their Jewish identity, see Baruch Braunstein, *The Chuetas of Majorca: Conversos and the Inquisition of Majorca*; and Kenneth Moore, *Those of the Street: The Catholic-Jews of Mallorca*.

31. José Gómez-Menor Fuentes, *El linaje familiar de Santa Teresa y de San Juan de la Cruz*; Narciso Alonso Cortés, "Pleitos de los Cepeda"; Homero Serís, "Nueva genealogía de Santa Teresa"; Américo Castro, *La realidad histórica de España*, p. 539; Francisco Cantera Burgos, "¿Santa Teresa de Jesús de ascendencia judía?"

32. Material on Toledo and Ávila as well as other converso communities is taken from Baer, *History of the Jews*; Caro Baroja, *Los judíos*, vol. 1; Domínguez Ortiz, *Los conversos*, pp. 145–51; and López Martínez, *Los judaizantes castellanos*, p. 112.

tax-collector and silk merchant who was reconciled by the Inquisition for Judaizing in 1485.[33] His brother Sancho was to have been prosecuted also before his death. The Carmelite founder had another great-uncle, Don Nuño Álvarez de Cepeda, who was considered to be a "típico representante del alto clérigo de origen converso" (typical representative of the prominent clergyman of converso origin).[34] Unfortunately, the sincerity of his Christianity became suspect, and when the Inquisition seized his goods in 1482, he found it necessary to seek refuge in Rome, where he died in 1491. Yet another uncle of the saint, Pedro de Cepeda, was condemned to life imprisonment by the Holy Office in 1530 when Teresa was fifteen.[35]

Although the founding mother of the Carmelites must have been aware of her Jewish descent and of the suspected Judaizing of her family members, she always avoided referring to her converso lineage. A separate question remains as to what extent she knew of Judaic and Cabalistic beliefs or customs. The studies cited herein testify to the persistence of such activities in seemingly Christian households well into the eighteenth century. Given the evidence of her own family's Judaizing, it is likely that she was familiar with some elements of Judaism and Cabala. The sincerity of her own Christianity is not in doubt, but the presence of Cabalistic imagery in her work points to the conclusion that she may have learned of Cabalistic elements from family and community members. Santa Teresa may never have realized that the concepts she absorbed were in fact Jewish or even Cabalistic; such is the character of material learned at the folk level. Cabala was an integral part of the popular culture and folk customs to which Teresa de Jesús was heir, as a descendant of conversos and as a member of Spanish society. We must recall that the popularity of Cabala made it volatile material that could have entered the dominant culture through contact between Christians and Jews at the folk level. In addition, Cabalistic elements could continue to be absorbed through the influence of conversos who maintained varied Judaic traditions. For those individuals, families, and communities who had to pass through the nebulous period of identity change that characterized the conversos' condition, Cabalistic imagery could serve as one more bridge between the old ways and the new. The blending of familiar Judaic—and perhaps Moslem—mystical imagery could help strengthen the awareness of oneself as a Christian. Such an approach would

33. Gómez-Menor Fuentes, *El linaje familiar*, pp. 30–33.
34. Ibid., pp. 25–29.
35. Ibid., p. 34.

benefit not only New Christians but also those of Old Christian stock for whom the religious imagery would have an appeal. In Santa Teresa's work, Cabalistic imagery is more than just a vestige of her ancestors' faith; it blends with and vitalizes her sincere Christian faith. Aided by Cabalistic symbolism, Santa Teresa's writings express with new intensity the Christian mystical experience.

Cabalistic Symbolism and the Structure of the *Moradas*

Any reader of Santa Teresa's works is struck by the seemingly unsystematic structure, the spontaneity of transitions, and the unpredictable transformation of imagery. In her rambling writing, the saint laid a maze of paths to spiritual development, which scholars continue to define, and a series of metaphors whose origin and interrelationship they attempt to explain. Their conclusion that her work is not original, but a synthesis of her sources and her natural élan, has left unsatisfactorily answered questions. Are there sources of her imagery other than those usually named? What is the relationship between the images? One relatively unexplored source of Santa Teresa's imagery is Cabala, and the richest display of that symbolism is to be found in her masterpiece *Moradas del castillo interior* (*Mansions of the Interior Castle*).[36] The *Zohar* in particular contains images strikingly similar to Santa Teresa's concepts of the Lord's palaces, the interior mansions, the palace of diamond, the silkworm, the mirror, and the nut or palm. The manner in which she transforms and interweaves these images is like that of Zoharic stylistics, in which mixing metaphors and interrelating simultaneous symbol systems is considered an art.[37]

The centerpiece of the imagery in Santa Teresa's *Moradas del castillo interior* is the concept of an interior castle of seven mansions or palaces. Several scholars have attempted to discover the probable origin of the seven-palace image, but few have offered a

36. The possible relationship of the *Zohar* to Santa Teresa's work has been briefly mentioned, but no specific textual comparison has been made. See Ariel Bension, *The "Zohar" in Moslem and Christian Spain*, pp. 28, 32, 37, 74; and Karl Kottman, *Law and Apocalypse*, p. 33. The title *Moradas del castillo interior* is the complete one as described by Efrén de la Madre de Dios and Otger Steggink in *Santa Teresa de Jesús: obras completas*, 6th ed. (Madrid: Biblioteca de Autores Cristianos, 1979). All further references to the works of the saint will be from this edition. The following abbreviations will be used for her writings: M, *Moradas*; V, *Vida*; and C, *Camino de perfección*. In general, the English translations of Santa Teresa's works were drawn from E. Allison Peers's *The Complete Works of Saint Teresa of Jesus*, 2 vols. (New York: Sheed & Ward, 1946).

37. David Blumenthal, *Understanding Jewish Mysticism*, 1:115.

plausible explanation that could account for all aspects of the symbol.[38] Some believe that the castle symbol is the legacy of medieval warfare and the chivalric tradition that had influenced Ramón Lull, Francisco de Osuna, Bernardino de Laredo, and other direct or indirect sources used by Teresa.[39] But none of these authors suggested as sources of the castle images refers to the all-important concept of the castle's seven mansions. In addition, the castle as a symbol of defensive warfare is minimal in Teresian works, and especially so in the *Moradas*.[40] Although Teresa admits to having been fond of novels of chivalry as a girl,[41] her knowledge of the texts does not explain the particular arrangement she chooses for the castle of the *Moradas*.

Other scholars have searched for contemporary architectural examples whose structures Santa Teresa might have regarded as models for her castle imagery. Robert Ricard thinks that the fortified walls of Ávila may have contributed to the image, but he recognizes that the seven-part element is missing from the medieval structure's design.[42] Dicken believes that San Juan de la Cruz may have described the structure of the Mota castle in Medina del Campo to Santa Teresa.[43] Neither of the supposed architectural prototypes is an exact match to the Carmelite mother's image. More importantly, the presence of an architectural model alone is not related to the concepts of the dwelling place of the Lord and the

38. For a survey of possible sources for Santa Teresa's castle imagery see Francisco Márquez Villanueva, "El símil del Castillo interior: sentido y génesis." A fine survey of the spiritual use of castle imagery is available in a new work by Luce López Baralt (see note 67 below). Other than Cabala, the literary tradition that may offer the most possibilities for discovering the source of the saint's castle imagery and related symbols in the *Moradas* is Sufism. See the seminal study by Miguel Asín Palacios in the series "Sadilies y alumbrados" in *Al-Andalus* 9 (1944) to 16 (1951). A recent and much closer comparison of Santa Teresa's imagery to Sufi traditions can be found in these fine studies by Luce López Baralt: "Simbología mística musulmana en San Juan de la Cruz y Santa Teresa de Jesús"; "De Nuri de Bagdad a Santa Teresa de Jesús"; and "Santa Teresa de Jesús y el Oriente."

39. Major studies of the chivalric tradition in Santa Teresa have been developed by Sister Miriam Thérèse Olabarrieta, *The Influence of Ramón Lull on the Style of Early Spanish Mystics and Santa Teresa*; by Fray Luis Urbano, *Las analogías predilectas de Santa Teresa de Jesús*; and by Gaston Etchegoyen, *L'amour divin; essai sur les sources de Sainte Thérèse*.

40. The reader can efficiently compare the uses of castle imagery in Santa Teresa's various works with the assistance of Fray Luis de San José's *Concordancias de las obras y escritos de Santa Teresa de Jesús*, pp. 251–52.

41. She is said to have written a book on chivalric themes as a young girl. See "Reseña biográfica" in the Efrón de la Madre de Dios and Steggink edition of her *Obras*, p. 2.

42. See his "Le symbolisme du *Château interior* chez Sainte Thérèse," and the updated version of that article in his *Études sur Sainte Thérèse*, pp. 21–38.

43. "The Imagery," pp. 201–9.

spiritual journey to the divine. In Cabala, however, there is just such a combination of both elements, as we will demonstrate in this study.

In order for scholars to explain Teresa's spiritual symbolism in a seven-part castle, they have had to imagine her combining an imperfect architectural prototype with varied spiritual motives. Among them are the general Judeo-Christian predilection for the number seven, Francisco de Osuna's idea of the human heart as a castle, and Bernardino de Laredo's interpretation of the soul as a walled holy city.[44] Other possible spiritual influences are Saint Augustine's admonition to seek the Lord in oneself and Christ's reported reference that "there are many mansions in the house of my Father" (John 14:2). For Santa Teresa to have combined all these factors—architectural as well as spiritual—for her conception of the seven-palaced castle would be plausible but more difficult than necessary. Mother Teresa did not have to depend on a chance combination of ingredients to produce the central image of the *Moradas* while a strikingly similar image was available. By means of popular Cabalistic traditions absorbed into the Spanish folk culture or through contacts with friends who were able to read Christian and Judaic Cabalistic texts, Santa Teresa could have learned of mystical tradition. The possible interrelationships of Cabalism and Sufism in Santa Teresa's *Moradas* will be discussed after examining the similarities between the Carmelite's mystical images and those of Cabala.

The first element of castle imagery that Cabala and Santa Teresa share is the course the aspiring mystic must take through seven chambers. As the Carmelite mother describes the *palacio*, she details the soul's spiritual trials and arduous journey through the *siete moradas* to the wondrous innermost chamber of the Lord. That inner chamber is "no una cosa arrinconada y limitada sino un mundo interior donde caben tantas y tan lindas moradas como havéis visto; y ansí es razón que sea pues dentro de esta alma hay morada para Dios" (not mean and insignificant but an interior world, wherein are the many and beauteous mansions that you have seen; and it is reasonable that this should be so, since within each soul there is a mansion for God; *M* 7.1.5). She adds that "primero se consuma el matrimonio espiritual, métela en su morada, que es la séptima . . . otro cielo [con] . . . otra luz" (before

<hr>

44. The apparent variety of sources that seem to converge in the *Moradas* is well summarized by Víctor García de la Concha, *El arte literario de Santa Teresa*, pp. 47–90; and Ricard, "Le symbolisme."

consummating the spiritual marriage, He brings the soul into this mansion of His which is the seventh . . . another heaven [with] . . . another light; *M* 7.1.3). Only the most pious can make the spiritual journey to the *séptima morada*: "No entran todos hasta su cámara" (They do not all get so far as to enter his chamber; *M* 3.1.6). They are the holy ones who "han vencido estos combates y con perserverancia entrado" (have overcome in these combats, and by dint of perseverance, entered; *M* 3.1.1). For those who finally reach the inner chambers of the King there are divine mysteries waiting. It is revealed that "es grande su hermosura y hay cosas tan delicadas que ver y que entender, que el entendimiento no es capaz para poder dar traza" (their beauty is great and there are such exquisite things to be seen and appreciated in them that the understanding is incapable of describing them; *M* 4.1.2).

In Cabala, as in the *Moradas*, there are seven mansions or palaces through which the aspirant must pass before learning the secrets of the inner chamber. The *Zohar* speaks of the prayers that raise one "into the seven Palaces, to wit, the Palaces of the King" (4.202a-b) and of the contrite souls who "enter the secret and hidden palace" (5.203a).[45] For the worthy there is "a secret entrusted to the keeping of the wise alone, and here is the substance thereof. . . . In the midst of a mighty rock, a most recondite firmament . . . there is set a Palace which is called the Palace of Love. This is the region wherein the treasures of the King are stored . . ." (3.97a). These Zoharic passages are later variations of the Merkavah opus *Pirqei Heikhalot* (*Work of the Palaces*), a Cabalistic interpretation of Ezekiel's ascent into the celestial palaces and of his heavenly vision (Ezekiel 1:26–27).[46] In the Merkavah, as in the *Moradas*, "YHVH, Lord of Israel, dwells in seven palaces, in the innermost room thereof."[47]

45. Unless otherwise indicated, all further references to the *Zohar* used in this study are from the edition of Harry Sperling and Maurice Simon (London: Soncino Press, 1949). Scholem attributes the *Zohar* to Moses of León; see *Major Trends in Jewish Mysticism*, pp. 156–204.

46. In addition to the *Pirqei Heikhalot*, there are also Cabalistic interpretations of Ezekiel's ascent by Akiba ben Joseph. See Scholem, *Major Trends*, pp. 78–79, and Warren Kenton, *The Way of Kabbalah*, p. 209. In a new study on rabbinical commentaries opposing Merkavah mysticism, David J. Halperin concludes that it does not "follow from this that non-rabbinic Jewish groups did not seek ecstatic experiences or claim to have attained them. We could not even exclude the possibility that certain rabbis secretly cultivated ecstatic technique without this being reflected in the rabbinic literature" (*The Merkabah in Rabbinic Literature*, p. 184). Halperin emphasizes that his study in no way discredits Gershom Scholem's model on Heikhalot mysticism.

47. Blumenthal, *Understanding Jewish Mysticism*, 1:62. His work includes an edition of the *Pirqei Heikhalot* that is cited in this study. In a recent brief study,

Like Santa Teresa, the Heikhalot mystic must struggle to enter each palace. The difficulty of the task is metaphorically represented by a series of fierce angel guardians of each palace's gates. "At the gates of each palace, there are eight guardians: four to the right and four to the left ... At the gate of the seventh palace, they stand angry and war-like, strong, harsh, fearful, terrifying, taller than mountains and sharper than peaks."[48] The Carmelite saint also describes the dreadful creatures, metaphors of impurity and temptation, which the soul must overcome before proceeding to other moradas. They are "sabandijas y bestias" (vermin and beasts; M 1.1.6), "culebras y víboras" (snakes and vipers; M 1.2.14), and "cosas emponzoñosas, unas lagartijillas" (poisonous creatures, some little lizards; M 5.1.5).

Other aspects of the castle imagery that Santa Teresa employs also resemble Cabalistic descriptions of heavenly palaces. She writes that the Lord's palace in heaven or in the soul is "de un diamante u muy claro cristal" (of a single diamond or of very clear crystal; M 1.1.1). This brings to mind her earlier comment that the palace was "de grandísimo precio, todo su edificio de oro y piedras preciosas" (very costly, all its structure of gold and precious stones; C 48.1). In Cabala, the heavenly palaces are also of precious stone, usually hard, diamondlike sapphire (from the Hebrew *sappir*, "radiance of God"). The identification of God with the celestial palaces is a development of the pre-Zoharic Merkavah tradition in which the throne—and by extension, the palaces—was the focus of mystic speculation.[49] The early Cabalistic mystics elaborated on Ezekiel's vision of the sapphire throne (Ezek. 1:26) to include all the heavenly chambers. Both Judaic and Cabalistic sources speak of sapphire as being diamondlike and white.[50]

Beyond the Heikhalot notion of the divine palaces as the stages through which one must pass in order to approach the Godhead, later Cabalistic works further identify the palace with the Divinity. The *Sefer Yezirah*[51] and the *Zohar* describe one of the three upper-most divine emanations, *Binah*, as a Palace. They also indicate how

---

"Saint Teresa of Avila and Heikhalot Mysticism," Deirdre Green has mentioned some of the similarities between Santa Teresa's *Moradas* and the Heikhalot account of the divine palaces.

48. Blumenthal, *Understanding Jewish Mysticism*, 1:62–63.

49. Scholem, *Major Trends*, pp. 43–57.

50. Ithamar Gruenwald, *Apocalyptic and Merkabah Mysticism*, p. 35, n. 21.

51. Knut Stenring has attributed the work to Akiba ben Joseph. See the English edition by Stenring, *The Book of Formation or Sepher Yetzirah* (London: William Rider & Son, 1923). See Scholem, *Kabbalah*, pp. 23–31, et passim; and *Major Trends*, p. 69, et passim.

Binah, the third *sefirah*, was called the divine Palace through which all the world was created and transformed into being from nothing. In this regard, it is important to remember that the highest *sefirot*—*Keter*, *Hokhmah*, and *Binah*—were identified with the Trinity by Christian Cabalists.[52] For Judaic and Christian Cabala alike, the lower seven *sefirot* were the less abstruse and more accessible of the divine emanations. *Binah*, the Palace, was the third of the most recondite emanations and the one through which the divine light would shine into the lower divisions.[53] Like the Cabalists, Santa Teresa also refers to the Divinity as the Palace. She writes that "es Dios como una morada u palacio muy grande y hermoso, y que este palacio—como digo—es el mesmo Dios" (God is like a very large and beautiful mansion or palace, and that this palace—as I say—is God Himself; M 6.10.4). Combining the concept of *moradas* with the Cabalistic idea of the Palace as a divine emanation, she writes, "que Su Majestad mesmo sea nuestra morada . . . pues digo que El es la morada y la podemos fabricar para meternos en ella" (that His Majesty Himself may be our mansion . . . I mean that He is the palace and we can construct it for ourselves and hide ourselves in it; M 5.2.5).

Santa Teresa's overall scheme for the *Moradas* depends on the assumption that not only does God reside in His heavenly palaces, but He seeks to dwell also in the spiritual palaces of men's souls. She asks the reader to "considerar nuestra alma como un castillo todo de un diamante u muy claro cristal, adonde hay muchos aposentos, ansí como en el cielo hay muchas moradas" (think of the soul as if it were a castle made of a single diamond or of very clear crystal in which there are many dwelling places, just as in heaven there are many mansions; M 1.1.1). But, we must recall that in the somewhat magical—perhaps "Zoharic"—symbol system the saint creates within the *Moradas*, there are sometimes subtle distinctions that can appear contradictory. Santa Teresa establishes that the soul is like a seven-chambered castle, but she clearly states that God Himself is also a chamber or palace. As related in the *Moradas*, the Carmelite mother carries her readers with her on a mystical journey through the seven divisions of the soul's castle to the innermost chamber where the Palace of the King/God is revealed. Santa Teresa's apparently mixed metaphors might be explained by comparing them with similar Cabalistic materials.

Two Jewish mystical traditions deal with the conception of Man

52. See, for example, Agostino Ricci's description of the upper *sefirot* as the Trinity in *De motu octavae sphaerae* as described in Chapter 1 above.
53. See also in this chapter the section "Light in the Seven Mansions."

having been made in the image of God and with the idea that Man and all Creation are a parallel lower world that complements the divine upper world. Santa Teresa uses similar terms in her attempts to describe the interior world of the soul as God's palace while continuing to speak of the heavenly world or the heavenly palace. In the same opening section of the *Moradas* in which she states that we can "considerar nuestra alma como un castillo . . . adonde hay muchos aposentos" (think of the soul as a castle . . . wherein there are many dwelling places; *M* 1.1.1), she also reminds us that God "nos crió a su imagen y semejanza" (created us in His image and likeness; *M* 1.1.2). Throughout the *Moradas* Santa Teresa refers to the interior castle in which God dwells, but she also continues to refer to His heavenly home. There is an exterior heaven or divine world as well as an interior one. We read that the soul is a *mundo interior* (an interior world; *M* 4.2.9, 6.9.10), and we also find that the soul is like another heaven for God. She writes that "como [Dios] la tiene en el cielo, deve tener en el alma una estancia adonde sólo Su Majestad mora y digamos, *otro cielo*" (just as [God] has a dwelling place in heaven, He needs to have one in the soul where His Majesty alone dwells, and let us call it another heaven; *M* 7.1.3). In addition to the heavenly world there is "este aposento de *cielo impíreo* que devemos tener en lo interior de nuestras almas" (this mansion of the empyrean heaven which we must have in the depths of our souls; *M* 6.4.8). The Carmelite mystic continues to blend the ideas of the interior and exterior palaces or heavens when she speaks of the mystic's journey. The soul simultaneously rises to the upper heavenly world as it struggles toward the interior heaven: "Dicen que el alma se entra *dentro de sí*, y otras veces que *sube sobre sí*" (It is said that the soul enters *within itself* and sometimes that it *rises above itself*; *M* 4.3.2).[54]

Santa Teresa's conception of parallel worlds or of interior and exterior heavens may have been influenced by Renaissance Neoplatonic ideas of macrocosm and microcosm.[55] However, her de-

54. The Biblioteca de Autores Cristianes edition of the *Obras completas* used for our study refers the reader to Francisco de Osuna's *Tercer abecedario*, tr. 9, c. 7. Osuna's concept of the soul that "se entra dentro de sí, y otras veces que sube sobre sí" could be examined for the possible Cabalistic significance of the phrase to his work as a whole.

55. Some Renaissance Christian Cabalists combined the medieval Pythagorean tradition with Hermeticism and Cabalism to produce a rich and complex view of macrocosmic and microcosmic relations. Giorgi, his French translator Guy Le Fèvre de la Boderie, and León Hebreo were particularly interested in the matter. See Yates, *Giordano*, p. 151; and George Perrigo Conger, *Theories of Macrocosms and Microcosms in the History of Philosophy*. León Hebreo also discusses universal harmony and the relationship of the macrocosm to the microcosm in his *Dialoghi d'amore*,

scriptions are similar to Cabalistic elements that may also have contributed to her scheme for the *Moradas*. As Scholem points out, the earliest work of Cabalistic literature, the *Sefer ha-Bahir*, "had spoken of the 'seven holy forms of God,' each corresponding to a part of the human body. From here it was only a short step to Adam Qadmon"[56] or to the Zoharic idea that the soul has been created out of the substance of the divine Throne or out of *Shekhinah*, the Divine Presence.[57] The Cabalistic accounts of the similarities shared by God and the Primordial Man, Adam Qadmon, are supported by the *Sefer Yezirah* and its description of the divine emanations of the *sefirot*.[58] Zoharic Cabalists considered that all Creation—the human world—was a reflection of the divine world and that everything that happened at the human level was a reverberation and a parallel of what occurred within the Divinity.[59] Human life as a mirror or parallel of the Divine is suggested by Cabalistic diagrams in which the sacred *sefirot* are superimposed over the figure of the Primordial Man (see Figure 1).

We have discussed the Heikhalot and *Zohar* notions of seven palaces or heavens as well as the descriptions of the divine attributes duplicated by Adam Qadmon that are found in the *Bahir*, *Yezirah*, and *Zohar*. Another Zoharic concept may also be shown to resemble Santa Teresa's description of the structure of the *Moradas* and her account of the parallel dwelling place for God: the heavenly palaces and the palace within the mystic's soul. For the Zoharic mystic the *sefirot* are the divine original of the Primordial Adam, the image in which Man was created. As the Spanish Cabalist Gikatilla wrote, "The human race has lost this nature, but if one were to purify himself, he would reconnect with the *sefirot* and become a vessel for them."[60] The similarities of *vessel* to *morada* and of *sefirot* to the seven *aposentos* of Santa Teresa's *castillo* is

---

dialogue 2. On the topic of the microcosm in Spanish literature, see Francisco Rico's *El pequeño mundo del hombre: varia fortuna de una idea en las letras españolas*.

56. *On the Kabbalah and Its Symbolism*, trans. Ralph Manheim, p. 104.

57. See Daniel Chanan Matt's edition of the *Zohar*, p. 219. Matt writes that in the Talmud, Shabbat 152b, "the souls of the righteous are said to be 'hidden beneath the Throne of Glory' after death . . . . The Zohar teaches that the soul has been created out of the substance of the Throne."

58. Scholem, *Kabbalah*, pp. 313–14; *On the Kabbalah*, pp. 103–4; and *Major Trends*, p. 215. See also Matt edition of *Zohar*, pp. 33–34.

59. The Cabalistic conception of parallel worlds or of Macroprosopus and Microprosopus is found in the Idra Rabba of the *Zohar*. See Dagobert D. Runes's English translation, *The Wisdom of the Kabbalah (As Represented by Chapters Taken from the Book "Zohar")*.

60. The translation from Gikatilla's *Sha'arei-Orah* is by Matt, from his edition of the *Zohar*, p. 34 and p. 201, n. 126. The italics are mine.

Figure 1. Adam Qadmon.

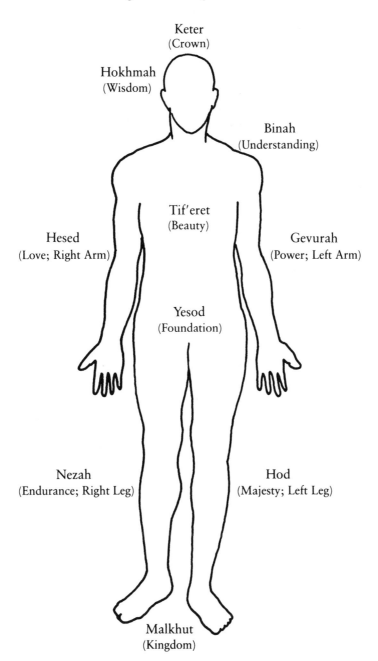

Keter
(Crown)

Hokhmah
(Wisdom)

Binah
(Understanding)

Tif'eret
(Beauty)

Hesed
(Love; Right Arm)

Gevurah
(Power; Left Arm)

Yesod
(Foundation)

Nezah
(Endurance; Right Leg)

Hod
(Majesty; Left Leg)

Malkhut
(Kingdom)

perceptible. As the mystic travels through the *sefirot*, each *sefirah* is encountered as an "opening within opening, level beyond level"—a Zoharic phrase which Daniel Matt explains as the process of revealing the *sefirot* "one by one as the mystic journeys within and beyond."[61] Again there is a discernible resemblance to Santa Teresa's mystical experience in the *Moradas*. In general, the *Zohar* is rarely explicit about the mystic's ascent or the glories of contemplating the Divinity in a unitive state. However, Matt has provided the following description of the Zoharic mystic's experience, which resembles Santa Teresa's account of her impression of the *moradas*, and the battles the soul must endure: "Once inside, the *sefirot* are no longer an abstract theological system; they become a map of consciousness. The mystic climbs and probes, discovering dimensions of being. Spiritual and psychological wholeness is achieved by meditating on the qualities of each *sefirot*, by imitating and integrating the attributes of God. The path is not easy . . . . From the Other Side, *demonic forces* threaten . . . ."[62] We are reminded of the Carmelite's "alma [que] entra dentro de sí, y . . . que sube sobre sí" (soul that enters within itself and . . . that rises above itself), struggling against demons while cultivating virtues (*M* 4.3.2, et passim).

A final comparison between the structure of the *Moradas* and that of the *sefirot* will illustrate a historically significant point of interaction between Judaic and Christian Cabala. For Santa Teresa the climax of the mystical journey toward the seventh *morada* is the vision of the sacred Trinity. She writes:

[El alma] metida en aquella morada por visión intelectual, por cierta manera de representación de la verdad, se le muestra la Santísima Trinidad, todas tres Personas, con una inflamación que primero viene a su espíritu a manera de una nube de grandísima claridad, y estas Personas distintas, y por una noticia admirable que se da a el alma, entiende con grandísima verdad ser todas tres Personas una sustancia y un poder y un saber y un solo Dios; . . . . Aquí se le comunican todas tres Personas y la hablan, y la dan a entender aquellas palabras que dice el Evangelio que dijo el Señor: que vernía El y el Padre y el Espíritu Santo a morar con el alma que le ama y guarda sus mandamientos. (*M* 7.1.7)

61. Ibid., p. 222. Also significant in the context of Saint Teresa's seven *moradas* are Sefirotic references to the number seven. Matt explains that the *sefirah Binah*, as the Divine Mother, "gives birth to the seven lower *sefirot*. Six of these flow into the seventh, *Shekhinah*, and manifest through her." In addition, the temple of Solomon, as it symbolizes *Binah*, contains seven years: the seven lower *sefirot*; cf. *Zohar* 2.31a (Matt edition, p. 227). On the septenary tradition and possible influences on Santa Teresa, see note 106 below.
62. Ibid., p. 37. The italics are mine.

([The soul] is brought into this Mansion by means of an intellectual vision, in which, by a representation of the truth in a particular way, the Most Holy Trinity reveals Itself, in all three Persons. First of all, the spirit becomes enkindled and is illumined, as it were, by a cloud of great brightness. It sees these three Persons individually, and yet, by a wonderful kind of knowledge which is given to it, the soul realizes that most certainly and truly all these three Persons are one Substance and one Power and one Knowledge and one God alone; . . . . Here all three Persons communicate Themselves to the soul and speak to the soul and explain to it those words which the Gospel attributes to the Lord—namely, that He and the Father and the Holy Spirit will come to dwell within the soul which loves Him and keeps His commandments.)

For the Jewish Cabalist, the Sefirotic equivalent of Santa Teresa's seventh *morada* would be the *sefirah* closest to the upper triad known as (1) *Keter*, the coeternal "no-thingness"; (2) *Hokhmah*, the beginning primordial point; and (3) *Binah*, the Womb or Palace that receives the seed from *Keter* and *Hokhmah* and then conceives the lower seven *sefirot*. The upper three *sefirot* are the Sefirotic Trinity, which produced the remaining seven divine emanations. The three are the head for which the lower seven are the body. The Zohar describes the relationship of the upper Sefirotic Trinity thus: "Three emerge from one; one stand in three; enters between two; two suckle one; one suckles many sides. Thus all is one."[63] Given such Zoharic references to a Sefirotic Trinity above the lower seven *sefirot*, it is not difficult to see the similarities to Santa Teresa's design of seven mansions culminated by a vision of the Three Divine Persons at the climax of the *Moradas*. It is easy to understand as well why Christian Cabalists also looked at the *sefirot* as seven sacred emanations crowned by the Trinity.[64]

Thus far in our examination of the Cabalistic aspects of the *Moradas*, we have demonstrated how the overall seven-part structure of the castle image resembles the seven-palace or seven-heaven concept of the Heikhalot. Moreover, we have shown that later Zoharic treatment of seven *sefirot* and the Sefirotic Trinity resembles Santa Teresa's scheme for the *Moradas*. There are indications that the prayers and meditations of Zoharic mystics could raise the soul through the seven palaces of the Heikhalot.[65] After rising

63. Ibid., p. 21. Matt notes that it was possible for the Jewish Cabalists to have rejected the Trinity while being influenced by its terminology. The ancient mythological image adopted by Christians was imitated by the author of the *Zohar*. In that work, the ten *sefirot* are sometimes grouped in three triads with the tenth *sefirah*, *Shekhinah*, including them all. See ibid., pp. 20–21.
64. See note 52 above.
65. Matt edition of *Zohar*, p. 38, and p. 202, n. 148.

through the lower palaces, the souls of the most devout might hope to proceed into the first seven *sefirot*—those seven emanations or divine attributes after which the individual soul is patterned. Beyond the seven lower *sefirot*, the vision of *Binah,* the Palace of the King, and of the most hidden divine secrets could be ecstatically anticipated although not completely revealed. We have seen how the Cabalistic concept of a journey through seven palaces and into the seven *sefirot* of the self or of the Divinity is similar to the Carmelite's struggle into the seven-chambered soul and upward through the seven palaces. In addition, we have found similarities in the comparisons of God and of the soul to a palace in Cabala and in the *Moradas.* The accumulation of similarities between the seven-part structure of the *Moradas* and equivalent aspects in Cabalistic mysticism provides stronger evidence for possible Cabalistic influences on Santa Teresa than for any known Christian source that might have influenced her.

We must consider, however, the relationship of possible Sufi influences on the castle imagery of the *Moradas.* The pioneering work of Miguel Asín Palacios has been recently expanded by studies on Santa Teresa and the Moslem mystics by Luce López Baralt.[66] She reports that the ninth-century Sufi Nuri of Baghdad described the adversities overcome and the grades of perfection he achieved as he traveled through seven concentric castles of his soul in a manner similar to Santa Teresa.[67] In López Baralt's study, the probable influence of the Judaic Heikhalot conception of seven palaces or heavens on the Sufis is recognized,[68] but the Arabist

66. I thank Professor López Baralt for so generously sharing with me the manuscript of chapter 4 from her new book, *Huellas del Islam en la literatura española: de Juan Ruiz a Juan Goytisolo,* before it became available in print. That chapter, entitled "El símbolo de los siete castillos concéntricos del alma en Santa Teresa y en el Islam," offers her most thorough discussion of the possible Sufi influences on the Carmelite's castle imagery. For works by Asín Palacios and other works by López Baralt on the topic, see note 38 above. J. A. Carpentier and Come Carpentier in a recent paper ("La experiencia y la escatología mística de Santa Teresa y sus paralelos en el Islam medieval de los sufís") point out similarities between medieval Sufi works and those of Santa Teresa. Unlike Asín Palacios and López Baralt, they do not draw conclusions about possible Sufi influences on Santa Teresa.

67. López Baralt, pp. 82–88.

68. Ibid., pp. 88–91. Jean Daniélou has described the pre-Islamic use of the concept of seven heavens or seven palaces in second-century Judaic thought. See *The Theology of Jewish Christianity,* ed. and trans. John Baker (vol. 1 of *A History of Early Christian Doctrine*), pp. 178–79. In this manner Daniélou supports Scholem's thesis that the origin of the idea of seven heavens or seven stages of the soul is pre-Gnostic. See Scholem, *Jewish Gnosticism, Merkabah Mysticism, and Talmudic Tradition,* and also *Major Trends,* p. 54, n. 51.

holds that Santa Teresa's conception of the castle-soul is closer to
the Sufi tradition than the Cabalistic. If, indeed, the early Heikhalot
elements were the only Cabalistic resemblances found in the *Moradas*, the Sufi case would appear to be a strong one. However, other
possible Cabalistic sources must be compared more closely to the
Sufi elements, and, moreover, the problems of access to Sufi mystical sources in sixteenth-century Spain must be considered.

First we must examine the term *castillo*. In the Sufi tradition the
soul is a fortified structure, a castle. For Santa Teresa it is often a
castillo but frequently it is a *palacio* in the Judaic manner, as our
study has shown. In addition, when Santa Teresa reaches the most
sacred *morada*, the seventh, she uses Hebraic-Cabalistic terminology: the experience in the final *morada* is compared to the holy
Judaic dwelling place—to Solomon's temple. The Carmelite writes
that "me parece es como en la edificación del templo de Salomón,
adonde no se havía de oír ningún ruido: ansí en este templo de Dios,
en esta morada suya, solo El y el alma se gozan con grandísimo
silencio" (I am reminded of the building of Solomon's temple,
where no noise could be heard; just so, in this temple of God, in this
Mansion of His, He and the soul alone have fruition of each other
in the deepest silence; *M* 7.3.11). With regard to the design of the
seven-part structure, the Sufis speak of their seven castles as being
concentric while both Santa Teresa and the Cabalists fluctuate in
their structural descriptions. When Teresa describes the castle's
structure at the beginning and at the conclusion of the *Moradas*, she
is clearly not outlining a precise concentric arrangement. At the
outset she invokes us, saying: "Pues consideremos que este castillo
tiene—como he dicho—muchas moradas, unas en lo alto, otras en
bajo, otras a los lados, y en el centro y mitad de todas éstas tiene la
más principal" (Let us imagine that this castle has—as I have said—
many mansions, some above, others below, others on the sides, and
in the center and midst of them all is the most important one; *M*
1.1.3). She concludes the work by reminding us, "de siete moradas,
en cada una de éstas hay muchas, en lo bajo y alto y a los lados" (of
seven mansions, in each one of these there are many below and
above and on the sides; *M* 7.4.22).

Our study has shown that, like Santa Teresa, Cabala refers to the
mystical journey from lower to upper palaces, but it also speaks of
going inward and beyond. The upward flight of the Cabalistic
mystic is especially evident in Heikhalot literature. We must remember that Santa Teresa also refers to the upward journey when
she writes of "los que *suben* a los aposentos" (those who *climb* to

the mansions; *M* 3.2.9, my italics), or when she says that they "no hayan miedo que *suban* a las moradas más juntas a el Rey" (should not be afraid *to climb* to the mansions most near to the King; *M* 3.2.4, my italics). The sense of upward motion is more striking when she writes of the anticipation of ecstasy as being a "vuelo de espíritu" (flight of the spirit; *M* 6.5.1, 7.3.12) or when she compares the soul's struggle to the *mariposica*'s (little butterfly's) attempts to fly upward (*M* 6.6.1–4).

While the early Heikhalot mystics spoke only of the upward journey, later Cabalists referred to the inward journey of contemplation of the seven *sefirot* of the soul. The latter Cabalistic development has more in common with the Sufi and the Carmelite sense of seven concentric structures of the soul. There is evidence that Zoharic Cabalists thought of Heikhalot palaces as being concentric. The seventh palace is called the most "hidden," the fourth palace is said to "enclose" all the others, and the second palace is described as being "enclosed" within the first.[69] Moreover, the early-sixteenth-century Cabalists of Safed sometimes drew diagrams of the *sefirot* in a concentric arrangement just as was done by the seventeenth-century Christian Cabalist Knorr von Rosenroth.[70] It is possible that the concentric concept of the *sefirot* had been developed by Spanish Cabalists on the Iberian peninsula before the Expulsion when the dynamism of Spanish Cabala nurtured the Lurianic Cabala of Safed.

Our study has shown that Zoharic Cabala, as opposed to early Heikhalot mysticism, expresses a sense of the personal identification of the soul with the seven *sefirot* in a manner similar to the Carmelite and the Sufi descriptions of the soul as seven dwelling places. In another aspect of the castle-palace imagery, Santa Teresa appears to be closer to the Cabalistic tradition. For her, as we have pointed out, "este palacio . . . es el mismo Dios" (this palace . . . is God Himself; *M* 6.10.4) and "El es la morada" (He is the mansion; *M* 5.2.5). The concept is similar to the Zoharic concept of the divine emanations as palaces and of the divine *sefirah Binah* as the Palace. At the same time, the Zohar speaks of the Divinity YHVH as being within the most inner Palace of the seven[71] just as Santa Teresa speaks of the "Rey *en* su palacio" (King *in* His palace; *M* 7.3.14). López Baralt has noted that for Nuri, "Dios también está visto como Rey que, rodeado de capitanes, habita en el centro del

    69. Ariel Bension, *The Zohar in Moslem and Christian Spain* (London: Routledge, 1932), pp. 198–209.
    70. See the edition cited of Scholem's *Kabbalah*, pp. 97 and 418.
    71. The italics are mine. See Blumenthal, *Understanding Jewish Mysticism*, 1:62.

alma" (God also is seen to be a King who, surrounded by captains, dwells in the center of the soul).[72] Clearly, there are similarities among the Carmelite, Cabalistic, and Sufi treatments of the imagery and spirituality associated with a sacred seven-part structure.

Since the Christian mystical tradition offers no examples as complete as the Cabalistic or Sufi models for the *Moradas*, the search for possible non-Christian sources of Santa Teresa's imagery becomes necessary. The question of sources is most problematic when attempting to find a connection between Santa Teresa and the Sufis.[73] Christian mystical works that mention Arabic texts differ significantly from Santa Teresa's *Moradas*, and extant works from the saint's *morisco* contemporaries do not reveal much similarity to earlier Sufi mystical traditions.

How then could Santa Teresa have learned of centuries-old Sufi mystical imagery? The remote possibility of some purely oral transmission or of some yet-unknown ascetic-mystic works exists.[74] However, the possibility of a Cabalistic source for Santa Teresa's imagery might be more likely. The persistence of Cabalistic practices among European Jews and Christians in the sixteenth and seventeenth centuries is well established. The indications that educated Spanish Christians used Cabala are becoming more evident through current investigations such as the present study. As we have shown, there is some likelihood that Cabala passed from Jewish to Christian society at the folk level long before the Expulsion and that it continued to interact with Christianity in the converso-influenced society of the fifteenth and sixteenth centuries.

Another speculative yet provocative possibility is that Zoharic Cabala was the vehicle by which elements of Sufi mysticism reached the society in which Santa Teresa was nurtured. Some possible influences of Sufism on Cabala have been indicated by recent studies,[75] and we have shown how ideas could be transferred from Moor to Jew to Christian and vice versa in Spain—especially during the period of cooperation between three cultures. The pos-

72. "El símbolo," p. 93.
73. Ibid., pp. 94–95.
74. On the question of oral transmission, it may be significant to remember that Ávila had in the fifteenth century a large number of Jews and Moslems. See Márquez Villanueva, "El símil del Castillo interior," pp. 497–98. See López Baralt, "El símbolo," p. 95, on the possibility of oral transmission and on the question of unknown ascetic-mystical works as Santa Teresa's source.
75. López Baralt, "El símbolo," pp. 88–93. In his edition of the *Zohar*, p. 259, Matt notes the Zoharic use of the Sufi phrase "Allah of the shining pearl." He also calls attention (p. 208) to the resemblance shared by the *Zohar*'s "dark flame" and the Sufi image of the "black light."

sibility for oral transmission at the popular level of ideas and images that could be easily adapted by any of the three religious groups cannot be dismissed.

The probability is strong that the *Moradas* represents a mingling of popular and more literate sources. There is in the *Moradas* an Hebraic—or perhaps a Semitic—sense of symbolic language. We see, for example, that her structure for the *Moradas* is not a clearly designed scheme, just as her symbol systems are not perfectly delineated. For the Carmelite, the soul is a garden, a tree, a butterfly, a castle, and so forth. In her own Zoharic-like wonderland the Carmelite writer floats between symbol systems, magically transforming them to suit her needs and to appeal to her readers.

Light in the Seven Mansions

Two particular images used by Teresa are closely related to her Cabalistic castle imagery: metaphors of light and mirror symbolism. Metaphors of light saturate most aspects of Cabalistic thought and of the *Zohar* in particular. That work is most concerned with God's light as the instrument of Creation, reaching out to touch all aspects of existence. *Ein Sof*, the Hidden God, is said to shine forth in the form of light from *Binah*, the Sefirotic Palace of the three upper *sefirot*, the sacred three whom the Christian Cabalists interpreted as the Trinity. From the upper three *sefirot* in the Palace, the Light passes to the lower seven *sefirot* or palaces.[76] This action in the Divine is also paralleled in the created world as God's light/power transcends all living creatures, giving them divine sustenance.

Santa Teresa also associates light with God's glory and power transmitted to man as wisdom and grace. In the *Moradas*, she speaks of the light that emanates from the seventh palace and out through the other six with decreasing intensity as the distance from the innermost chamber increases. She says, "Havéis de notar que en estas moradas primeras aun no llega casi nada la luz que sale del palacio donde está el Rey" (You must note that the light which comes from the palace occupied by the King hardly reaches these first mansions at all; M 1.2.14). Although light imagery is also common in Christian mysticism, Santa Teresa's reference to light shining from the most-central palace is unique in Christianity and suggests a Cabalistic influence. In another example of her light

76. Scholem, *Kabbalah*, pp. 90, 95–96.

symbolism, she uses a Christian tradition that is reinforced by Cabalistic, Gnostic, and Platonic concepts of divine lights. She writes, "también dice el Señor que es luz" (the Lord also says that He is light; *M* 6.7.6).

Closely related to light imagery in Cabala and in the *Moradas* is that of the mirror. Mirror symbolism is a common Judeo-Christian heritage, but there are peculiarities in the Carmelite founder's approach to the mirror concept that have a Cabalistic coloration. Most Christian mystics use the mirror as a symbol of the human soul that was made in the image of God.[77] Teresa employs a variation of that mirror concept that is not known in Christian mysticism.[78] She speaks of the degree of clarity in a mystic's mirror as a symbol of his soul's capacity to benefit from the divine word. In the *Moradas*, she compares a mirror covered by a cloth to the impure or unworthy soul (*M* 1.2.3). The case is stated more clearly in *Vida*: "estar un alma en pecado mortal es cubrirse este espejo de gran niebla" (when a soul is in mortal sin, it is a mirror covered by a thick fog; *V* 40.5). From the time of the Merkavah, Cabalistic mystics have spoken of similar variations on a mirror's or a soul's reflective power.[79] The *Zohar* states that "our teachers have laid down that Moses derived his prophetic vision from a bright mirror, whereas the other prophets derived their vision from a dull mirror" (3.82b), and speaks of the "luminous glass" of Moses as compared to the other prophets' vision, "a glass that did not illumine" (5.268b–269a). In another Zoharic reference, a mystic prophet is said to be capable at times of seeing with "a dim glass only" while on other occasions he sees with a "clear glass" (1.120a). In another Spanish Cabalistic work, the *Sha'arei Zedeq*, a Cabalist describes the advanced mystical stage when "that which is within will manifest

---

77. See *The Works of Bonaventure*, vol. 1, *Mystical Opuscula*, trans. José de Vinck, p. 28; Ruysbroeck's *Le miroir du salut éternel*, in *Oeuvres de Ruysbroeck l'admirable*, trans. the Benedictines of Saint-Paul de Wisques, 1:89, 129–30; Eckhart's sermons in *Meister Eckhart*, ed. James Clark, pp. 178, 183–84, 200; *The Sermons and Conferences of John Tauler*, trans. Walter Elliott, p. 145; and Francisco de Osuna, *Tercera parte del libro llamado tercer Abecedario espiritual*, in *Escritores místicos españoles*, 1.10.11, p. 433; 1.21.5, pp. 567–78.

78. Helmut Hatzfeld, *Estudios literarios sobre la mística española*, p. 60.

79. Louis Jacobs, ed., *Jewish Mystical Testimonies*, pp. 11, 33. Jacobs is citing an unspecified page from Ithamar Gruenwald. The Cabalistic use of the mirror to symbolize the soul's reflective power is thought to antedate Islam's use of the rusty mirror versus the clear mirror as discussed by R. C. Zaehner in *Mysticism, Sacred and Profane*, p. 194, and *Concordant Discord*, pp. 288–89. We should recall the possible influence of Cabala on Muslim mysticism. See Bension, *The "Zohar" in Moslem and Christian Spain*, pp. 40–41, on the similarities between pre-Zoharic or Zoharic mirror symbolism and that of Ibn Arabi.

itself without, and through the power of sheer imagination will take on the form of a polished mirror."[80]

Perhaps the use of mirror imagery that most divorces Santa Teresa from Christian mirror symbolism and allies her with the Cabalistic is her reference to God as an *espejo*. Of her mystical experience she writes, "Parecíame en todas las partes de mi alma le veía [al Señor] claro como en un espejo, y también este espejo . . . se esculpía todo en el mesmo Señor" (I seemed to see Him in every part of my soul as clearly as in a mirror, and this mirror . . . was wholly sculptured in the same Lord; *V* 40.5). In Cabala also, God's divine emanations, the *sefirot*, are sometimes referred to as a mirror.[81] *Tif'eret*, the *sefirah* of Beauty, is often called the luminous mirror of the other *sefirot*, and Shekhinah as the lowest *sefirah* is the "vision" and "mirror" that reflects all the *sefirot* for the gaze of the prophet/mystic.[82]

The references to mirrors in Spanish Cabalistic works suggest that some of Santa Teresa's Spanish Christian predecessors may have employed similar images in their mystic works. However, none of her Spanish mystic masters who used mirror symbolism display the Cabalistic sort of mirror found in her work. Her mystic master Francisco de Osuna writes of the soul as a clear or a clouded sky but not as a mirror.[83] Osuna and Alonso de Madrid speak of one's soul being polished like a shield/mirror to best receive light or grace.[84] However, their mirrors are either used as martial images or they are not as closely related to Santa Teresa's mirrors as hers are to Cabala. Just as with her castle imagery in the *Moradas*, the mirror symbol is much closer to Cabala than to any militaristic symbolism or chivalric legacy. This study has shown that the mirrors, the interior castle, and the seven mansions, rather than being loosely tied to the medieval tradition, have more in common with the symbolism and spiritual depth of Cabala.

The Silkworm, the Nut, and the Tree

Throughout the *Moradas*, the author's line of thought frequently hops to other sets of metaphors that may seem incongruous with the central conception of seven interconnected mansions. The abrupt jumps to other symbol systems lend an Alice-in-Wonder-

80. From an anonymous disciple of Abraham Abulafia, *Sha'erai Zedek*, trans. Scholem, in *The Secret Garden*, ed. David Meltzer, p. 145.
81. Scholem, *Kabbalah*, p. 100.
82. Kenton, *The Way of Kabbalah*, p. 53; Matt edition of *Zohar*, p. 229.
83. *Tercera parte del libro llamado Abecedario espiritual*, 10.2, p. 433.
84. Olabarrieta, *The Influence of Ramón Lull*, pp. 102–3.

land quality to the work that is quite Zoharic. One such group of metaphors in the *Moradas* deals with the silkworm. Virtually all uses of the term *gusano* (worm) in her work occur in the *Moradas* and apply to the same little *gusano de seda* (silkworm).[85] Nearly all the accompanying references to a *mariposa* (butterfly) apply to the transformed *gusano de seda* and are found in the *Moradas*. The silkworm images, then, appear to be especially closely related to the mystic experience as described in the *Moradas*. And, like the palace/castle imagery, they are Cabalistic metaphors. The Christian Cabalist Guy Le Fèvre de la Boderie, her younger contemporary, was also fond of the silkworm symbolism.[86] Fray Luis de Granada uses a *gusano de seda* image he may have adapted from the *Zohar*. Scholars do not agree that Santa Teresa knew all of this mystic predecessor's work,[87] but it is possible that the Cabalistic image came to her indirectly through Luis de Granada.[88]

In Cabala, the silkworm is initially used as a symbol of the inner workings of the Divinity, which are later paralleled in the universe as a whole. The book *Zohar* tells us that the brightness (*Zohar*) of divine Light caused the Primordial Point (of all Creation) to shine and that "this 'beginning' then extended, and made for itself a palace for its honour and glory. There is sowed a seed which was to generate for the benefit of the universe. . . . Again there was Zohar [brightness], in that it sowed a seed for its glory just as a silkworm encloses itself, as it were, in a palace of its own production which is both useful and beautiful" (1.15a). The creation of the palace of the *sefirot* was thought to be paralleled by the creation of man's earthly home. Similarly, the silkworm of the divine *sefirot* and that of the soul's *sefirot* enclose themselves and begin to grow, to unfold. Here again we see the macrocosm/microcosm parallel so prominent in Cabala, in Renaissance thought, and in Santa Teresa's analogy of the interior palace of the *Moradas*.

Like the author of the *Zohar*, Santa Teresa is fascinated by the

85. *V* 19.2 and *C* 3.9 give a late-medieval view of the worm as vile and foul like man's mortal condition. This is also seen in two instances in the *Moradas* (2.1.4, 1.1.3). On the worm as an element of medieval imagery of man's mortality, see J[ohan] Huizinga, *The Waning of the Middle Ages*, trans. F. Hopman, p. 141. See also Dante Alighieri, *Inferno*, 3.69.

86. See above, p. 32.

87. See García de la Concha on the problem, *El arte literario de Santa Teresa*, pp. 62–63. Louis Oeschlin, in *L'intuition mystique de Sainte Thérèse*, p. 116, feels that the saint may have been familiar with Luis de Granada's *Guía de pecadores*, but Oeschlin is not sure of the edition. Urbano, *Las analogías predilectas*, p. 101, does believe that Santa Teresa used the *gusano* image like Luis de Granada.

88. The use of the silkworm image may indicate a Cabalistic influence on Luis de Granada. In his case, we must also consider whether his sources were a Christian Cabalistic transformation of a Sufism's silkworm concept.

simple creature's remarkable handiwork and its ability to be transformed. She writes, "Ya havréis oído sus maravillas en como se cría la seda, que sólo El pudo hacer semejante invención . . . ; [los gusanos] con las boquillas van de si mesmos hilando la seda y hacen unos capuchillos muy apretados, adonde se encierran; y acaba este gusano, que es grande y feo, y sale del mesmo capucho una mariposica blanca muy graciosa" (You will have heard of the wonderful ways in which silk is made—a way which no one could invent but God . . . ; and [the silkworms] with their tiny mouths start spinning silk and making themselves very tight little cocoons, in which they enclose themselves. Then finally the worm, which is (was) large and ugly, comes out of the cocoon a beautiful white butterfly; M 5.2.2). For Santa Teresa, the *gusano* is like the human soul whose earthly labor—spiritual development—prepares the way (i.e., "sows the seed") for its eternal glory. Here we find a slight distinction between purely Judaic Cabala and Christian Cabala. For the latter, the silkworm symbol and mystical symbolism in general focus on the achievement of the individual's soul or of the Church. In Judaic Cabala, the individual's mystical ascent is often expressed as a part of the spiritual development of the Community of Israel. Thus we read in the *Zohar* that "Israel are called 'worm.' " Or again, as the silkworm, that precious creature which produces from itself a fine thread out of which is woven the costliest kingly raiment, leaves behind before it dies a seed out of which it comes to life as before; so Israel, although they seemingly die, always re-emerge and persist in the world as before" (2.177b–78a). If we substitute the Christian Church for the position of Israel as the silkworm, a more Christian Cabalistic version is achieved. That substitution is, of course, the sort of interpretation more scholarly Christian Cabalists were apt to make. (The experience of Luis de León and those who influenced him to substitute the Church for Israel in Cabalistic contexts will be discussed in Chapter 4.)

Santa Teresa does make another interesting use of the *gusano* image that more specifically suggests the Church as a whole—not just the individual soul—is a silkworm. The Carmelite mystic emphasizes the Zoharic "death" or metamorphosis of the creature. She writes that "crecido este gusano . . . comienza a labrar la seda y edificar la casa adonde ha de morir. Esta casa querría dar a entender aquí que es Cristo" (once the silkworm is grown . . . it starts to spin its silk and to build the house where it is to die. This house may be understood to mean Christ; M 5.2.4). Here the Judaic and Christian parallels are interesting. The *sefirah Binah* (Palace) is a silkworm's cocoon of its further glory, i.e., the emanation of the other *sefirot* and the creation of the universe with all its creatures reflecting and partaking of the Divine. Similarly the Christian soul finds its greatest glory in the Mystical Body of Christ—His Church—and in the spiritual development that, after death and "transformation," will yield for the soul a share of His eternal glory. The Teresian soul is freed from its material bonds and is transformed into a *mariposa*. Through the symbol of this beautiful yet delicate creature, Santa Teresa emphasizes that the mystic's soul must continue to struggle against sin and temptations. She explains that "no acaba esta mariposica de hallar asiento que dure" (the little butterfly can find no lasting repose; M 6.6.1). Eventually, however, the mystic soul like the *mariposa* achieves the long-desired union when "la mariposilla que hemos dicho, muere [en matrimonio espiritual], y con grandísimo gozo, porque su vida es ya Cristo" (the little butterfly to which we have referred dies [in spiritual marriage], and with the greatest joy because Christ is now its life; M 7.2.6).

In her Zoharic style, Santa Teresa sometimes alternates the term *mariposa* with *paloma* to refer to the struggling soul. Eventually, when the soul achieves divine union,[89] she joins the two images and praises "todas estas mercedes que ha hecho el Esposo a el alma para que la palomilla u mariposilla está satisfecha" (all these favors which the Bridegroom has granted the soul so that this little dove or little butterfly may be satisfied; M 6.11.1). Like Santa Teresa, the author of the *Zohar* also uses the silkworm/butterfly and the dove to refer to the same principle. While the Christian Cabalist may use them to describe the individual soul, for the Hebrew Cabalist the dove and the silkworm are Israel. The *Zohar*, in a Midrash on one of the Canticles (2.14), states that "the 'dove' here is the Community of Israel, which like a dove never forsakes her mate, the Holy One" (5.61a). A contemporary of Santa Teresa, Cardinal Egidio da Viterbo, also used the dove symbol in a Zoharic manner to refer to the Divine Presence, the *Shekhinah*.[90]

A variation of the seven-palace imagery in the *Moradas* is that of the nut or palm shrub. It is a symbol not found in any of Teresa's mystic masters but one known to Christian Cabalists like Ambrogio Fiandino, an Augustinian hermit monk and one-time bishop of Mantua.[91] The nut or palm shrub has a rough exterior and a series of layers similar to the structure of the seven-mansioned

---

89. Concerning the use of Cabalistic symbolism to describe the Christian mystical union, see Chapter 6 below.
90. Secret, "Le symbolisme de la kabbale chrétienne dans la *Scechina*," p. 144.
91. Secret, "Notes sur Paulus Ricius," p. 186, and *Les kabbalistes*, pp. 266–67.

palace. Santa Teresa asks the reader to consider the "pieza u palacio a donde está el rey, y considerad como un palmito,[92] que para
llegar a lo que es de comer tiene muchas coberturas, que todo lo
sabroso cercan" (chamber or palace where the King is, and consider it like a nut with many rough surrounding layers which must be
removed before the savory center part can be eaten; M 1.2.8). We
are reminded that "es Dios como una morada u palacio" (God is
like a mansion or palace) and that "este palacio—como digo—es el
mesmo Dios" (this palace—as I say—is God Himself; M 6.10.4).

In a very similar manner the *Zohar* holds that the sacred names
YHVH and *Elohim* are equated with the Palace of the *sefirah Binah*[93] and that the nut is the Holy Chariot, another aspect of the
Divine Presence or *Shekhinah* (3.15a–b). The fact that Elohim is a
plural ("Gods") further adds to the image of several palaces or
layers of the nut. The entire Zoharic nut or palm image is a Midrash
of the sixth Canticle (v. 2): "I went into the garden of nuts." The
Zohar interprets the verse, saying, "for, as the nut has a shell surrounding it and protecting the kernel inside, so it is with everything
sacred: the sacred principle occupies the interior, whilst the 'other
side' [coarse, evil] encircles it on the exterior" (4.233a–b). This is
strikingly similar to Santa Teresa's "muchas coberturas, que todo
lo sabroso cercan" (many layers that surround all the savory center). For her, the "coberturas" (layers, husk) of the palm/nut are
also like the evil "cosas esteriores . . . savandijas y bestias que están
en el cerco del castillo" (exterior things . . . vermin and beasts that
are in the center of the castle; M 1.1.6). In a like manner, the term
husk or *shell* (*qelipah*) is a symbol of evil or impurity in Cabala.[94]
Every aspect of existence has its less perfect exterior, from the husk
guarding the fruit, to the cranium surrounding the brain, to the
Tabernacle housing the *Shekhinah* (*Zohar* 3.69b, 108b, 140b–
41a). It is a concept found in creatures of the universe and in every
paired macrocosm and microcosm. The same is true in the palace of
the King and the palace of the soul as in the nut/palm of the celestial
world and that of the human soul. From the Zoharic point of view,
the seven-palace imagery and the nut/palm symbolism of the *Moradas* are one and the same. And that, indeed, is the manner in which
Santa Teresa treats them.

92. The *palmito* is a Castilian shrub with a nutlike structure, as noted by Santa
Teresa's editors Steggink and Madre de Dios in *Obras completas*, p. 369. A series of
layers surround the hidden core or kernel of the shrub.

93. See Figure 2.

94. Georges Vajda, *Recherches sur la philosophie de la kabbale dans la pensée
juive*, p. 189; Scholem, *Kabbalah*, pp. 138–39, et passim.

Figure 2
Cabalistic Correspondences

Sefirotic Number	Sefirotic Name	Zoharic Names	Divine Names	Biblical Figures
1	Keter (Crown)	Supreme Crown of God; Most Mysterious and Recondite King	Ehieh	
2	Hokhmah (Wisdom)	Point; Beginning; Primordial Idea of God	Asher; Asher Ehieh	
3	Binah (Understanding)	Palace; Womb; Mother	YHVH; Elohim	
4	Hesed (Love/Mercy)	Love; Greatness; Right Kindness; Right Hand	El Gadol	Abraham
5	Gevurah (Power)	Din; Judgement; Rigor; Punishment; Left Arm	Elohim	Isaac
6	Tif'eret (Beauty)	Rahamin (Compassion); Blessed Holy One; Heaven; Sun; Harmony; Central Column; Truth; Peace	Jehovah	
7	Nezah (Endurance)	Prophecy; Right Leg; Lasting Endurance	Zebaot	Moses
8	Hod (Majesty)	Prophecy; Left Leg	Shaddai	Aaron
9	Yesod (Foundation)	Zaddiq (Righteous One); Covenant; Phallus		Joseph
10	Malkhut (Kingdom of God)	Shekhinah (Presence); Keneset (Communion) of Israel; Earth; Moon; Justice; Queen; Daughter	Adonai	King David

Another image that the Carmelite mystic relates to the *castillo* symbolism in the *Moradas* is the tree of life. In her Zoharic treatment of the *castillo*, she established the palace as a symbol of the human soul, as a microcosm of the heavenly dwelling place of the Lord, and as a symbol of God Himself. Now she Cabalistically transforms the *castillo* symbolism, saying "este castillo . . . este árbol de la vida que está plantado en las mesmas aguas vivas de la vida, que es Dios" (this castle . . . this tree of life, planted in the living waters of life, namely, in God; *M* 1.2.1). This image of the tree of life in a life-giving water seems to recall the garden imagery of *Vida* and *Relaciones* in which the soul is equated with the *huerto/a* (garden) and God with the *hortolano celestial* (heavenly gardener). But those works, predecessors of the *Moradas*, contain no mention of any tree of life or stream of life. Some of Santa Teresa's mystic masters had mentioned a tree of life, perhaps relying on the biblical saying, "She is a tree of life to them that lay hold upon her" (Prov. 3:18).[95] Only Alonso de Orozco had spoken of the double symbol of the tree of life and the fountain of life in his *Verjel de oración* and *Monte de contemplación*. As we show in Chapter 4, Orozco the Blessed used Christian Cabalistic imagery that probably influenced Fray Luis. It is possible that Santa Teresa knew of Orozco's use of the Cabalistic tree-fountain image through his works or through a third party, but the image may represent an independent yet similar reliance on Cabalistic tradition in both Santa Teresa and Alonso de Orozco.

In Cabala, the divine emanations of the *sefirot* have a formalized structure that takes the shape of a tree growing downward from its roots in the first three *sefirot*: *Keter, Hokhmah,* and *Binah*.[96] More importantly for a comparison with Santa Teresa, the Cabalistic tree of life is a symbol of the life-giving powers of the divine emanation of Light, the *Tif'eret*. Indeed, all souls are said to be part of the tree and are thought to enter the world through it. The Merkavah and its apocalyptic tradition hold that the tree of life could be a place on which God rests, just as He does on His throne.[97] The *Zohar* states that "in the midst of the Garden stands the Tree of Life . . . . The fruit of the Tree gives life to all . . . . Within this Tree is a light [Tif'eret]" (3.2a). The Garden itself is another reference to divine powers since it is the celestial Garden of Eden, which is equated with the *Shekhinah*.[98]

Thus, like Santa Teresa, Cabala identifies the tree of life symbol with God. In addition, the close relationship of the saint's "árbol de la vida" (tree of life) image to the "aguas mesmas de la vida" (living

95. Ricard, "Quelques remarques sur les *Moradas* de Sainte Thérèse," p. 192.

96. Scholem, *Kabbalah*, p. 106. The same Scholem edition includes an illustration taken from the title page of Paolo Ricci's 1516 translation of Gikatilla's *Sh'arei Orah*. The woodcut pictures a man holding a tree with the ten *sefirot* (p. iii). In *Les kabbalistes* (figure 15), Secret presents an engraving of "L'arbre de la cabale." It is a rare remnant from *L'interprétation de l'arbre de la Cabale, enrichy de sa figure tirée des plus anciens auteurs hebreiux*, originally published in 1625. I can find no evidence that the Sefirotic tree was called the "Tree of Life" in the sixteenth century. Some twentieth-century students of the occult have used the phrase. See Gareth Knight, *A Practical Guide to Qabalistic Symbolism*; and Aleister Crowley, *Seven, Seven, Seven*.

97. Gruenwald, *Apocalyptic and Merkabah Mysticism*, pp. 50–51.

98. Scholem, *Kabbalah*, p. 112, and the *Zohar*, 3.60a-b.

waters of life) is also found in Cabala. The *Zohar* speaks of the tree
being within the House of the World, i.e., in the divine emanations
forming the world. The *Zohar* explains that "from this Tree the
house is watered" (2.172a–b). Here the tree and water connection
is made in the manner found in the *Moradas* but not in any of Santa
Teresa's mystic mentors. The *Zohar* further describes the sacred
identity of the life-giving water as the "ever-flowing celestial river
whence all the souls emerge" (2.197a–b). It explains that "Israel's
God is called 'fountain of living waters.' For the perennially flowing Stream waters all the Garden and replenishes every place"
(5.266a). Although none of the Carmelite's established sources
spoke of the divine waters in the same manner, Cardinal Egidio da
Viterbo did so. Like Santa Teresa, he had also been interested in the
Zoharic celestial stream. The Augustinian Cabalist equates the divine waters with the *Shekhinah*.[99]

In speaking of the Cabalistic sources of Santa Teresa's images of
the *gusano de seda* and the *árbol de la vida*, it is important to recall
the possibility of Sufi influences. The silkworm was a prominent
image in thirteenth-century Sufism, and the tree in the waters of life
was known in the work of the ninth-century Sufi mystic Nuri.[100]
The early influence of Sufis in Spain may have had some bearing on
the development and use of the silkworm and tree-of-life imagery in
the *Zohar*. Santa Teresa could have learned of the Zoharic-Sufi
symbols through popular culture. Her use of such varied metaphors for the soul indicates her desire to convey her mystical experience to her "hijas" (daughters) or "hermanas" (sisters) by whatever
symbolic devices may have been at her disposal.[101] She drew upon
the teachings of her confessors and mystic masters, but the significance of folk traditions and the influence of popular culture cannot
be denied. The Carmelite selected images that would explain her
mystical experience to those with whom she shared a common
heritage in the converso-influenced culture of her era. Therefore, in
a sense, Teresa de Jesús's Cabala-like metaphors take on a Christian apologetic function in her work, making her Christian mysticism more intelligible and attractive to those familiar with some
aspects of the Judaic legacy of converso society. The use of Cabala
may have served a similar function in the works of Fray Luis de
León and San Juan de la Cruz, as Chapters 4 and 6 indicate. The
two friars were better educated and thus, perhaps, more conscious
of their roles in Christian apologetics. But their works and those of

99. Cited in Secret, "Le symbolisme," p. 143.
100. See López Baralt, "Simbología mística," pp. 76–79.
101. For example, in the first Morada alone, the following references to her nuns
appear: 1.2; 1.4; 1.7; 1.9; 2.2; 2.5; 2.11; 2.15; 2.18.

Santa Teresa can all be seen as part of the apologetic tradition of Christian Cabala.

Sacred Names, Messianism, and the Occult

Thus far our study has concentrated on the elements of Cabalistic symbolism in Santa Teresa's writings—the *Moradas* in particular. Like other Christian Cabalists she employed Cabalistic imagery to enhance her work and to serve, perhaps, an apologetic purpose. Another area in which the saint's writings reflect the concerns of Christian Cabalists is the problem of heresy and Inquisitional accusation. The chief concerns were the danger of demonic influences in doctrine and the fine line of differentiation between religion and magic.[102] Two of the accusations of the Inquisition against Santa Teresa's work were that she was deceived by demons and that she espoused doctrines similar to those of Giovanni Pico della Mirandola.[103] It is possible that her spiritual advisors informed her of the Christian Cabala of Pico or other Italian Cabalists, although she would not have needed such sources. In Yitzhak Baer's view, the Cabala of Pico and other humanists interested in Judaic thought, "together with certain parts of the Cabala which had become common property, were fused into a single body of culture in *converso* Spain."[104] Sebastián Cirac Estopañán, in his study of Inquisitional processes on magic and witchcraft, points to "paganized humanist" sources and Judaic tradition as two major forces in Spanish magic of the era.[105] He also notes that Judaizing was a common accusation against a supposed necromancer. Among the examples of conjury included in his study are magical prayers or chants with Cabala-like use of divine names and a preference for the number seven.

In this regard, it is interesting to consider Santa Teresa's choice of the seven-mansion scheme for the *Moradas*. Not only was there a

---

102. Benjamin F. Kimpel in *The Symbols of Religious Faith*, pp. 172–83, has discussed the problem of religion and magic. See also Keith Thomas, *Religion and the Decline of Magic.*

103. Llamas Martínez, *Santa Teresa*, pp. 385, 436, 471.

104. *History of the Jews*, 2:72. Further evidence that Pico's occult works were known in Spain is found in a 1487 brief from Innocent VIII to the Catholic kings. The Pontiff informed the Spanish monarchs of Pico's errors and the dangers his ideas had presented to the faith. See Fidel Fita, "Pico de la Mirándola y la Inquisición española," p. 315.

105. Cirac Estopañán also designates the Arabic influence, residual ancient magic, North European pagan traditions, and natural science as influences on Spanish magic. See his *Los procesos de hechicerías en la Inquisición de Castilla la Nueva.*

Cabalistic model for the seven palaces, but there were Christian and traditional magical beliefs in the power of the number seven.[106] Christian Cabalistic contemporaries of Santa Teresa combined Zoroastrian, Pythagorean, and other ancient systems of thought on numbers with Judaic-Cabalistic and Christian numerology. Agrippa's *De occulta philosophia* is a combination of such varied sources on the values and powers of numbers. Perhaps it is significant that Agrippa the Christian Cabalist devoted more pages to the number seven than to any other and that he concluded by saying, "Lastly, this number [seven] is the most potent of all."[107]

A possible similarity between the Carmelite mother and the magical interests of her Christian Cabalistic contemporaries is her preoccupation with demons. Like Pico and Agrippa, she was concerned about demonic interference in her quest. Her goals were more purely spiritual than Pico's or Agrippa's, but she was nonetheless as concerned about the power of devils to create her mystical visions or to cause her to sin. Demonic powers were also a major concern of Inquisitors of the era for interiorized religion[108] and for magical practices.[109] Santa Teresa wrote that "las visiones imaginarias dicen que son adonde puede meterse el demonio más que en las intelectuales" (the imaginary visions are said to be where the devil interferes more frequently than in intellectual ones; *M* 6.9.1). She warned her Carmelite nuns about the demons' powers, saying, ". . . es mucho menester no nos descuidar para entender sus ardides y que no nos engañe, hecho ángel de luz" (. . . it is most important that we not cease to be watchful against the devil's wiles lest he deceive us in the guise of an angel of light; *M* 1.2.15). Teresa's Carmelite brother, San Juan de la Cruz, demonstrated similar concerns that his mystical experiences were affected by demons. He warned that "puede también el demonio causar estas visiones en el alma" (the devil also can cause these visions in the soul), and he spoke of those who had "pacto oculto con el demonio (porque muchos de estos por este oculto pacto obran estas cosas)" (a secret pact with the devil [and many of them do in fact perform these

---

106. A recent study by Raquel Sajón de Cuello, "La tradición esotérica del Septenario y las siete *Moradas*," has surveyed the septenary tradition from the time of Pythagoras with possible reference to Santa Teresa. Sajón mentions Cabalistic and other Hebrew uses of the number seven, but her focus is on patristic septenary sources. She concludes that the saint's confessors or her own readings taught her something of the traditional reverence for the number seven.

107. *Three Books of Occult Philosophy*, trans. J[ohn] F[rench], book 2, p. 202.

108. Llamas Martínez, *Santa Teresa*, p. 25.

109. Cirac Estopañán, *Los procesos de hechicerías*, p. 224.

works by such secret pacts]).[110] Agnes Moncy Gullón has studied both Carmelites' extensive references to demons, and she states that Santa Teresa, like San Juan de la Cruz, ultimately regarded the demons as divinely ordained functionaries in man's earthly trial,[111] a view of the devil found in the Gnostic tradition of Cabala[112] and Jewish Christianity in general.[113]

Another aspect of Santa Teresa's works should be compared to the writings of well-known Christian Cabalists: her use of divine names. The Carmelite founder was not educationally prepared to discuss the sacred numerical values of the names of God. And while she did not have an elaborate theory of divine names like Reuchlin or Luis de León, her application of Cabalistic symbolism constitutes a unified series of designations or attributes of God. It is an essential element of Christian Cabala used by Santa Teresa in her efforts to explain the ineffable mystical experience.

Almost all of the Teresian Cabalistic images discussed in this study relate to the inner workings of the Divinity, to His glory and greatness, and to His transcendence in His created world.[114] These images are like a Teresian vocabulary of Christian Cabalistic names of God. She equates Him with the King (the Sefirotic *Keter* or Crown) and with His Palace (*Binah*). The sacred Palace is of diamond or crystal (like *Sappir*/Divine Light), and it is also like a nut or palm (the *Shekhinah*). God is called a Mirror (like all the *sefirah*, especially *Tif'eret*). He is also the Tree (*Tif'eret*), the Water (God of Israel), and the Oriental Pearl (*Tif'eret*). He is the Primordial Point which, like the silkworm, created the divine emanation *Binah*/Palace. These names are symbols of the divine macrocosm. They are reflected in the microcosm, the imagery of the human soul partaking of the Divine. The soul of man is like a seven-chambered castle in which the Lord may dwell. The soul or the Church is also

110. *Subida del Monte Carmelo* in *Vida y obras de San Juan de la Cruz*, ed. Crisógono de Jesús et al., 2.24.7, p. 543; 3.31.5, p. 600. See also the friar's references to demons in *Llama de amor viva*, 3.63, p. 958; 3.64, p. 959.

111. "Santa Teresa y sus demonios," pp. 151, 161.

112. Scholem, *Kabbalah*, pp. 320–26, et passim.

113. Daniélou, *The Theology of Jewish Christianity*, pp. 189–92. The author also notes that most aspects of Christian demonology stem from Jewish apocalyptic roots (p. 187). In a paper given recently, Guzmán Álvarez writes that Santa Teresa's *demonios* have more in common with the Satan of the Old Testament than with medieval concepts of the devil as an adversary. See his "En el texto de *Las Moradas*," pp. 346–47.

114. Concerning God's transcendence, Santa Teresa shares another point in common with Cabala: both have been called pantheistic. Américo Castro denies that label for the saint in *Santa Teresa y otros ensayos*, pp. 45–46. Scholem denies that same accusation for Judaic thought in *Kabbalah*, pp. 144–52.

like the silkworm, spinning threads of hope for its future glory.

Nicole Pélisson has studied the use of divine names from the Bible and the Church Fathers in Santa Teresa's works.[115] Although she does not examine the names for their Cabalistic significance, her study reports the frequency with which the saint uses traditional biblical and Christian names for God. Apparently, Santa Teresa most commonly evokes the names of or references to God the Father with emphasis on His majesty and glory. The names and attributes she uses are largely Spanish equivalents of Hebraic terminology. In addition, when she does evoke names of Christ, they are appellations of His glory and justice. The emphasis on God's glory and Christ's joyful Resurrection bespeaks a rather Hebraic concern for God's covenant with His Chosen People and their victorious triumph through His Messiah. Santa Teresa, unlike many other Christian mystics, deemphasizes the Passion, seeing it as but a part of the glorious Resurrection and the subsequent Redemption of all. She seems to be expressing sympathy for the apocalyptic and millenarian enthusiasm of her contemporaries. The Carmelite mother may have been anticipating the Second Coming. Other Christians had used Cabalistic speculation for a similar purpose, as our study of Fray Luis's messianism will show in Chapters 4 and 5.

Admittedly, Santa Teresa's messianic concerns are veiled in Augustinian terms stressing a more spiritual and less material fulfillment of the ancient Judaic and Christian prophecies and eschatologies.[116] However, she has much in common with the messianic reformers of her era, and if her messianism or millenarianism is more covert, it should be remembered that many of her predecessors had suffered Inquisitional pressures that she sought to avoid. The Carmelite mother was a Spanish Church reformer in the tradition of Cardinal Ximénez de Cisneros, who sought to restore spiritual values to the monastic orders as part of broader reform goals. Marjorie Reeves summarizes Cardinal Cisneros's messianic interests as a dream "of *renovatio mundi* in which, after the final crusade led by Spain, there would be 'unum ovile et unus pastor.'"[117] Like his Cabalistic contemporaries, Cisneros was also receptive to the idea of a great reforming pope. The cardinal's views

115. See Pélisson's "Les noms divins dans l'oueuvre de Sainte Thérèse de Jésus."
116. See Jean Daniélou, *The Theology of Jewish Christianity*, pp. 377–85, on the Judeo-Christian apocalyptic traditions and their interrelationship.
117. Reeves's conclusions in *The Influence of Prophecy in the Later Middle Ages*, p. 446, are based on Marcel Bataillon. See Bataillon, *Erasmo y España*, trans. Antonio Alatorre, pp. 62–71, on Cisneros's messianic chaplain who had a large following of conversos and visions of church reform after the Second Coming.

were similar to those expressed by Egidio da Viterbo in his Cabalistically supported appeal to Carlos V for reform, the *Scechina* (1530).

Other possible messianic and millenarian influences on Santa Teresa stem from the Christian converso culture in which she was raised. López Martínez holds that a strong spirit of the messianic remained with the conversos.[118] The Spanish *alumbrados*, many of whom are thought to have been conversos,[119] were often accused of eschatological excesses.[120] José Nieto has studied Spanish Franciscan *alumbrados* who espoused "drastic and fantastic dreams of reform" and whose converso heritage offered special coloring to the general European interest in apocalyptic reformation of the Church in that era.[121] He points out that, despite their outlandish ideas, they were never accused of anything because they did not challenge the Church's doctrine or structure. Other Franciscans were more politically involved: in 1523, Francisco de Ocaña prophesied a great reforming mission for Carlos V which, after twelve years, was to have set a Spaniard on the chair of Saint Peter.[122] The Franciscan tendency toward messianic and apocalyptic concerns is well-known.[123] The degree to which Santa Teresa's Franciscan masters Laredo and Osuna partook of their order's predilection has not been studied, but the possibility of their eschatological interest is strong, given the tradition of the order and the intellectual climate of the period. In addition, Osuna was known to have been an early associate of those who were later called *alumbrados*,[124] and he is thought to have been of converso stock.[125]

Jean Daniélou has revealed the debt that Christian millenarianism owes to the symbolism of Jewish apocalyptic accounts and has demonstrated the close relationship of eschatology to mystical visions in Jewish Christianity.[126] The Merkavah tradition to which Cabalistic mysticism was heir is particularly rich in apocalyptic

118. *Los judaizantes castellanos*, pp. 157–59.

119. Antonio Márquez, *Los alumbrados*, pp. 86–89; Andrés Martín, "Tradición conversa y alumbramiento."

120. Márquez, *Los alumbrados*, p. 265.

121. "The Franciscan Alumbrados and the Prophetic-Apocalyptic Tradition," p. 15.

122. Reeves, *The Influence of Prophecy in the Later Middle Ages*, pp. 359, 447.

123. Several chapters of Reeves's book deal with the Franciscans' role in European apocalyptic movements. Another study on the same theme that discusses the Franciscans is Norman Cohn's *The Pursuit of the Millennium*.

124. Márquez, *Los alumbrados*, pp. 63–64.

125. Andrés Martín, *Los recogidos*, p. 111.

126. *The Theology of Jewish Christianity*, pp. 377–90.

meaning, as Ithamar Gruenwald has shown.[127] We should recall that Santa Teresa's conception of God's seven palaces or seven-chambered home is remarkably similar to the Merkavah view of God dwelling within the innermost of seven enclosed heavens.

Teresa de Ávila's life and work should be considered against the background of apocalyptic reform interests in Spain and in other Christian Cabalists. The emphasis on God's glory and on Christ's triumph in her writings, the Carmelite reforms she accomplished, and the enormous pietistic influence she had on the faithful are variations of the same themes espoused by other Christian Cabalists. Ricci, Reuchlin, Egidio, Seripando, and Luis de León were all concerned with spiritual and other reform, and they all used Cabala to support their points of view. Due to her lack of education and to the times in which she lived, Santa Teresa did not explicitly tie Cabala to millenarian prophecies as did some of her Christian Cabalistic predecessors like Egidio. But the apocalyptic concerns are implied in her reforms, her emphasis on the spiritual life, her choice of divine names, and her use of Cabalistic imagery to describe her mystical experience. As we have shown in this study, Teresa de Jesús used symbols remarkably similar to Cabala's imagery, and she reflected the superstitious preoccupations of Christian Cabalists of her era. Her work is a manifestation of Egidio da Viterbo's belief that the sacred names and letters were "not merely symbols of divine reality, but [that God] gave them power to penetrate the minds of the pious and humble to make themselves understood there."[128] It is the pious yet vivacious Teresa, the Christian Cabalist, who uses sacred names and symbols in hope of informing and inspiring others.

127. This is Gruenwald's thesis in *Apocalyptic and Merkabah Mysticism*, which frequently refers to the books of Enoch and their relationship to mysticism and Apocalypse. It is interesting to recall that the Carmelite Order's legendary founder was the prophet Enoch. See Gerald Brenan, *Saint John of the Cross*, p. 10.

128. O'Malley, *Giles of Viterbo*, p. 91.

4

fRay luis de león: christian
cabala in de los nombres de cristo

Seldom has the name Luis de León (1527–1591) been mentioned in a Cabalistic context. The friar has been considered to be the prime example of the humanistic spirit in Castilian poetry and prose.[1] His work as a biblical scholar and theologian has supported his reputation as a very Christian humanist.[2] Most attempts to define Fray Luis's thought have focused on its Hellenic character. Scholars such as Aubrey Bell have found an eclectic Aristotelianism in Fray Luis's work.[3] Marcelino Gutiérrez has found a Stoic quality in Fray Luis, while Marcelino Menéndez y Pelayo, Alain Guy, Dámaso Alonso, and others have emphasized the Neoplatonic and Pythagorean elements.[4] Although the recognition of Hellenistic facets of the friar's work is beneficial, it ignores other valid elements.

Most literary critics have also sustained George Ticknor's statement that Luis de León had a "Hebrew soul."[5] Only in recent years, however, have scholars gone beyond citing Luisian Old Testament references or mentioning vague similarities to rabbinical works to show the extent of Fray Luis's Hebraic traits. Studies by José Millás

1. Marcelino Menéndez y Pelayo, *Historia de las ideas estéticas en España*, vol. 3, and his article "Las obras latinas de Fray Luis de León"; James Fitzmaurice-Kelly, *Fray Luis de León*; Aubrey Bell, *Luis de León*; Alain Guy, *La pensée de Fray Luis de León*; Karl Vossler, *Fray Luis de León*, trans. Carlos Clavería; Dámaso Alonso, *Poesía española*; and Manuel Durán, *Luis de León*.
2. Most Luisian scholars emphasize this point of view. One of the most precise studies of Fray Luis's Christianity is Salvador Muñoz Iglesias's *Fray Luis de León, teólogo*. Two more general works on the subject are Robert Welsh's *Introduction to the Spiritual Doctrine of Fray Luis de León*; and Gustavo Vallejo's *Fray Luis de León: su ambiente, su doctrina espiritual, huellas de Santa Teresa*.
3. Bell, *Luis de León*, pp. 257–58 in particular; also Guillermo Quintana Fernández, "Las bases filosóficas de la teología de Fray Luis de León"; Ernst Robert Curtius, *European Literature and the Latin Middle Ages*, trans. Willard R. Trask.
4. Gutiérrez, *Fray Luis de León y la filosofía española del siglo XVI*; Guy, *La pensée*; Alonso, *Poesía española*.
5. *History of Spanish Literature*, vol. 2, pt. 1, p. 104.

Vallicrosa on Hebraic motifs in Fray Luis's poetry[6] and Alexander
Habib Arkin on rabbinical sources in the Luisian commentaries on
Canticles and Job[7] have helped to document the "Hebrew soul" of
Fray Luis. These studies, as well as the work of François Secret,
Jules Piccus, and Ariel Bension, have occasionally mentioned
Cabala with reference to Luis de León's work, but none have pursued the matter.[8] It is as though many scholars—with the possible
exception of Secret—have feared to explore an unorthodox side of
the converso Fray Luis and have therefore accepted his denial to the
Inquisition of ever having read rabbinical works.[9] Arkin in his
rabbinical study fails to mention that many of the Midrashim reflected in Fray Luis's *Cantares* and *Libro de Job* are also Cabalistic
sources.[10] Although Arkin's study is well documented, it should be
noted that a humanistic scholar with Luis de León's ability had only
to read *Christian* Cabalistic works to garner many of those same
Hebraic elements.

Karl Kottman is the first to study significantly Christian Cabala
as a major Luisian source. As we discussed in Chapter 1, Kottman

6. "Probable influencia de la poesía sagrada hebraico-española en la poesía de
Fray Luis de León."

7. "La influencia de la exégesis hebrea en los comentarios bíblicos de Fray Luis de
León"; Arkin later amplified his thesis in a monograph of the same title. We should
also recognize a pioneering work on the rabbinical sources by José Llamas, "Documental inédito de exégesis rabínica en antiguas universidades españolas."

8. Secret, *Les kabbalistes*, p. 137; Bension, *The "Zohar" in Moslem and Christian
Spain*; Piccus, "Fray Luis de León y la figura del tetragrámaton en *De los nombres de
Cristo*."

9. These writers take Fray Luis at his word despite their suspicions to the contrary:
David Gutiérrez, "Fray Luis de León y la exégesis rabínica"; and Mariano Revilla,
"Fray Luis de León y los estudios bíblicos en el siglo XVI." Fray Luis's great-
grandmother and his great aunt were reconciled by the Inquisition in 1512 after
having been condemned for practicing Jewish rites. This point was made public at
his Inquisitional hearings in 1572. He was also denounced for having translated the
Song of Songs into Castilian, using rabbinical interpretations of Scripture, question-
ing the authority of the Vulgate, believing (supposedly) in justification by faith
alone, and not having denounced heretical positions. The friar was incarcerated for
five years by the Inquisition. The testimonies of numerous distinguished colleagues
were instrumental in securing his release. See Bell, *Luis de León*, pp. 145–46; Luis
Alonso Getino, *Vida y procesos del maestro Fray Luis de León*; and Miguel de la
Pinta Llorente, *La Inquisición española y los problemas de la cultura y de la
intolerancia*.

10. Rabbinical sources frequently cited by Arkin in his studies of the *Exposición
del Cantar de los Cantares* and of the *Exposición del Libro de Job* include Rashi,
David Kimhi, and Ibn Ezra. In *Kabbalah* (pp. 155, 224, et passim), Scholem states
that the *Zohar* used the writings of these biblical commentators. In *A Short Survey
of the Literature of Rabbinical and Medieval Judaism*, pp. 227–28, W. O. E.
Oesterley and G. H. Box write that Cabala and the Midrashic works of Kimhi,
Rashi, and Ibn Ezra acted and reacted on each other. The two were seen as complementary forces in opposition to the excesses of Maimonidean exegesis.

finds Fray Luis's Cabalism most strongly linked to Paolo Ricci, a converso like the Augustinian friar. In relating Cabala to Aquinas's writings on law, Ricci held that Christians as well as Jews were bound to both natural law and the Ten Commandments. Ricci concluded that "the essence of Christian mysticism must include Cabala, since it, like the Decalog, is based on divine law, as must be all Christian moral practice."[11] In discovering evidence of this principle in the work of Luis de León, Kottman has examined the friar's theological tractates. He occasionally mentions Cabalistic matters in *De los nombres de Cristo* when there is an echo of the Latin treatises, but Kottman does not thoroughly explore the Cabalistic elements of *Nombres* or other Castilian works by Fray Luis. He is mainly interested in the ramifications of Christian Cabalistic thought in Luisian moral and social theory.

It is, then, the purpose of this chapter to trace the influence of Christian Cabala in one of the most praised models of Renaissance Castilian prose: *De los nombres de Cristo*. In *Nombres*, poetics and theology become one, with Cabala providing an appropriate bridge between the two. This unity of purpose is not found in the works usually cited as literary precursors of *Nombres*; it has been customary to look to Dionysius the Areopagite's *De divinis nominibus* (4th century) as a distant forerunner in its concern with sacred appellations, or to patristic sources such as Origen, Basil, Gregory of Nazianzus, and Isidore of Sevilla.[12] Such works reveal the apologetic and syncretic nature of the names of Christ.[13] (This trait, found in both Fray Luis and the early Spanish Christian Cabalists, will be discussed in greater depth later in this chapter.) Bernard of Clairvaux and Ramón Lull are mentioned as possible medieval sources of *Nombres*, but as a whole, the theological commonplace of *nomina Christi* was not greatly developed in that period.[14] As Ernst R. Curtius recognizes, not until the appearance of the *Nombres* of Luis de León did this "*locus theologicus* enter general literature."[15]

Indeed, Fray Luis de León popularized as he embellished and interpreted Christ's names. But something must be said of the con-

11. *Law and Apocalypse*, p. 36.

12. Walter Repges, "Para la historia de *Los nombres de Cristo*."

13. See Wilhelm Bousset, *Kyrios Christos*, trans. John Steely; Vincent Taylor, *The Names of Jesus*; Ferdinand Hahn, *The Titles of Jesus in Christology*, trans. Harold Knight and George Ogg; Leopold Sabourin, *The Names and Titles of Jesus*, trans. Maurice Carroll; Gaza Vermes, *Jesus the Jew*; Irénée Hausherr, *The Name of Jesus*, trans. Charles Cummings.

14. Repges, "Para la historia de *Los nombres de Cristo*," p. 341.

15. *European Literature*, p. 226, n. 24.

tribution of a fellow Augustinian, Alonso de Orozco (d. 1591), and his *De nueve nombres de Cristo*. The controversy surrounding the authorship of *Nueve nombres* and its possible impact on Luis's *Nombres*[16] has been partially solved by Edward Schuster's study of parallels between an unedited Latin declamation by Orozco and Fray Luis's *Nombres*.[17] Schuster concluded that Fray Luis was initially influenced by Orozco's *Declamationes* if not by the *Nueve nombres*. Kottman has pointed out common Midrashic designations found in the Castilian works of both authors, and he has recalled that Orozco was a ranking Augustinian during the visitation of Christian Cabalist Girolamo Seripando, disciple and successor to Cardinal Egidio da Viterbo.[18] In this connection, it has not been mentioned that Egidio, the renowned Augustinian Cabalist, also wrote an onomastic treatise entitled *Opus contra hebraeos de adventu Messiae et de divinis nominibus*.[19] We should also recall that Egidio, as the Augustinian general, had been closely involved in the reform of the Spanish Augustinian houses just prior to the era of Alonso de Orozco and Luis de León. Both friars may have been educated under a program that included uses of Christian Cabala.[20]

There are also indications that Orozco was familiar with Reuchlin's Cabalistic treatment of the names YHVH and YHSVH in *De Verbo Mirifico* (1494). As we discussed in Chapter 1, Reuchlin had stressed that the addition of the letter *S* (ש/*shin*) to the name YHVH made the powerful and wonder-working name YHSVH (*Yehoshuah* or *Jesus*).[21] Reuchlin was probably familiar with the belief from Judaic Cabala that the letter *shin* was the one missing from the Judaic understanding of the Torah in earlier centuries and that with the coming of the deficient *shin*, the revelation would be clarified and the new interpretation of the Torah would herald in a new age.[22] Reuchlin held that the addition of the *shin* in the center of the Tetragrammaton rendered the ineffable YHVH

16. See Pinta Llorente, "Autores y problemas literarios en torno a Fray Luis de León," and his *Estudios y polémicas sobre Fray Luis de León*; and Ángel Custodio Vega, *Cumbres místicas: Fray Luis de León y San Juan de la Cruz*.

17. "Alonso de Orozco and Fray Luis de León."

18. *Law and Apocalypse*, p. 97.

19. This lost work is remembered in the Angelica Library, Rome, MS. 1001, fol. 253r. See Eugenio Massa, "Egidio da Viterbo e la metodologia del sapere nel cinquecento," p. 185.

20. See Chapter 1, n. 107.

21. Pico had also spoken of *shin* and the change in the Tetragrammaton in his conclusions 6 and 14. See Secret, *Les kabbalistes*, p. 36. Reuchlin's work may have been more widely known to Christian Cabalists in the sixteenth century.

22. Scholem, "The Meaning of the Torah in Jewish Mysticism II," pp. 90–91.

pronounceable for man, just as the Incarnation of Christ brings
God's grace and a New Law to mankind. Discussing the prediction
of Moses in this regard, he wrote, "When the Tetragrammaton
shall become audible, that is effable . . . it will be called by the
consonant which is called *shin*, so that it might become YHSVH,
which will be above you, your head and your master."[23] He also
noted the similarity of the shape and form of the Hebrew letter *shin*
(שׁ) to a lamp with all of its accompanying sacred symbolism of
divine light and fire. In a like manner, Christ Incarnate is the new
Light of the world. Reuchlin wrote that "a torch in its shape and the
figure of the consonant letter *shin* . . . are equal and similar . . . In the
element *yod*, which designates Deity to the Hebrews, a lamp shines
. . . Oil among the Hebrews begins with the letter *shin*, therefore
shin is the sign of oil: that is, the coming together of the uttered and
speakable name shows a sign which thus the character of Christ
conceives."[24]

Alonso de Orozco conveys a similar message in a more con-
densed form: "It should be observed that that ineffable name
YHVH, as certain people say, was made effable through the letter
S, which the Hebrews call *shin* . . . where a miraculous work of
incarnation is shown. At the very moment as *shin* was uttered, God
became man and was called Jesus. Besides, *shin* among the
Hebrews has the form of a torch, for which reason it signifies
Incarnation."[25] Further similarities between Orozco and Reuchlin

23. The original reads thus: "hoc est, quando Tetragrammaton fiet audibile, id
est, effabile, tunc nomen Tetragrammaton vocatum per שׁ Schin, erit super te, haud
secus atque si diceret, Si nomen ineffabile Tetragrammaton oporteat fieri effabile,
necessario vocabitur per consonantem quae appelatur שׁ Schin, ut fiat יהשוה qui erit
supra te, caput tuum & dominus tuus." Johannes Reuchlin, *De Verbo Mirifico*
(1494), in Johannes Pistorius, ed., *Ars cabalistica* (1587; facsimile rpt. Unveranderter Nachdruck/Frankfurt: Minerva GMBH, 1970), 3.14, pp. 968–69. All further
references are from this edition. I thank Pamela Draper for her assistance in verifying
the English translations made of some of Reuchlin's works in this chapter.

24. "Videamus nunquid lampas in effigie sua & figura consonantis שׁ Schin literae,
circumductis lineamentis corporalibus par & consimilis est, in quae instar ' Iod
elementi, quod deitatem Hebraeis designat, lychnus splendet. Oleum eius lampada
& lychnum, ita igni coniungit, ut absque omnibus ijs simul iunctis splendor lampadis tenebras exire nolit. Quare Salomon cecinit: Oleum effusum nomen tuum.
Oleum aunt apud Hebraeos a שׁ Schin incipit litera, igitur שׁ Schin olei nota: id est,
effusi & effabilis nominis conveniens extat signaculum quod ita Christi personam
imbibit, ut quicquid de una in illo natura dicitur, de alia quoque verum esse per-
hibeatur" (*De Verbo*, 3.14, p. 970).

25. After discovering the citation in a selection of the *Declamationes* edited by
Schuster in his study "Alonso de Orozco," p. 268, I consulted an early edition of the
work. See *Declamationes* (Mantua, 1569), 349v. The original Latin citation reads:
"Adhaec notandum quod nomen illud ineffabile, ut quidam aiunt, effabile factum
est per literam. *S.* quam Schin Hebraei vocant. In cuius pronuntiatione maxillam
inferiorem superiori iungimus. Ubi incarnationis mirabile opus ostenditur. Ibidem

will be noted later in this study with reference to Fray Luis's
Nombres. For the present, we can conclude that Alonso de Orozco
used Cabalistic elements in his *Declamationes*. He may have been
influenced by Judaic works or by Christian Cabalists such as
Reuchlin, Egidio, and Seripando. The fact that Fray Luis would use
Cabalistic elements in his *Nombres* makes it seem more likely that
he was familiar with Orozco's work on Christ's names, which also
used Cabala.

Cabala and a Theory of Language and Names

Fray Luis introduces the *Nombres* with a discussion among three
interlocutors on the nature and origin of names and of language in
general. Most scholars see a Platonic influence in this section, while
affirming that Luisian language theory surpasses the Academics' in
complexity. Recent critical works have seen the friar's theory as a
foreshadowing of Descartes, Locke, Hume, Berkeley, Kant, and
Hegel, but in particular they have noted the "modern" character of
Fray Luis's theory and compared it to Saussure's analysis of the
signifiant in relation to the *signifié*.[26] Perhaps Schuster has best
summed up these views that in Fray Luis, there are intermingled

> linguistic, semantic, and theological interpretations . . . [and] language
> appears as the means which not only assimilates subjective and objective
> reality, but [is] also the bridge which connects perceptible phenomena or
> objectivity with the internal world of the subject. If the theological idiom
> is employed of set purpose, this also has linguistic significance, as in the
> repeated references to the marriage and union, including the mystical
> union of the soul with God.[27]

What Schuster has defined but not identified in his description is
the Cabalistic quality of Luisian language theory. In Cabala, all the
created world and therefore all "named" things are themselves
participants in the divine act of creation, which is itself a linguistic
activity. In the *Zohar*, the various letters and sacred names con-

---

Deus homo factus est, & vocatus Iesus, praeterea, Schin, apud Hebraeos figuram
lampadis habet, quam ob rem incarnationem significat. Iuxta illud Essaie. Et Salvator ut lampas accendatur. Lampas Christum denotat, nam intus habet lumen divinitatis, & oleum effusum quod est nomen benedictum Iesum." Pamela Draper
translated the passage to English.

26. Guy, *La pensée*, 163–70; Schuster, "Fray Luis de León and the Linguistic
Approach to Epistemology"; Eugen Köhler, "Fray Luis de León et la théorie du
nom"; and Carlos Noreña, "Fray Luis de León and the Concern with Language."
Noreña mentions (pp. 207, 209) that Fray Luis's language theories have Cabalistic
connections, but he makes no comparative study.

27. "Fray Luis de León," p. 198.

nected with the *sefirot* are the shining instruments of light with which God created the world. As Scholem says,

> The secret world of God is a world of language, a world of Divine names which, in their own way, develop out of each other. The elements of the Divine language appear as the letters of the Holy Writ. The letters and the names are no conventional means of communication. They are much more than that. Each of them represents a concentration of energy and expresses some fullness of meaning which may not be translatable into human language, or, at least, not exhaustively.[28]

Fray Luis recognizes the secret essence of words, and, similar to a Cabalist concentrating and meditating on the qualities of Hebrew words,[29] he tries to explore all their qualities. He writes that "todos los nombres que se ponen por orden de Dios traen consigo significación de algún particular secreto que la cosa nombrada en sí tiene, y que en esta significación se asemejan a ella; que es la primera de las tres cosas en que, como diximos, esta semejança se atiende. Y sea la segunda lo que toca al sonido . . . Y la tercera es la figura" (all names that are given by God's decree carry with them the meaning of some particular secret which the thing named holds within itself, and that in this meaning they are like it, which is the first of the three things in which, as we said, this likeness is to be noted. And let the second be what concerns the sound . . . . And the third is the form . . .).[30] With regard to the "figura" of divine letters we should recall Orozco's analysis of the letter *shin* in YHSVH and similar comparisons by Reuchlin and other Christian Cabalists. Reuchlin, echoing the *Zohar* in his *De arte cabalistica*, remarked that for the Cabalist, "single words . . . syllables, long marks and points are full of secret meanings."[31]

Not only does Cabala explain the theological-mystical quality of Fray Luis's language, but it also accounts for some of the more mundane elements of his theory. He recognizes that ideally every

28. "The Meaning of the Torah I," p. 39. See also "Bereshit," *Zohar* 1, on Creation unfolding through the power of divine light and letters.

29. See Scholem, *Kabbalah*, pp. 174–82, on prayer and meditating with sacred words.

30. *De los nombres de Cristo*, ed. Cristóbal Cuevas García (Madrid: Cátedra, 1977), pp. 162–63. All further references are to this edition. I have maintained Cuevas's capitalization pattern with the exception of my use of *Él* to refer to the Deity. Translations from the *De los nombres de Cristo* are by Audrey Lumsden-Kouvel, from her forthcoming complete annotated translation of the work.

31. Reuchlin, *De arte cabalistica* (1517), in Pistorius's facsimile edition (1:639). All further citations of *De arte* are from this edition. The original Latin of the citation reads: "Hic est solus verae contemplationis campus, cuius singula verba, singula sunt sacramenta, & singula sermones, syllabae, apices, punctaque eius plena sunt arcanis sensibus . . . ."

word should be "cabal," i.e., complete, exact, perfect in its correspondence to the thing named (p. 168). The most perfect appellations are those designated and inspired by God. Fray Luis gives
examples of the names originating with Adam and of the divinely
assigned names of Abraham, Sarah, Jacob, and Joshua. Because the
names were Hebrew, i.e., divine in origin, their perfection was
safeguarded: "Pero si queremos dezir la verdad, en la primera
lengua de todas casi siempre se guarda. Dios, a lo menos, assí lo
guardó en los nombres que puso" (But if we wish to speak truth, in
the first language of all it is almost always safeguarded. God, at
least, kept it so in the "name" which he gave; p. 159). It is interesting to note that these same examples of the perfection of Hebrew
and the names assigned by Adam or given to Abraham and others
are also cited by another Christian Cabalist, Francesco Giorgi of
Venice, in his *De harmonia mundi* (1525).[32] Giorgi does not develop such a unified theory of names and language as Fray Luis
does, but the examples given are an integral part of a work in which
the significance of sacred epithets is of prime importance.

After discussing the appearance and essence of letters, Luis de
León alludes to his familiarity with Cabalistic techniques of
gimatriyya, *notarikon*, and *temurah*. His mouthpiece Marcelo
says, "Pues lo que toca a la figura, bien considerado, es cosa maravillosa los secretos y los misterios que ay acerca desto en las letras
divinas. Porque en ellas, en algunos nombres se añaden letras, . . . y
en otros se quitan algunas . . . [y] . . . en otros mudan las letras su
propria figura . . . y se trasponen y desfraçan" (For with regard to
the form, if duly considered, it is a marvellous thing the secrets and
mysteries there are concerning this in the Holy Scriptures. In them,
in some names, letters are added . . . and in others, some are taken
away . . . . In others, the letters change their very form . . . and are
transposed and disguise themselves; p. 163). But Fray Luis/Marcelo shows himself to be a cautious converso and former defendant
before the Inquisition, and he stops this discourse short, saying, "Y
no pongo ejemplos de esto porque son cosas menudas, y a los que
tienen noticia de aquella lengua como vos, Iuliano y Sabino, la
tenéys, notorias mucho, y señaladamente porque pertenecen propiamente a los ojos; y así, para dichas y oýdas, son cosas oescuras"
(And I am not going to quote examples of this because these are
trivial matters and very well known to those who, like you, Juliano
and Sabino, are familiar with that language, and chiefly because

32. *De harmonia mundi* (Paris: Andreas Berthelin, 1545), 3.8.2, 446v-447v. All
references to the work are from this edition, and the translations of its citations are
my own. The citations were translated by Pamela Draper and myself.

they rightly pertain to the eye, and are difficult things to be spoken of and listened to; p. 163). To a Cabalist this statement would refer not only to the difficulty involved in explaining these techniques in a dialogue structure, but also to the fact that true understanding of the sacred words and letters would come from prayer and not discussion.[33]

Next Fray Luis, in the guise of Marcelo, leads the discussion to the most important of all sacred names, "el nombre propio de Dios, que los hebreos llaman *ineffable*, porque no tenían por lícito el traerle comúnmente en la boca; y los griegos le llaman *nombre de quatro letras*" (the proper name of God, which the Hebrews call *Ineffable*, because they did not hold it lawful to carry it on their lips; and the Greeks call it the *four-letter name*; p. 164). He adds, "si attendemos a la condición de las letras hebreas con que se escrive, tienen esta condición, que cada una dellas se puede poner en lugar de las otras, y muchas vezes en aquella lengua se ponen; y así en virtud, cada una dellas es todas, y todas son cada una; que es como imagen de la sencillez que hay en Dios . . . y de la infinita muchedumbre de perfectiones" (if we pay attention to the character of the Hebrew letters with which it is written, they have this quality, that each one of them can be put in place of the others and often they are so put in that language; and so, in truth, each one of them is every one and every one is each; which is like an image of the singleness which there is in God . . . and of the infinite multitude of perfections; p. 164). By this declaration the Augustinian friar demonstrates his knowledge of *temurah* and his probable familiarity with the permutations of the Tetragrammaton found in *Sha'arei-Zedeq*, or *The Gates of Justice* (see Figure 3),[34] a Spanish Cabalistic work of the late thirteenth century by an anonymous disciple of Abraham Abulafia. It is also possible that Fray Luis knew this work on justice and other qualities of the Godhead since he elaborates his *temurah*-like description of YHVH, saying that "la perfecta sabiduría de Dios no se differencia de su justicia infinita; ni su justicia de su grandeza, de su misericordia . . ." (the perfect wisdom of God does not differ from His infinite righteousness; nor His righteousness from His greatness, nor His greatness from His mercy . . . ; p. 164). Another Christian Cabalist, Johannes Reuchlin, also refers to the *Sha'arei-Zedeq* in *De arte cabalistica*, and he lists twelve possible variations of the order of the Tetragrammaton (3:710).

33. Scholem, *Kabbalah*, pp. 174–82.
34. In the collection *The Secret Garden*, ed. David Meltzer, pp. 136–53. On the *Sha'arei Zedeq*, see Scholem, *Major Trends*, pp. 146–47, and *Kabbalah*, passim.

Figure 3
Permutations of the Tetragrammaton

YHVH יהוה
YHHV יההו

| VHYH והיה | | YVHH יוהה |
| YVHH יוהה | | HVHY הוהי |

| HVYH הויה | | VHHY וההי |
| HHYV ההיו | | HYHV היהו |

HYVH היוה
HHVY ההוי

Immediately after mentioning the varied arrangements of YHVH, Fray Luis turns to another sacred figure that he feels clearly illustrates the equality and perfection of each Person of the Trinity: an arrangement of three identical letters drawn in the sand by Marcelo. Fray Luis's spokesman says, "Porque, en las letras chaldaycas este sancto nombre siempre se figura assí. Lo qual, como veys, es imagen del número de las divinas personas, y de la igualdad dellas y de la unidad que tienen las mismas en una essencia, como estas letras son de una figura y de un nombre" (For in Chaldean letters this holy name is always formed thus, which, as you see, is an image of the number of the divine Persons, and of their equality and the unity the same have in one Being, as these letters are of one form and one name; p. 165).

Before analyzing the Cabalistic connotations of this Luisian citation it would be useful to recall the significance of triads in Cabala. Scholem describes the tendency to consider the Sefirotic tree in groups of threes, with the supreme Trinity consisting of the first three *sefirot Keter* (Crown), *Hokhmah* (Wisdom), and *Binah* (Understanding).[35] Christian Cabalists were particularly struck by this triad, which they equated with the Father, Son, and Holy Ghost, respectively.[36]

The triad of "letras chaldaycas" Fray Luis had his Marcelo draw in the sand is an application of Judaic traditions—Cabala in par-

35. *Kaballah*, pp. 106–7. See also the Spanish Cabalist Moses of León's "The Doctrine of Ether," trans. George Margoliouth, in *The Secret Garden*, pp. 158–61.
36. Blau, *The Christian Interpretation*, p. 15.

ticular—for Christian purposes. However, before examining the Cabalistic significance of the letters, their identity must be established. In this matter, the twentieth-century editions of the *Nombres* vary considerably, and none of the modern editors uses the same Hebrew letters found in the *Nombres* of Fray Luis's lifetime.[37] The three editions printed before his death in 1591 employ the Hebrew letter *yod* in a triangular arrangement ׳ ׳ , or, less frequently, in a straight line ״׳.[38] It is therefore reasonable to assume that the three-letter formation Luis de León intended to use consisted of three *yod*.

The friar might have become familiar with applications of the three-*yod* symbol in several ways. The figure was frequently used in medieval rabbinical commentaries on the Bible to replace the Tetragrammaton יהוה.[39] Jules Piccus has pointed out that ׳ ׳ ,

37. Piccus ("Fray Luis de León y la figura del tetragrámaton," pp. 851–53) correctly pointed out the discrepancy in the choice of letters used by modern editors of the *Nombres*. However, he did not examine the earliest editions, those of Fray Luis's era, in order to determine which letters were used when the friar would have had some influence over what was printed. For the present study, all of the early editions of the *Nombres* available at the Biblioteca Nacional, the Biblioteca de Palacio, and the Biblioteca de la Facultad de Filología in Madrid were consulted. I thank Audrey Lumsden-Kouvel for comparing her findings with the results of my examination of the same early editions. See note 38 for a summary of conclusions about the *yod* based on our examination of the early editions.

38. The Salamanca edition of 1583 by Juan Fernández uses the straight-line pattern of three letters. In their Salamancan editions, Mathias Gast (1585) and Guillelmo Foquel (1587) use the triangular disposition of three *yod*. The 1587 Barcelona editions of Hieronymo Genovés and Pablo Marieschal also use three *yod*, but the Hebrew font they used for the Hebrew letters was of poor quality. Their *yod* are almost like modern commas or single quotation marks: ׳׳. Some Spanish printers of the period may have had difficulty acquiring the Hebrew fonts needed or they may not have been accustomed to using them correctly. We find, for example, in the Gast edition that one of the *yod* is positioned upside-down ، ׳ . There may have been problems with the use of the *yod* in the earliest edition of the *Nombres* also. Some copies of the Fernández early edition show three *yod* ״׳ while others use three *lamed* ללל. It is quite possible that the printer had difficulty distinguishing between the *yod* and the *lamed* in manuscript form. An enlarged *yod* does resemble a *lamed* just as a reduced *lamed* resembles a *yod*. Luis de León may have had his Salamancan printer correct the early use of *lamed* in the later 1583 editions. That would explain the different choice of Hebrew letters in editions published the same year. The probability is strong that Fray Luis intended the printer to use the *yod* rather than the *lamed*, because all the other editions of the friar's lifetime employ the *yod*. In the first copies of the 1583 edition, the printer could have easily mistaken the friar's handwritten *yod* for a small *lamed*. When examining the autograph manuscript of the *Exposición del Libro de Job*, the only extant Luisian autograph containing Hebrew characters, I found that the friar's *yod* does indeed resemble a small *lamed*. It appears that Luis de León was inclined to put an upper curl on his *yod* which made the letter therefore resemble a small *lamed*. I thank Professor Dwayne E. Carpenter for initially suggesting to me that the *lamed* could have been taken for a *yod*.

39. "Names of God," in *The Jewish Encyclopedia*, 9:164. Daniel Matt—in a letter

was used in the *Sarajevo Haggadah*, an Aragonese manuscript in Hebrew and Aramaic, and that it appeared in inscriptions for Spanish synagogues and other Hebrew monuments.[40] We can add that another Hebrew and Aramaic work from fourteenth-century Spain, the *Kaufmann Haggadah*, frequently uses the ׳ י׳ .[41] Piccus has also suggested that Fray Luis might have encountered the ׳ י׳ abbreviation from a targum such as the Targum *Onkelos* because the friar mentions "letras chaldaycas," i.e., Aramaic—the Hebrew dialect in which such biblical paraphrases were frequently written.[42] Indeed it is quite possible that Luis de León knew the Targum *Onkelos*, at least through its appearance in the Complutensian Bible. The symbol ׳׳׳ appears, for instance, on the first folio of Genesis in the Complutensian polyglot Bible.[43]

Other factors also link the three-*yod* figure, the *Onkelos*, and Cabala. Scholem has noted that the Targum *Onkelos* was a main source of the *Zohar*, the masterpiece of Cabalism.[44] Christian Cabalists such as Reuchlin were familiar with the *Onkelos*. In *De arte cabalistica*, he says that the *Onkelos* refers to Christ as the anointed Messiah (1:627). More importantly for Christian Cabalistic purposes, however, is the fact that Reuchlin, like the author of the *Onkelos*, uses the triangular three-*yod* symbol as an abbreviation for the Tetragrammaton. For Reuchlin the *yod* figure has special mystical meaning that he specifically identifies as Cabalistic. He writes that the Cabalists "because of the mystery [of the Tetragrammaton] write the name with three *yod*s, as shown here ׳ י׳ ."[45]

We have seen that the three-*yod* symbol found in the early edi-

to me of 3 October 1985—writes that the earliest triple-*yod* source known to him is the "eleventh-century Midrash entitled *Lekakh Tov* by Tobias ben Eliezer in the Balkans. At the end of his commentary on Torah portion *Naso* (Numbers 4:21–7:89), he mentions the custom of writing the divine name with three *yod*s. He connects this to three verses in that Torah portion: Numbers 6:24–26, each of which begins with a *yod*. These verses constitute the famous priestly blessing transmitted by God to Moses, to Aaron, to the Children of Israel."

40. "Fray Luis de León y la figura del tetragrámaton," p. 854.

41. See *The Kaufmann Haggadah* (Budapest: The Hungarian Academy of Sciences, 1957). In his introduction to the *Haggadah*, Alexander Scheiber establishes that the work is almost certainly Spanish (see pp. 8–11). I thank Professor Norman Roth for his comments on the frequent appearance of ׳ י׳ in Jewish medieval works such as the *Kaufmann Haggadah*.

42. "Fray Luis de León y la figura del tetragrámaton," p. 854.

43. *Vetus Testamentum, multiplici lingua nunc primo impressum. Et imprimis Pentateuchus hebraico greco atque chaldaico idiomate. Adiuncta unicuique sua latina interpretatione* (1517), vol. 1.

44. *Kabbalah*, pp. 223, 226–28.

45. The Latin passage reads: "Cabalistae . . . quod ad mysterium hoc scribunt nomen tribus Iod, uti hoc ׳ י׳ " (3:712).

tions of the *Nombres* was usually represented as ، ’ ، but that in the Fernández edition of 1583 the *yod*s are written side-by-side: ’’’. While Reuchlin's arrangement of the three *yod*s in *De arte cabalistica* was ، ’ ، we saw that the Complutensian Bible used ’’’. In addition to the Targumic and Christian Cabalistic uses of the three-*yod* symbol, Fray Luis could have known either the ، ’ ، or the ’’’ from Judaic Cabalistic sources. One of the earliest Provençal Cabalists, Isaac the Blind (fl. early thirteenth century), wrote the three *yod*s side-by-side, while others wrote them in the familiar pyramid shape.[46] In either pattern, the three-*yod* symbol for the Tetragrammaton was important in Zoharic works. Moses de León's *Zohar* cites the eleventh-century use of the three *yod*s in the *Lekakh Tov*, and there are several references to the symbol in the early *Zohar* imitation, the *Ra'aya Meheimna*—attributed to a student of Moses de León. One passage from that work points out that there are three *yod*s in one of the full Hebrew spellings of the Tetragrammaton: יוד הי ואו הי.[47] Such an illustration of three *yod*s in the Tetragrammaton was, of course, the sort of manipulation of Hebrew letters that would appeal to Christian Cabalists.

For Christian Cabalists the three-*yod* figure would be an appropriate way of demonstrating the unity of the Trinity while simultaneously maintaining Hebrew traditions connected with the most sacred name of God. It is quite possible that Luis de León was familiar with a similar Trinitarian approach to the Tetragrammaton found in the *Declamationes* of Alonso de Orozco, his Augustinian contemporary. Orozco provides another symbol for the Tetragrammaton as he explains that the addition of the letter *shin* to the name YHVH produces the effable and marvelous name YHSVH (*Jesus*). He writes that the Hebrews "did not wish to write this name outside biblical texts, and thus they were sometimes compelled to produce the name through the figure ∴.."[48] Based on the evidence we have established on the uses of three-*yod* to refer to YHVH in Spanish Hebrew texts and in Christian Cabala, we may state that Orozco could have intended to use ، ’ ، rather than the ∴ his Mantuan editor printed. There is also a possibility that Orozco

46. In his letter to me of 3 October 1985, Daniel Matt describes Isaac the Blind's use of the three *yod*s as "according to the *Explanation of the Secrets of the Ramban*, written apparently by Joshua ibn Shu'ayb, on Exodus."

47. See *Zohar* 3.246b in the *Ra'aya Meheimna*. For this and all the information on the use of three *yod*s in the Zoharic era, I thank Daniel Matt. He pointed out the following instances of the three-*yod* figure in the *Ra'aya Meheimna*: 2.158a, 2.180a, and 3.247b.

48. *Declamationes*, 348v. The Latin reads: "Nec scribere hoc nomen extra libros biblicos volebant, coacti aliquando per figuram sic exarabant . . . . "

was familiar with the manner in which the three points in a triangular disposition had been used by Jewish Cabalists.

The three-dot formation was used by an anonymous Spanish Cabalist of the second half of the fourteenth century to represent the vowel points of the Tetragrammaton.[49] It was seen to symbolize the unity of the creative powers of the name YHVH and thus to stand for the unity of all creatures with the divine source. For the Cabalist engaged in meditation, the three points would appear as inner sparkling lights. This meditation technique is described in the Cabalistic work *Berit Menuhah*. Since the three-point formation symbolized the Tetragrammaton, it was perfect for use as a Trinitarian symbol by Christian Cabalists. In addition, the Judaic Cabalistic concept that one of the three points or three illuminations would come to rule over the day of Redemption[50] could be used to emphasize Christ's role as the Word Incarnate. The Cabalistic significance of the three points may explain why Reuchlin's Tübingen printer used the formation as part of his mark.[51]

There are also indications that the very physical appearance of the *yod*—namely its similarity to a point—could have caused the ∴ to take on some of the same connotations as the ׳ ׳ ׳ . In the *De arte cabalistica*, Reuchlin mentions that the *yod*, because of its shape as an indivisible point, became an appropriate symbol for the Tetragrammaton (3:712). Reuchlin does not describe the Cabalistic sources for his characterization of the *yod* as a point, but it is possible that he was relying on traditions maintained by Spanish Cabalists. In the *Doctrine of the Ether* by Moses of León, for instance, we find the following description of *yod* as the origin of all

49. On the Spanish Cabalist and this aspect of his work, see Louis Jacobs, *Jewish Mystical Testimonies*, pp. 87–91; Scholem, *Kabbalah*, pp. 65, 105, 181–82, and *Major Trends*, p. 146.

50. Jacobs, *Jewish Mystical Testimonies*, pp. 90–91.

51. Secret (*Les kabbalistes*, p. 51) had noted that the mark was included in Théophile Beaudoire's *Genèse de la cryptographie apostolique et de l'architecture rituelle du premier au seizième siècle*, p. 7. As the title suggests, the work attempts to show evidence of the continued yet transformed usage of Hebrew letters and other symbols in Christian imagery from the days of the early church to the Renaissance. Beaudoire writes that "le triangle △, symbole de Jehovah ou Dieu dans le judaisme et le christianisme est un des principaux motifs architectoniques des synagogues, des anciennes églises et autres monuments chrétiens . . ." (p. 5). He also shows that "le symbole de Iehovah sous la forme de trois Points ∴ ou ∴ fut très couramment employé pendant les quinze premiers siècles de notre ère" (p. 9). While Beaudoire hesitates to explore the Cabalistic significance of the signs described in his work (p. 268), he does agree with the Cabalists that the *yod* was used to signify Iehovah (p. 5). René Allendy saw a link between Masonic use of the three points ∴ and the Judaic-Cabalistic ׳ ׳ ׳ . He wrote, "Les trois points massoniques ∴ sont un rappel des trois *iods* qui désignaient Dieu chez les Juifs . . . ." See Allendy's *Le symbolisme des nombres*, p. 64.

Creation: "It is also the beginning of the unique divine name, which is raised and exalted over all blessing and praise. This is the mystery of the letter *yod*, which is the same as the mystery of the 'hidden point,' the beginning of all beginning."[52]

In *Apologia*, Paolo Ricci also discusses the *yod* as a point in a manner similar to Reuchlin and Moses of León. Ricci, however, draws a more Christian Cabalistic conclusion as he writes:

> Some say that the *yod*, first letter of the Tetragrammaton, which refers to the indivisible point and the Unity, designates the individual essence of the supreme Unity. Others hold that it designates the ten, the ten *sefirot* as a unity, which includes the whole series of numbers and signifies the beginning and the end. Still others judge that the *yod* is placed in the first place, because, by its little point scarcely noticed, it designates the divine essence as indivisible and incomprehensible. Truly, the ten signifies the ten *sefirot*, that is to say the three Persons of divine essence and the seven gifts of the Holy Spirit.[53]

We have already noted in this study that Fray Luis's Latin tractates use Cabala in ways similar to those of Ricci, so it is interesting to observe Ricci demonstrating an interest in the *yod* and the Tetragrammaton similar to that of Fray Luis. We have also shown the likeness of Luis de León's and Francesco Giorgi's descriptions of Hebrew names. It should be pointed out with regard to the possibility of a triangular *yod* figure in *Nombres* that the Venetian friar elaborates on the significance of the *yod* in a manner much like Ricci does. In *De harmonia mundi*, Giorgi concludes that "God who is designated by that letter is the beginning, He is ternary, from whom, in whom, and by whom all things are."[54] Like Reuchlin and Ricci, Giorgi uses the *yod* to stand for the whole Tetragrammaton. As Fray Luis seems to do with the three-*yod* formation in *Nombres*, Giorgi speaks of using the *yod* as part of a "ternary" or Trinitarian symbol. There are other similarities between Giorgi's work and *Nombres*, as we will continue to show in this study.

A final relevant point should be made concerning the probability of the *yod* figure in *Nombres*. It is a Christian Cabalistic point, that

52. In *The Secret Garden*, ed. Meltzer, p. 159.
53. My translation of Secret's French, cited in *Les kabbalistes*, p. 91. Secret is citing Ricci's *Apologeticus sermo* (f. 115), a defense of Cabala against the attacks of Jacobus van Hoogstraten.
54. The entire phrase from *De harmonia* reads, "Hinc dixere reconditissimi theologi Hebraeorum illam literam divinitatis, quae est ׳, significans principium & finem, cum sit finis numerorum, & principium est ipce denariorum, habere sex spinulas: quoniam in ea ratione, qua principium est ipse Deus signatus per literam illam, ternarius est: a quo, in quo, & per quem omnia" (3.5.1, 383v). The translations of *De harmonia* in this chapter are mine.

is, one unifying Judaic and Christian views. The *Zohar* tells us that
the *yod*, as the primal point of Creation, is a representation of the
second *sefirah, Hokhmah* or Wisdom (1.3b). Of course, to Christian Cabalists, *Hokhmah* represented the Second Person of the
Trinity. In *De occulta philosophia* (1533), Agrippa ties all the
Cabalistic ends together and states that *Hokhmah* is the *yod* or
Tetragrammaton as well as Wisdom, the Son, and the Divinity Full
of Ideas.[55] Agrippa's latter point probably refers to the comparisons of Christ to the *sefirot*, a matter we will consider later in
this study. But Agrippa's conclusion does summarize the Christian
Cabalistic position Fray Luis espouses through his discussion of
YHVH and the Aramaic abbreviation for the Tetragrammaton:
י ,י ,י . For Fray Luis to choose three *yod* for the three-lettered formation described in *Nombres* is to fulfill a dual function. In one symbol he simultaneously illustrates the importance of Christ (the *yod*,
the *Hokhmah*) and the unity of the Trinity, demonstrating through
Cabalistic principles the truth of Christianity. That is the essence of
Christian Cabala and an underlying motivation of *Nombres*. The
friar's discussion of these Cabalistic elements was probably as overt
as possible in a work meant for the general public. The re-
membrance of his previous imprisonment by the Inquisition and
the suspicious religious climate of Spain in the 1580s made an
expanded examination of the Cabalistic elements in YHVH or the
three-*yod* symbol too dangerous.

Fray Luis continues to show his cautious Christian Cabalism as
he concludes the introductory section of *Nombres* with a discussion on the propriety of the names of God. The arguments the friar
develops in the course of the dialogue are ones that attempt to
diminish excessive concern for the exterior representation of the
Deity in a name. He is doubting not so much the propriety and
power of the name as he is the human capacity to understand the
essence that the name is supposed to represent. He writes:

> Algunos dizen que este nombre, como nombre que se le puso Dios a sí
> mismo, declara todo aquello que Dios entiende en sí, que es el concepto y
> verbo divino, que dentro de sí engendra entendiéndose; y que esta pa-
> labra que nos dixo y que suena en nuestros oýdos, es señal que nos
> explica aquella palabra eterna e incomprensible que nasce y vive en su
> seno; . . . Pero, como quiera que esto sea, quando dezimos que Dios tiene
> nombres proprios, o que aqueste es nombre proprio de Dios, no
> queremos dezir que es cabal nombre, o nombre que abraça y que nos

55. *Three Books of Occult Philosophy*, trans. J[ohn] F[rench] (London: [Printed
by R.W.] for Gregory Moule, 1651), 3.10, p. 368. All future citations are from this
edition.

declara todo aquello que ay en Él. Porque uno es el ser propio, y otro es el ser igual o cabal . . . Y assí a Dios, si nosotros le ponemos nombre, nunca le pondremos un nombre entero y que le iguale, como tampoco le podemos entender como quien El es entera y perfectamente; porque lo que dice la boca es señal de lo que se entiende en el alma. Y assí, no es posible que llegue la palabra *adonde el entendimiento no llega.* (pp. 168–69; my italics)

(Some say that this name, as a name God gave Himself, sets forth all that God understands in Himself, and that it is the concept and divine Word which he engenders within Himself in understanding Himself; and that this word which he spoke to us and which sounds in our ears is a sign which explains to us that eternal unknowable word which is born in and lives in His breast; . . . . But be this as it may, when we say that God has proper names, or that this is the proper name of God, we do not mean that it is the complete name, or a name which embraces and expresses for us all that there is in Him. For it is one thing to be appropriate and another to be equivalent or complete . . . . And so if we give a name to God, we shall never be able to give Him a name that is whole and which matches Him, just as we are not able either to understand what He is entirely and perfectly; because what the mouth speaks is a sign of what is understood in the soul. And so it is not possible for the word to reach *where the understanding does not reach.*)

It is important to note the significance of the phrases "tampoco le podemos *entender*" and "adonde el *entendimiento* no llega." Fray Luis denies that a superficially understood divine name will ever be truly *cabal*. In Cabalistic terms, Luis de León disapproves of the misuse of divine names found in the magical aspects of practical Cabala. He promotes the refinement of the *entendimiento*, that is, the mystical use of names to bring one close to God. He writes:

Quiero dezir que [Dios] está presente y junto con nuestro ser, pero muy lexos de nuestra vista y del *conoscimiento claro que nuestro entendimiento apetece* Por lo qual convino, o por mejor dezir, fue necesario que entre tanto que andamos peregrinos de Él en estas tierras de lágrimas . . ., tuviéssemos . . . en el entendimiento alguna figura suya, como quiera que ella sea imperfecta y escura, y como S. Pablo llama, enigmática. Porque, quando bolare de esta cárcel de tierra, en que agora nuestra alma, presa, trabaja . . . y saliere a lo claro y a lo puro de aquella luz, Él mismo, que se junta con nuestro ser ahora, *se juntará con nuestro entendimiento* entonces; . . . y *no será entonces su nombre otro que Él mismo.* (p. 166; my italics)

(I mean that [He] is present and close to our being, but very far from our sight and from *the clear knowledge that our understanding craves.* Therefore it is fitting, or better said, it was necessary that while we are absent from Him in these regions of tears . . . that we should have . . . in

our understanding some form of His, however imperfect and dim, or as
St. Paul calls it, enigmatic. For when our soul flies from this earthly
prison in which it now labors . . . and emerges into the brightness and
purity of that light, He Himself, Who unites Himself with our being
now, will then *unite Himself with our understanding*; . . . and *His name
will then be no other than His own.*)

Only in death or through mystical experience can one hope to
have such an *entendimiento* and such unity with God. Fray Luis
certainly approved of the mystical way, as is witnessed by his defense of Santa Teresa[56] and by the numerous semi-mystical elements in his *Cantares* and his poetry. Most Luisian scholars hold
that either he had a profound mystical longing or he was himself a
true mystic.[57] Mysticism is the ground on which the Christian and
Cabalist can meet. As Scholem has said in a manner very similar to
Fray Luis's conclusion on the divine name, "Kabbalah may be
considered mysticism insofar as it seeks an apprehension of God
and creation whose intrinsic elements are beyond the grasp of the
intellect."[58] As a very Christian Cabalist, Fray Luis recognized the
value of sacred names as a means of greater understanding of God.

Christian Cabala and the Apologetic Tradition

As a Christian humanist, Fray Luis was aware of the historical
significance of writing a work on the names of Christ. It was an
early Christian and patristic-apologetic tradition, not only a medieval one. He knew the Old Testament sources of such names, and
he relied on them heavily, citing them more frequently than New
Testament or patristic sources.[59] The Augustinian friar was also
aware of Judaic Cabala's uses of sacred names, as he reveals in the
introduction to *Nombres*. Judging from the parallels with Christian Cabalistic usage of divine onomatology we have demonstrated
in this study, Fray Luis was probably aware of his contemporaries'
efforts to use Cabala in establishing Christianity as the rightful
successor to Judaism.

56. Not only did Fray Luis edit Santa Teresa's works, but he also urged Felipe II to
publish the papal decree on Carmelite reform. He wrote an *Apología* and *Dedicatoria* on her works. See his *Obras completas castellanas*, pp. 1291–94, 1321–46.
57. Among scholars who argue most convincingly on Fray Luis's mystic status are
David Gutiérrez, "Fray Luis de León, autor místico"; Félix García in his edition of
the *Obras*, pp. 1–20, et passim; E. Allison Peers, *Studies of the Spanish Mystics*,
1:257–79. It is interesting that Marcelino Gutiérrez uses Fray Luis's works as
models of orthodox Christian mysticism in *El misticismo ortodoxo*.
58. *Kabbalah*, p. 3.
59. In the Félix García edition, I have counted approximately 299 Old Testament
references and 216 for New Testament or patristic sources.

Thus Fray Luis was aware of the company with which his *Nombres* would be compared and of the patterns of association that would be set up in the minds of contemporary Spanish readers. As we have shown in Chapters 1 and 2, Spain had a reputation as a source of Cabalistic and other occult materials. The chapter on Santa Teresa's Cabalistic symbolism revealed the persistence of Cabalistic elements—if not their deliberate retention and conceal-ment—in the converso subconscious. For Fray Luis to write a work on the names of Christ, to include Cabalistic materials, and to express his views in contemporary Castilian was to appeal to a general public with converso awareness if not converso sympa-thies. In effect, Luis de León was writing a Christian Cabalistic apology in the tradition of Ramón Martín and the Spanish conver-sos who used similar techniques. But he spared the harsh rhetoric and wrote a softened, humanistic, and Christian Cabalistic appeal that became a widely read magnum opus.

Before commenting on additional Cabalistic elements in *Nombres*, it would be useful to point out the historical importance of onomatology in apologetic literature. Traditionally, the use of divine names is a major facet of Christian apologies. Theologian Wilhelm Bousset has stated that "the whole body of apologetic literature is a continuation of the argument with polytheism which the Jewish Diaspora had begun in polemic and apologetic."[60] Stud-ies by him and others describe the long process by which non-Judaic and non-Christian elements eventually became part of Christianity through the inclusion of new names and attributes into Christology.[61] It was a development somewhat similar to the Re-naissance humanists' syncretic approach to Christianity, which also relied on the similarities of divine names in varied philosophi-cal and theological traditions. The names Fray Luis selects for *Nombres* hearken back to that earlier syncretic tradition. All of his choices have Old Testament roots, but several of their final Christological uses were products of that time of great cross-cultural fertilization (65 to 900 A.D.).[62] This fact is evident in the

60. *Kyrios Christos*, p. 385.
61. See also Taylor, *The Names of Jesus*; Sabourin, *The Names and Titles of Jesus*; and Hausherr, *The Name of Jesus*.
62. See Taylor, *The Names of Jesus*, pp. 170–75, on the influence of varied cultural influences on names for Christ. Although all of the names Fray Luis chose have Hebraic roots, it is also true that most names used for Christ do have Judaic connections. Significantly, however, Luis de León could have chosen many names that do not have Hebraic roots. Among them are "Bread," "Spirit," "Only," and "Advocate" from Saint John; "Newborn" from Luke; "Child" and "Humble" from Matthew; and "Sanctification" and "Redemption" from Paul. These names are found in the list described in n. 63 below.

appearance of all the Luisian names in an anonymous Greek collection of some 187 titles for Christ from the seventh century.[63] It is interesting to note that Scholem says the seventh century commenced a particularly syncretic period in early Cabala, during which it absorbed Christian, Gnostic, and assorted Middle Eastern influences.[64]

Cabalistic Elements of the *Nombres* in General

If we consider that an important aspect of Renaissance Christian Cabala is apologetic, it is significant to survey the general similarities between Luis de León's *Nombres* and works of other Christian Cabalists. Like Reuchlin's *De Verbo Mirifico*, the *Nombres* is a three-part dialogue cast in the Renaissance "Platonic" mold of refined language, style, and setting. Like the German humanist, Fray Luis also employs three well-educated spokesmen in the discussion of divine names. Unlike Reuchlin, the Augustinian friar only treats names for Christ. Both writers, however, draw the same dramatic conclusion: that the most wonderous, powerful, and sacred name is YHSVH or *Jesus*.

There are also notable points of general comparison between the *Nombres* and Giorgi's *De harmonia mundi*. Both authors paint a peacefully and beautifully ordered picture of the universe in which Christ's role is all-important. The Christocentrism is naturally more clearly outlined within the precisely defined framework of *Nombres* than it is in Giorgi's all-encompassing opus. However, the Venetian friar goes beyond Reuchlin's discussions of names for the Godhead in general and provides, in a manner quite similar to Fray Luis, ample reference to the many attributes of Christ as symbolized by His various names.

A notable point of difference between the Augustinian friar's *Nombres* and the works of Giorgi and Reuchlin is the choice of language. Luis de León used Castilian in order to bring his message to a wider audience and not to an elite set of educated Latinists alone. His Cabalistic treatment is therefore somewhat simplified, but it is sufficient to strike a familiar chord or to establish valid principles in the general reader, whose ignorance and confusion on matters of Christian faith greatly concerned the friar. This is the essence of his *Dedicatoria* to the *Nombres*, which he concludes by

63. Father F. Diekamp published the list in *Doctrina Patrum de Incarnatione Verbi*, in 1907. Sabourin's English edition includes a translation of the list (*The Names and Titles of Jesus*, pp. 315–17).
64. *Kabbalah*, pp. 30–35.

saying, "Y desseando yo agora escrivir alguna cosa que fuese útil al pueblo de Christo, hame parecido que començar por sus *Nombres*, para principio, es el más feliz y de mejor anuncio, y para utilidad de los lectores, la cosa de más provecho, y para mi gusto particular, la materia más dulce y más apacible de todas" (And being desirous now of writing something which would be useful to Christ's people, it seemed to me that to begin with His Names as a starting point is the happiest, most auspicious, and for the benefit of readers, the most profitable thing; and for my personal taste, the sweetest and most soothing of all; p. 146).

Throughout the *Nombres* the frequent use of the pronoun *Él* to refer to God or Christ is striking. One would not ordinarily think so since the *Él* is the appropriate pronoun to apply in this case. But the application of the *Él* in a Cabalistic wordplay in the introductory section of *Nombres* places the frequent employment of the pronoun in an interesting light. In the section of the discussion on man's *entendimiento* of God in mystical experience or the afterlife, Fray Luis writes that "Él por sí, y sin medio de tercera imagen, estará junto a la vista del alma; y no será entonces su nombre otro que Él mismo, en la forma y manera que fuere visto; y cada uno le nombrará con todo lo que viere y conociere de Él, esto es, con el mismo *Él*" (He Himself, without the mediation of any third image, will be present to the sight of the soul; and His name will then be no other than His own, in the form and manner in which He will be seen; and each one will name Him with all that he sees and knows of Him, that is, with His very own name; p. 166). This final *Él* is not the pronoun but one of the sacred Hebrew names of God. It is found in the *Zohar* as well as Christian Cabalistic works such as Agrippa's *De occulta philosophia* (3.17.121), Giorgi's *De harmonia mundi* (2.6.6, 287r-289v), and Reuchlin's *De Verbo Mirifico* (2.21.946) and *De arte cabalistica* (3:697, 710). Throughout the *Nombres*, the frequent appearance of the pronoun *Él* in carefully structured sequences would be striking to one familiar with the Hebraic use of the name *Él*. A random glance at the text, for instance, reveals this example: "Obra Él y obramos con Él y por Él y lo que es devido al ser suyo que en nuestra alma está puesto, y a las condiciones hidalgas y al nascimiento noble que nos ha dado, y hechos assí otro Él, o por mejor decir, envestidos en Él, nasce de Él y de nosotros una misma obra" (He does His work and we work with Him and through Him and what is due to that being of His which is placed in our soul, and to the noble qualities and high birth which He has given us. Thus we are made into another Christ [literally Him] or rather, by taking on His mantle, there is born of Him and of us one and the same work; p. 452). Thus we see that for Luis de León, Cabala provides another dimension to his stylistics.

Another curious stylistic quirk is the choice of the term *cabal* (*complete*) to refer to names that most properly and adequately signify their respective objects. After *cabal* is defined and applied in the section on *Los nombres en general*, it occurs in noticeable selections of the rest of the text. What is significant is that Fray Luis was probably aware of the two accepted etymologies of the word in his era. Covarrubias writes of *cabal* in his *Tesoro de la lengua castellana* (1611) that "dezimos estar la cosa justa y cabal, porque se ajusta con su medida y peso, y quando en esta forma se dize estar de dar y tomar. Y por esso algunos entienden ser vocablo hebreo del verbo קבל cabal, en piel, *recipere, accipere*" (We say that something is exact and complete, because it is adjusted exactly according to its proportion and weight, and when in this form it is said to be in a state of exchange. And for that reason some understand it to be a Hebrew term for the word קבל, apparently, *recipere, accipere*; p. 249). Of *Cábala*, Covarrubias says, "Es cierta dotrina mística entre los judíos, la qual no se escribe, sino que de uno en otro se va conservando, tomándola de cabeça, y los que professan se llaman cabalísticos, de la dicha raíz קבל, *in piel*, קבל, *suscipere, recipere*, etc." (It is a certain mystical doctrine among the Jews, which is not written, but rather which one passes to another, conserving it and keeping it in his head, and those that profess are called Cabalists, from the root קבל, it appears, *suscipere, recipere*, etc.; p. 249). With this current usage of the term in mind, Fray Luis's applications of *cabal* can be seen to take on another Cabalistic layer of meaning. He writes that God is "infinito y cabal en sí mismo" (infinite in perfection and complete in His own person; p. 513) and that through Christ He "comunicó cabalmente" (communicated completely; p. 622). Christ is "el parto de Dios cabal y perfecto" (the complete and perfect offspring of God; p. 519) because "no engendra a su *Hijo* el Padre entendiendo a bulto y confusamente su essencia, sino entiéndola apuradamente y con cabal distinción" (the Father does not beget His Son understanding His essence haphazardly and confusedly, but understanding it precisely and discriminating completely; p. 524). In quotations like these it almost seems that Fray Luis is inviting the reader to take a "Cabalistic look" at his Christocentric *Nombres* and the Christocentric world he portrays therein.

Finally, in examining Fray Luis's selection of names for their Cabalistic content, it is significant to consider the relationship of those names to the *sefirot*. Of course Christian Cabalists commonly associated the upper three *sefirot* (*Keter*, *Hokhmah*, and *Binah*) with the Trinity. But other than the comparisons of the *Tif'eret* (Beauty/Glory) to Christ Incarnate, there was no general consensus on which emanations compared to which Persons of the Godhead.[65] There is, however, the suggestion that all the *sefirot* as the collective emanations of God, i.e., the means through which He becomes manifest, are made visible in the Incarnation. This concept is graphically demonstrated by an engraving from the *Liber Sacrosancti Evangelii de Iseu Christo*, published in Vienna in 1555.[66] The engraving (see Figure 4) pictures the Sefirotic tree as a vision of Saint John, and it draws lines of comparison from each *sefirah* to the crown of thorns, stigmata, and other parts of the body of the crucified Christ. The overall impression created by the illustration reminds the careful reader of Luis de León's sensitive balance of Old Testament sources, Cabalistic symbolism, and the message of the Gospels in the *Nombres de Cristo*. Given its early publication date, it is possible that Fray Luis knew this edition of the New Testament although he would certainly not have had to see the engraving to use Cabala in the Christian manner that is such a constant substratal motif of *Nombres*. But like that engraving, Fray Luis employs Cabala to demonstrate that the Second Person of the Trinity became incarnate and that as man His human qualities are further manifestations of His divinity.

Several of the names selected by the Augustinian friar to portray Christ's perfection in His humanity are also names that historically the Cabalists used to refer to the *sefirot*. Scholem notes that these alternative references to the emanations are drawn from Cabalistic sources outside the *Zohar*.[67] From his listing we can compare them to some of the *nombres*: sprouts (*Pimpollo*), inner faces (*Faces*), mirrors (*Verbo*), crowns (*Rey de Dios* and *Príncipe de Paz*), limbs (*Brazo*), and shepherds (*Pastor*).

Pimpollo

The name the Augustinian humanist chose to discuss first is a prime example of his marriage of Christian Cabalistic interpreta-

65. Blau, *The Christian Interpretation*, p. 15. In addition, see my Figure 2.

66. Guillaume Postel had directed the preparation of special delicate types for the Viennese edition of 1555. In Antwerp, a 1571 Syriac New Testament was also edited by Guy Le Fèvre de la Boderie, the French Christian Cabalistic disciple of Postel and translator of Giorgi's *De harmonia mundi*. Le Fèvre de la Boderie used the text Postel had brought from Damascus. See the *Historical Catalogue of Printed Editions of the Holy Scripture in the Library of the British and Foreign Bible Society*, 2:1531. See also Secret, *Les kabbalistes*, p. 201.

67. *Kabbalah*, p. 100.

Figure 4. The Sefirotic Vision of St. John. From *Liber Sacrosancti Evangelii de Iesu Christi Domino & Deo nostro* (Vienna, 1555), folio 102. Used courtesy of the University of Chicago Library, Department of Special Collections.

tions to Old and New Testament sources. The "sprout" or "fruit" is the promised Messiah. Fray Luis writes:

> Porque dezirle a David y prometerle que le nacería o fructo o *Pimpollo* de justicia, era propria señal de que el fructo había de ser Iesuchristo, mayormente añadiendo lo que luego se sigue, y es que este fructo haría justicia y razón sobre la tierra: que es la obra propia suya de Christo y uno de los principales fines para que se ordenó su venida, y obra que Él solo y ninguno otro enteramente la hizo. (p. 174)

> (For to tell David and promise him that from him would be born either the fruit or the Offshoot of righteousness was a sign in itself that the fruit was to be Jesus Christ, especially when he adds what follows, which is that this fruit would execute justice and righteousness in the land, for this is the very task of Christ Himself, and one of the principal ends for which His coming was ordained, and the task that He alone and no other accomplished.)

Scholars have noted the similarity of Fray Luis's *De Incarnatione* and *Pimpollo* to Duns Scotus's unsanctioned doctrine that Christ would have become incarnate even if man had not sinned, since Christ was the final cause of Creation.[68] But the scholars also have commented that Fray Luis's elaboration of this theme has a more profound notion of Christ's Incarnation than does Scotus's account. Kottman has demonstrated that that notion may stem from the friar's Christian Cabalistic sources. He shows that Fray Luis differs from Scotus and complies with Pico della Mirandola's *Apologia* (1486) and especially with Galatino's *De arcanis* (1516) in his treatise *De Incarnatione* and, by extension, in *Pimpollo*.[69] Pico, Galatino, and Fray Luis used rabbinical sources to show that the Jewish authorities seemed to defend the Christian doctrine of the Incarnation.

There are other possible Cabalistic connections with *Pimpollo*. One is that the *sefirot*, as Scholem and Georges Vajda have explained, were the agency through which all created things came into being, and they contain the root of all change. In other words, they are the first cause as well as the final cause of Creation.[70] These

---

68. Muñoz Iglesias, *Fray Luis de León, teólogo*, pp. 101–7, 111–12; Welsh, *Introduction to the Spiritual Doctrine of Fray Luis de León*, 112–13; and Enrique Rivera de Ventosa, "El primado de Cristo en Duns Escoto y Fray Luis de León," pp. 494–500. Noreña, "Fray Luis de León and the Concern with Language," p. 162, remarks that this view of the Incarnation is closer to Neoplatonism than to Christianity. We might also add that it is closer to a syncretic, Christian Cabalistic view.

69. *Law and Apocalypse*, pp. 71–77.

70. Scholem, *Kabbalah*, p. 100; Georges Vajda, *Recherches sur la philosophie et la kabbale dans la pensée juive*, p. 182.

qualities of Christ as God and Redeemer Incarnate are present in *Pimpollo* and throughout the *Nombres*.

Other Christian Cabalists also use the term *sprout*. Giorgi speaks of the "Filial Sprout" in *De harmonia* (1.7.7). Alfonso de Zamora, the sixteenth-century apologist who sometimes used Christian Cabalistic sources, speaks of the term *Pimpollo* for Christ and cites the *Bere'shit Rabba*.[71] This Midrash on Genesis was a major source of the *Zohar*.[72]

The Anthropomorphic Symbols: *Faces* and *Brazo*

Two of Fray Luis's names for Christ, *Faces* and *Brazo*, will be considered together because of their common ties to the anthropomorphic tradition of Cabala. Anthropomorphic symbols were a common Hebrew usage before some early pre-Cabalists concentrated on body metaphors to interpret the Bible—Genesis and Canticles in particular.[73] It merged with other Cabalistic currents in the *Zohar*, especially in the section known as the *Idra Rabba*, in which exaggerated anatomical and physiological symbolism was used to describe the Godhead. The comparison of God to man's body is paralleled by the Zoharic conception of man being composed of all ten *sefirot*. In fact, the Cabalistic diagram of primal man, Adam Qadmon, has been overlaid on the diagram of the Sefirotic tree to emphasize that man is a microprosopus of the divine Macroprosopus (see Figure 1). The similarity of the Adam Qadmon engraving to the engraving of Christ's body and the *sefirot* from the 1555 Syriac New Testament is striking (see Figure 4).

Another interesting anthropomorphism from Cabala is the belief that the entire Torah is a manifestation of YHVH and that it is also the Mystical Body of *Keneset Israel* (the Community of the Chosen People).[74] Therefore, the Torah and the *Keneset Israel* with its individual members are seen to represent the "members" (body parts) of the *Shekhinah* or Divine Presence. Kottman has shown that in Luis de León's Latin treatises, the friar, like other Christian

---

71. *El manuscrito inédito de Alfonso de Zamora*, ed. Federico Pérez Castro, pp. 67–68.

72. Scholem, *Kabbalah*, p. 223.

73. See P. E. Dhorme, "L'emploi métaphorique des noms de parties du corps en hébreu et en akkadien." In addition, see the general comments on anthropomorphic terms in Scholem's *Kabbalah* and *Major Trends*.

74. Scholem, "The Meaning of the Torah I," pp. 43–47, and *Kabbalah*, pp. 170–71.

Cabalists, transfers Hebrew doctrines of the Mystical Body to the Christian view of the Church as the Mystical Body of Christ.[75] Fray Luis suggests in his treatises, and in *Nombres* as we shall see, that the Jews are therefore to be included in the Christian Mystical Body, which is the heir of the Cabalistic one. In this regard, it would be wise to reconsider Bataillon's assumption that the converso attraction to the Mystical Body concept was a reaction against the Judaic past and an attempt to *encastillarse* in Pauline-Erasmian Christianity.[76] Instead, the attraction may have been the result of Christian Cabalistic apologetics.

Cabala allowed for the change in man's conception of the Torah and thus for the changes in concepts such as the meaning of the Mystical Body. Cabalists held that the Torah would be known differently and interpreted in new manners in each succeeding age or *shemitah*.[77] In other words, this Cabalistic view could assist conversos in accepting the New Law of Christianity. Fray Luis draws on this point in *Brazo* by stressing that "otro es su Brazo, y otra su fortaleza" (His Arm is other, and other His might; p. 524) in order to show that Christ's power is not purely physical force as it was thought to be in the earlier readings of the Law. He defines that new power as love and grace. Like Luis de León, Giorgi also notes that Christ's "arm is . . . virtue with power" (in *De harmonia* 2.1.1, p. 338).

The Cabalistic motif of the new *shemitah* and the new view of the Law is also present in Fray Luis's other main anthropomorphic name, *Faces*. The Torah is said to have "occult faces" that are revealed in different ages and times.[78] Thus Luis de León is again using a name for Christ whose Cabalistic significance has direct bearing on the friar's apologetic concerns for conversos and for Spanish Christians in general. We should also point out that he uses the more Hebraic plural form *faces* with all its Cabalistic implications instead of using the more traditionally Christian and Castilian singular *faz*. Alfonso de Zamora had also used the plural form in his apologetic work.[79]

It is interesting that Fray Luis does not limit his description to the divine face alone, but, like the *Idra Rabba*, he expands from the face to include the whole body: "Pues pongamos los ojos en aquesta acabada beldad, y contemplémosla bien, y conoceremos que

75. *Law and Apocalypse*, chapters 4 and 5 in particular.
76. *Erasmo y España*, p. xv.
77. Scholem, *Kabbalah*, pp. 112–21, and "The Meaning of the Torah II."
78. Scholem, "The Meaning of the Torah II," p. 82.
79. *El manuscrito*, p. 14.

todo lo que puede caber en Dios en un cuerpo, y quanto le es possible participar dél, y retraerle y figurarle y asemejársele, todo esso con ventajas grandíssimas, entre todos los cuerpos resplandece en aqueste; y veremos que en su género y condición es como un retrato bivo y perfecto" (Then let us set our eyes upon this perfect beauty and let us contemplate it well, and we shall know that all that can be contained of God in a body and as much as it is possible for Him to participate in it, portray it and take its form and incorporate itself in it, all this, with the greatest advantage over other bodies, shines in that one; and we shall see that in its kind and nature it is like a living, perfect portrait; pp. 199–200).[80] In essence, Fray Luis is saying that Christ in His human nature ought to be the object of devotion. Kottman has shown how the friar demonstrated that belief in his Latin glosses on Canticles, in his Castilian commentary on them, and in references to Canticles in *Nombres*. He has also pointed out similarities between Fray Luis's glosses and those of the *Idra Rabba* and Archangelo de Burgonuovo's explanation of Pico's Cabalistic *Conclusiones*.

Another aspect of *Faces* is its relationship to the *sefirah Tif'eret*— otherwise known as Beauty, Glory, Mirror, Image of God, and Word of God. Christian onomastic scholar Vincent Taylor informs us that the translation of the Hebrew to the English word *Image* does not convey its additional and all-important meaning of *Word* or *Logos*, a meaning found to a certain extent in Plato or in the *Corpus Hermeticum*.[81] Taylor also states that in the face or image of Jesus, we see the *Shekhinah* present in visible form. It is this same sense of Christ as the *Faces* and the *Verbo* as well as the glorious and beautiful presence of God that is evident in Luis de León's portrayal. He describes Christ as the long-awaited divine manifestation of the *Ein Sof* (the Hidden God of the prophets). He then concludes that, "para dezirlo en una palabra, dezimos que Christohombre es Fazes y Cara de Dios porque como cada uno se conoce en la cara, assí Dios se nos representa en Él, y se nos demuestra quién es claríssima y perfectíssimamente" (and to sum up in a word, we are saying that Christ in human form is the Face and Countenance of God, because as each person is known by his face, so God is represented to us in Him, and is shown most clearly and perfectly; p. 198). Somewhat similarly, in *De harmonia*, Giorgi also calls Christ the *Tif'eret*, Virtue, Beauty, Glory, Word, and *Hokhmah* (2.2.6, p. 511; 2.8.1, p. 582).

---

80. Kottman, *Law and Apocalypse*, pp. 93–94, and n. 23.
81. *The Names of Jesus*, pp. 125–27.

Monte, Pastor, and *Cordero*

These names could almost be termed pastoral because of their similarity to the classical commonplaces so esteemed in Renaissance literature. The names the Augustinian humanist selected, however, rely on Judeo-Christian tradition more than on classical antiquity. All three relate to the concept of future peace, harmony, and justice in which Christian Cabalists like Egidio, Giorgi, and Fray Luis believed so intensely. The peace/harmony/justice theme is found throughout his Latin works[82] and, as this study reveals, in *Nombres* and in his poetry.

Luis de León introduces a rather complicated metaphor of the peaceful New Law in *Monte.* The term is closely related to another epithet of Christ, Stone, since Daniel topped a graven image with a stone and thereby created a mountain of rubble from which a new "monte de la casa del Señor" (mountain of the house of the Lord [New Law]; p. 242) would be established. In addition to the Old Testament significance of the name *Monte,* Cabala gave its own special meaning. It was said that the new reading of the Torah (New Word, New Law) would be founded on the stone rubble of which the previous *shemitah*'s "edifice" had been constructed.[83] To the Christian Cabalist the *Monte* of rubble from which the new temple and the New Law will be built is Christ. Fray Luis must have been aware of the Cabalistic significance of the name *Monte* and its role within the apologetic tradition of writers like Egidio da Viterbo and Giorgi.

Part of the metaphorical attraction of the name *Monte* is its significance as a source of all things peaceful, natural, fruitful, and virtuous in life. The *montes* are richly "preñados ... con árboles ... frutas ... yerbas ... fuentes ... y ríos" (pregnant ... with trees ... fruits ... plants ... springs ... and rivers; pp. 246–47). Also, *Monte* "en la Escritura y en la secreta manera de hablar de que en ella usa el Espíritu Santo, significa todo lo eminente o en poder temporal, como son los príncipes, o en virtud y saber espiritual, como son los prophetas y los prelados" (in Scripture and in the secret manner of speaking that the Holy Spirit uses in it, it means all that is eminent either in temporal power, like princes, or in virtue and spiritual wisdom, like prophets and prelates; p. 244). The sense of virtue, peace, and plenitude in which Fray Luis portrays the name *Monte* is

82. Saturnino Álvarez Turienzo, "La ley y vida en el pensamiento moral de Fray Luis de León"; José María Becerra Hiraldo, "La personalidad de Fray Luis a través de sus obras latinas"; Guy, *La pensée*; Kottman, *Law and Apocalypse.*

83. Scholem, "The Meaning of the Torah II," p. 89.

also found in Giorgi's *De harmonia* (1.7.9, 133r-135v; 1.7.30, 156r). Both authors also juxtapose the names *Monte* and *Pastor* and associate the virtuous life of the shepherd with the examples of Moses, David, and other prophets. Both conclude that Christ is a shepherd in the biblical tradition, but that he brings a new order and new special care and feeding for His flock. Fray Luis writes, "Mas si Christo es *pastor*, porque rige apastando y porque sus mandamientos son mantenimientos de vida, también lo será porque en su regir no mide a sus ganados por un mismo rasero, sino atiende a lo particular de cada uno que rige . . . Más Christo, nuestro *pastor*, porque es verdaderamente *pastor*, haze paz y rebaño" (But if Christ is Shepherd because he rules by pasturing and because His commandments are the sustenance of life, He must be so also because in His ruling He does not measure His flocks by the same yardstick, but pays attention to the particularity of each one he rules . . . . But Christ our Shepherd, since He is truly a Shepherd, brings about peace and one flock; pp. 233, 239).

The emphasis on the peaceful and protective rule under the Shepherd's law suggests that Luis de León might have been familiar with the *Ra'aya Meheimna* (*The Faithful Shepherd*).[84] This Spanish text, one of the earliest Zoharic-era works to use the term *Kabbalah*, treats the *sefirot* as instruments of God as well as His essence. In addition, it deals with the Cabalistic significance of the commandments and with Moses as the shepherd. The *Ra'aya Meheimna* is also especially concerned with the layers of meaning in the Torah and the progressive revelation of the Law through its exegesis in succeeding ages or through mystical contemplation. This message of *The Faithful Shepherd* has much in common with the image Fray Luis creates of Christ in the name *Pastor*. Christ the Good Shepherd is seen to bring forth the full meaning of the Torah and of the New Law. Hebrew mysticism, i.e., Cabala, is a tool to help bridge the old and the new traditions. Cabala reveals that Christianity is the true Judaism.

The final pastoral element, *Cordero*, is used in both *Nombres* and *De harmonia* as a symbol of the gentle and peaceful New Law. Giorgi describes the lamb as the appropriate sacrifice of the Old Testament while the sacrifice of the Lamb/Christ is seen as the most perfect ever possible. The Lamb removed the stain of sin from the whole world for all time (2.7.22, 321v-322r). Similarly, Fray Luis writes that "y, ni más, ni menos, es la víctima y sacrificio acceptable

84. Scholem, *Kabbalah*, pp. 101–2, and "The Meaning of the Torah II," pp. 70–71, 77–80.

y suficiente a satisfazer por todos los pecados del mundo, y de otros
mundos sin número" (He is no less than the victim and acceptable
sufficient sacrifice for all the sins of the world, and of countless
other worlds; p. 573). Fray Luis's emphasis on universal peace
through the *Cordero* and the New Law is also similar to Giorgi's.
The Augustinian friar continues,

> Y es puntualmente en este nuestro *Cordero*, lo que en el cordero antiguo,
> que dél tuvo figura, que todos le comían y despedaçaban y con todo él se
> mantenían . . . . Ansí que es sin medida el amor que Cristo nos tiene . . . .
> Y ansí, la misma naturaleza de las cosas pide, y la razón del govierno y
> mando, que quanto uno es mayor señor y govierna a más gentes, y se
> encarga de más negocios y officios, tanto sea más sufrido y más manso.
> (pp. 569, 571)

> (And it is precisely with this our Lamb that there came to pass what
> happened with the old Lamb, which prefigured Him, that all ate of it and
> divided it up and sustained themselves with the whole of it . . . . Thus it is
> that the love Christ has for us is measureless . . . . And so the very nature
> of things demands, as does the purpose of government and command,
> that the greater lord one is, and the more affairs and duties one is in
> charge of, the more patient and meek one is.)

Padre del Siglo Futuro, *Rey de Dios*, and *Príncipe de Paz*

Fray Luis's pastoral appellations with their emphasis on a transition to a new order of peace and harmony through Christ are an
integral part of the whole scheme of *Nombres* and of the monarchi-
cal and rather eschatological names found therein. Both the pastoral names and the ones to be discussed in this section stress that
the New Law is legally, morally, and mystically linked to the Old
Testament. Fray Luis employs Cabala to support that view rather
explicitly in his Latin works, whose resemblance to the works of
Ricci, Galatino, Pico, and Judaic Cabala has been noted. In the
main body of the text of *Nombres*, that Cabalistic view is an underlying motif that must be understood in relation to the more clearly
Cabalistic introduction and closing of the *Nombres* and in view of
the Cabalism of his Latin works. The eschatological/monarchical
names Fray Luis uses for Christ must be examined in that context.

The Salamancan humanist had opened *Nombres* with Cabalistic
references to sacred language, YHVH, and other sacred names,
which would strike a familiar chord with converso readers in the
general public. Then he used a series of appellations with Sefirotic
and Zoharic significances, which would also be familiar to his

audience. All the while, the friar firmly established the Old Testament origins of those names and demonstrated their importance to Christianity. Now, in the names we have called eschatological/monarchical, Fray Luis draws on his own prophetic views and the messianic fervor so widespread in his era—particularly among conversos.[85] In his tractate called *In Abdiam prophetam explanatio* (1582), Fray Luis says that all present signs indicate that the end of the world will come in 1656 A.D.[86] He bases his position on the interpretation of Elijah's prophecy by Christian Cabalists Galatino, Pico, and Giorgi as well as on the Sibylline Books, Hermes Trismegistus, Origen, and three principal Doctors of the Church—Augustine, Irenaeus, and Jerome. Two key elements in Fray Luis's declarations on Abdias's prophecy are the conversion of the Jews and the role of Spain. He held that the conversion of the Spanish Jews was prophesied and was momentous in terms of the events to follow. That the Spanish Jews were thought to be from the most select of all Israel became significant in a world threatened by Islam. Fray Luis thought that the Spanish Christians (Old and New) had a special role to play with regard to that threat and to the predicted conversions of Gentiles in new lands—America, for example.[87]

In view of this Latin treatise, Fray Luis's apocalyptic and apologetic concerns in *Nombres* take on special meaning. Titles like *Brazo* and the pastoral names of Christ are an integral part of those concerns, but the friar especially stresses the apocalyptic-apologetic motifs in the names *Padre del Siglo Futuro*, *Rey de Dios*, and *Príncipe de Paz*. He comments on the Jews—and perhaps their Spanish descendants—with a few of the expected references to their sins and "la mayor ofensa que se hizo jamás, que fue la muerte de Jesucristo" (the greatest offense that was ever committed, which was the death of Jesus Christ; p. 314). But what is striking is the compassion that the converso friar shows toward the Jews. He writes:

> Porque, dexando aparte el perdimiento del reyno y la ruyna del templo y el assolamiento de su ciudad, y la gloria de la religión y verdadero culto de Dios traspassada a las gentes; y dexados aparte los robos y males y muertes innumerables que padescieron los iudíos entonces, y el eterno captiverio en que viven agora en estado vilíssimo entre sus enemigos, hechos como un exemplo común de la ira de Dios; assí que dexando esto

---

85. See the introductory and concluding pages of Chapter 3.
86. Kottman, *Law and Apocalypse*, pp. 79–80.
87. Ibid., pp. 16, 108–9; Noreña, "Fray Luis de León and the Concern with Language," pp. 159, 189.

aparte, ¿puédese imaginar más desventurado sucesso que, habiéndoles prometido Dios que nascería el Messías de su sangre y linaje, y aviéndole ellos tan luengamente esperado, y esperando en Él y por Él la summa riqueza, y en duríssimos males y trabajos que padescieron, aviéndose sustentado siempre con esta esperança, quando le tuvieron entre sí, no le querer conoscer, y, cegándose, hazerse homicidas y destruydores de su gloria y de su esperança, y de su sumo bien ellos mismos? A mí, verdaderamente, cuando lo pienso, el corazón se me enternesce en dolor. (pp. 314–15)

(For, setting aside the loss of the kingdom and the ruin of the temple and the destruction of their city, and the glory of their religion and the true worship of God passing over to the gentiles, and setting aside the robberies and ills and countless deaths that the Jews suffered then, and the most miserable state of endless bondage in which they now live amid their enemies, as a public example of the wrath of God; leaving this aside, then, can any more unhappy event be imagined than, after God had promised them that the Messiah would be born of their blood and lineage, and after they had for so long waited and hoped in Him and through Him for the supreme riches, and, in the worst hardships and troubles they suffered, had always sustained themselves with this hope, when they had Him in their midst, that they should refuse to recognize Him, and in their blindness, become themselves the murderers and destroyers of His glory and their hope and their supreme good? In truth, for my part, when I think of it, my heart is moved to sorrow.)

Fray Luis finds solace and a hopeful future for the Jews—as well as all mankind—in the name *Padre del Siglo Futuro*. He writes, "Cierta cosa es y averiguada en la Santa Escriptura, que los hombres, para bivir a Dios tenemos necessidad de nascer segunda vez . . . . De manera que si los fieles, nasciendo de nuevo, començamos a ser nuevos hijos, tenemos forçosamente algún nuevo padre cuya virtud nos engendra; el cual padre es Christo. Y por esta causa es llamado *Padre del Siglo Futuro*" (It is a certain thing and one proven in Holy scripture that, in order for us men to live in God, we need to be born a second time . . . . So that, if we faithful, being born again, begin to be new sons, we needs must have some new Father whose power engenders us, and this Father is Christ. For this reason He is called *Father of the World to Come*; pp. 265–66).

This *Padre* is also called *Rey*, but, as Luis de León points out, he is quite different from any known earthly king. Therefore the friar—quite independently—calls Him *Rey de Dios*.[88] However, in

88. None of the major Christological onomastic studies cites this exact title or any similar English translations. I do not find any reference to this particular form of the

a manner reminiscent of Giorgi, Fray Luis states that "sus obras las annuncia el cielo estrellado" (the firmament declares the work of His hands) and that "como en la música no suenan todas las bozes agudo, ni todas gruesso, sino gruesso y agudo devidamente, y lo alto se tiempla y reduze a consonancia en lo baxo, assí conosció que la humildad y mansedumbre entrañable que tiene Christo en su alma, convenía mucho para hazer armonía con la alteza y universalidad de saber y poder con que sobrepuja a todas las cosas criadas" (and just as in music all the voices do not sound high, nor all low, but low and high, as is appropriate, and the high part is modulated and brought into tune with the low, so He knew that the lowliness and inner meekness of the soul of Christ were very well suited to harmonize with the loftiness and universality of wisdom and power in which He surpasses all created things; pp. 358–59). This *Rey*, then, is to be a true *Príncipe de Paz*, as Fray Luis calls Him. Peace, the universally admired good, flows from Christ: "Y si la paz es tan grande y tan único bien, ¿quién podrá ser *príncipe* de ella, esto es, causador de ella y principal fuente suya, sino esse mismo que nos es el principio y el autor de todos los bienes, Iesucristo, señor y Dios nuestro?" (If peace is such a great and unique good, who can be the Prince of Peace, that is, its first cause and its chief source, save that same one who is the origin and author of all good, Jesus Christ, our Lord and God?; p. 407). The *Príncipe de Paz* brings true peace that must also be "sosiego y orden . . . y concierto" (calm and order . . . and harmony; pp. 408–9).

Fray Luis's words are remarkably similar to these of Giorgi in *De harmonia*: ". . . He was King of Salem, that is to say of peace, designating Christ our Pontiff and King of the true peace: who has come to give us and to leave us that true peace which the World cannot give us."[89] Reuchlin also speaks of Peace as a name for Christ; Peace is included along with the sixth *sefirah Tif'eret* as a designation for the Messiah in *De arte cabalistica* (1:628; 2:704).

In his treatment of the names *Príncipe de Paz*, *Rey de Dios*, and *Padre del Siglo Futuro*, Luis de León distinguishes between natural law, Mosaic Law, and the New Testament's rule of grace and enlightenment in a manner similar to Reuchlin in *De Verbo*

---

epithet *King* in the other Christian Cabalistic sources referred to in this study either. Fray Luis seems to have been emphasizing the spiritual quality of Christ's kingship. Perhaps he was also suggesting the divine king of the *sefirot*, the *Keter* or Crown, since he calls Christ "King of God."

89. ". . . fuit rex Salem, id est pacis, Christum nostrum pontificem, & regem veram pacis significans: qui venit dare, & relinquere eam veram pacem nobis: quam mundus dare non potest" (*De harmonia mundi*, 2.3.10, 230v).

Mirifico (3.19.977–78) and Agrippa in *De triplici ratione cognoscendi Deum* (1515).[90] The Nettesheimer writes that on Mount Sinai, Moses received a secret revelation in addition to the Decalog. Agrippa then gives a classic explanation for Cabala, saying that the complete exposition of the true law hermetically contained in the written law was passed by word of mouth for generations. Hence, the secret meaning of the law, that is, the spiritual law, was called "Cabala" for "reception." The Christian Cabalists saw this secret spiritual law as the one that would be revealed in a new *shemitah* with its new and Christian interpretation of the Torah. That idea was an important aspect of Fray Luis's association of natural law, the Decalog, and Christianity. The Cabalistic, mystical understanding of the Old Law would be a common ground on which the Jews—and hesitant conversos—could be brought to Christianity, to a law more "mystical" in that its essence is grace. Although that aspect is discussed more clearly in his Latin tractates, Fray Luis makes an implied reference to it when he writes in *Rey de Dios* that "la segunda es dicha *ley de gracia y de amor* . . . y es dulcíssima por estremo, porque nos haze amar lo que nos manda, o por mejor dezir, porque el plantar y enxerir en nosotros el desseo y la afición a lo bueno, es el mismo mandarlo" (the second is the so-called *Law of Grace and Love* . . . and it is surpassingly sweet, because it makes us love what is commanded of us, or, rather, because it plants and grafts in us the desire and affection for good, it is the same as commanding it; p. 384).

Esposo and *Amado*

Perhaps the most sublime and poetic symbols for the New Law of grace Luis de León describes in *Nombres* are the titles *Esposo* and *Amado*. In his application of these names, Fray Luis could have looked beyond the Judeo-Christian tradition and recalled a more broadly syncretic one. For instance, the Gnostics were concerned with the marriage of the soul with the Savior-Deity.[91] Although both Judaism and Christianity would speak instead of the marriage of the Deity and the Chosen People or the Church, the similarity with other religious sects was an added point of interest to humanists like Fray Luis.

Luis de León was, of course, chiefly interested in analyzing the

90. Blau, *The Christian Interpretation*, p. 83.

91. Bousset, *Kyrios Christos*, pp. 268–72. See also Taylor, *The Names of Jesus*, pp. 87–88, and Sabourin, *The Names and Titles of Jesus*, pp. 87–91, on the origins of the term.

Hebraic roots of the name and applying it to Christianity. The title *Esposo* to refer to Christ was not widely used in the New Testament,[92] and the friar relies heavily on rabbinical and Cabalistic sources to explain it in his Latin treatises on Canticles.[93] In *Nombres* he repeats much of the same sensuousness of his literal exegesis as well as the essence of the metaphorical interpretations. To choose the name *Esposo* with all its connotations from Canticles—one of the most lyrical of the Old Testament books—was to appeal to a set of concepts long-revered in Cabala.[94] The emphasis on the Song of Songs was one of the notions of Cabala which, through the *Zohar* and the popular diffusion of Cabala, came to enjoy a wide appreciation among the Jews of Spain and—it is thought—continued to be held in varied esteem by the converso population.[95] Thus, Fray Luis's selection of this name and his concentration on its translation and interpretation can be seen as one more apologetic aspect of *Nombres*.

In addition, the name *Esposo* carries an eschatological promise that all Jews and Gentiles would join in the mystical union of the *Esposo*/Christ and His *Esposa*/The Mystical Body of the Church. Fray Luis reveals his sensitivity to those apocalyptic aspects of *Cantares* when he writes that

> aunque siempre por manera llena de amor y de regalo, como se vee claramente en el libro, de quien poco antes dezía, de los *Cantares*, el qual no es sino un debuxo bivo de todo aqueste trato amoroso y dulce que ha avido hasta agora, y de aquí adelante ha de aver entre estos dos, *esposo y esposa*, hasta que llegue el dichoso día del matrimonio, que será el día *quando se cerraren los siglos*. (p. 478; my italics)

> (although always in an extremely loving and affectionate way, as is clearly seen in the *Song of Songs*, of which I spoke a short time ago, which is nothing but a living picture of all this sweet and loving communication there has been up till now, and from now on will be, between these two, *Bridegroom* and *Bride*, until the happy wedding day, which will be the day *when human history comes to an end*.)

A similar regard for Canticles is expressed in the *Zohar*:

> Solomon, however, was gifted with a still greater knowledge of that song: he penetrated into the essence of wisdom, and so he wrote many proverbs and made a book of the song itself. This is the meaning of his

92. Taylor, *The Names of Jesus*, pp. 87–88.
93. Kottman, *Law and Apocalypse*; see chapters 4 and 5 as well as appendices 1 and 2.
94. Scholem, *Kabbalah*, passim.
95. See the previous chapter on the continuation of Judaic customs and beliefs.

words, "I gat me men singers (*sharim*) and women singers" (Eccl. II, 8); that is to say, he acquired the knowledge of the hymn sung by heavenly and terrestrial beings. And on account of this he called his book "The Song of Songs": the song of the supernal songs, the song containing all mysteries of the Torah and of Divine wisdom; the song wherein is power to penetrate into things that were and things that will be; the song sung by the supernal princes. (3.18b)

The *Zohar*, like Fray Luis's work, treats the union of *Esposo* and *Esposa* mystically, but it also expresses that union in more explicit physical terms. We find it written, for instance, that

> if, however, [a man] guards the [holy imprint on his soul], then the *Shekhinah* does not depart from him. He cannot be sure of it until he is married, when at last the sign enters into its place. When the man and wife are joined together and are called by one name, then the celestial favour rests upon them, the favour (*Hesed*) which issues from the supernal Wisdom and is embraced in the male, so that the female also is firmly established . . . . For the *Shekhinah* is always present whenever marital intercourse is performed as a religious duty; and whoever obstructs such a performance causes the *Shekhinah* to depart from the world. (1.94a; 2.176a)

For Fray Luis the physical union is a beautiful and sacred symbol of union with Christ. He writes, "Y no sólo en las palabras, mas en el hecho es assí nuestro *esposo*, que toda la estrecheza de amor y de conversación y de unidad de cuerpos, que en el suelo hay entre dos, marido y mujer, comparada con aquella con que se enlaza con nuestra alma este *esposo*, es frialdad y tibieza pura" (And not only in words but in fact our *Bridegroom* is such that all the closeness of love and communication and physical union which on earth exists between the couple who are husband and wife is coldness and mere lukewarmness compared with that which binds this *Bridegroom* to our soul; p. 450). While always pointing out that the real union is the one with Christ, he never hesitates to use the full physical sense of words to achieve the spiritual goal. In this sense, the methods of Fray Luis and the *Zohar* are similar.

Luis de León's treatment of *Amado* also extensively uses the Canticles and *Zohar*-like symbolism even though the term did not originate with the Bridegroom image from the Song of Songs and was really a "typically Johannine" title.[96] Fray Luis cites Isaiah (5:1) as his Old Testament source, but in his own interpretation of *Amado* he quotes Canticles (pp. 732–33). In so doing, the friar

96. Taylor, *The Names of Jesus*, p. 160.

Cabalistically legitimizes the epithet and brings it closer to the powerful attachment evoked by the name *Esposo*.

The Cabalistic connections of the appellation *Esposo* are more extensive than has been demonstrated in this chapter. The heritage of the term *Esposo* in Cabala will be more appropriately discussed in relation to the mystical symbolism of San Juan de la Cruz in Chapter 6.

Hijo de Dios and the *Verbo, Jesús*

Traditionally, Christ's titles as *Hijo de Dios* and *Amado* are considered integral parts of one another, as Fray Luis explains in linking his two chapters on these names: "Y el mismo Padre celestial . . . le nombra su *Amado* y su *Hijo*" (And the same heavenly Father . . . names Him His *Beloved* and His *Son*; p. 588). As the Son, Christ is Beloved of His Father. The two names appear in the third and final book of *Nombres*, in which the friar sums up the qualities manifested by all the previously discussed titles with some of the most prominent names applied to Christ.[97] The work then climaxes with Luis de León's presentation on the name *Jesús*.[98]

The name *Hijo* provides Fray Luis with an opportunity to re-emphasize a belief he had espoused in the chapter on *Pimpollo* and had supported with Christian Cabalistic interpretations: Christ's Incarnation was not the result of man's sin. The friar expands on the Scripture (Prov. 8:22–31) and writes that "[Cristo] nos es nacido, esto es, el engendrado eternalmente de Dios ha nacido por otra manera differente para nosotros, y el que es *Hijo*, en quien nació todo el edificio del mundo, se nos da nacido entre los del mundo como *Hijo*" ([Christ] is born to us, that is, He that is eternally begotten by God has been born in another different way for us; and He that is *Son*, in Whom is born all the structure of the world, is given to us born as a *Son* among those of the world; p. 528).

Scholars tell us that the concept of the divine Son of God has

97. Ibid., pp. 172–75, lists *Son of God* and *Jesus* among the most stable of names for Christ and predicts their future endurance.

98. In the 1585 edition of *Nombres*, the definitive one of the author's lifetime, *Jesús* is given as the final name. It is clear from the comments Fray Luis made at the close of *Cordero* (p. 790) that he wished this latter name to be inserted just prior to the title *Amado*. That would have maintained the scheme of the 1585 edition in which the friar appropriately culminated the work in the name *Jesús*. The posthumous addition of *Cordero* after *Jesús* destroys Fray Luis's carefully ordered structure and lessens the effect he had intended to achieve with the name *Jesús*.

Hellenic roots as well as Judaic ones. The Egyptian descendants of the sun-god Ra were held to be divine.[99] This was the sort of religious belief that interested Renaissance syncretists, including Christian Cabalists. Our Salamancan humanist might be seen to express poetically his knowledge of the Egyptian myth when he describes the *Hijo de Dios* in a sun/ray metaphor. The friar writes that "assí como el sol engendra su rayo—que todo este bulto de resplandor y de luz que baña el cielo y la tierra, un rayo solo es que embía de sí todo el sol—, assí Dios engendra un solo *Hijo* de sí, que reyna y estiende por todo" (just as the sun engenders its ray—for all this mass of radiant light which bathes the sky and the earth is one single ray emitted by the entire sun—so God engenders of Himself one single Son who reigns and extends over all; p. 522).

Another syncretic reference to Christ, but one much more closely associated with Christianity, is the name *Verbo*. Fray Luis introduces the title in connection with the name *Hijo*, but he develops it more thoroughly with the name *Jesús*. Scholarship has revealed that the roots of this name are diverse. In the Old Testament, the Word was seen as the "extension of the Personality of Yahweh."[100] In more Cabalistic terms, the Word was associated with the *Shekhinah* and the *sefirah Hokhmah* (Wisdom), the one Christian Cabalists used for Christ.[101] Ultimately, the Church Fathers combined the Judaic notion with the Hellenic concept of Hermes, the Egyptian god Thoth, and the Stoic ideas of world-governing divine reason in the term *Logos*.[102] Fray Luis, with the name *Hijo de Dios*, acknowledges the Logos concept:

> Y por la misma razón aquesta biva imagen [de Cristo] es sabiduría puramente, porque es todo lo que sabe de sí Dios, que es perfecto saber, y porque es el dechado y . . . el modelo de quanto Dios hazer sabe; y porque es la orden y la proporción y la medida . . . y la compostura y la armonía y el límite y el propio ser y razón de todo lo que Dios haze y puede; por lo qual San Iuan en el principio de su Evangelio le llama *Logos*. (p. 518)

> (For the same reason, this living image [of Christ] is wisdom in its pure form, because it is all that God knows of Himself, which is perfect knowledge, and because it is the pattern and . . . the model of all that

99. Taylor, *The Names of Jesus*, p. 54.

100. Aubrey Johnson, *The One and the Many in the Israelite Conception of God*, p. 20. Taylor, *The Names of Jesus*, pp. 163–64, also quotes Johnson.

101. Bousset, *Kyrios Christos*, p. 389; Scholem, *Kabbalah*, pp. 53–55.

102. Bousset, *Kyrios Christos*, pp. 385–400. Not all scholars agree with Bousset's thesis that Logos was a totally formed concept when it was absorbed by Christianity. See Taylor, *The Names of Jesus*, pp. 47–49.

God can do; and because it is order and proportion and measure ... and the structure, harmony, the bounds and proper being and reason of everything that God does and can do; for which reason St. John in the beginning of his Gospel calls it *Logos*.)

More interesting, however, is Luis de León's Cabalistic treatment of Logos in conjunction with *Jesús*. He says, "Christo, assí como tiene dos naturalezas, assí también tiene dos nombres proprios; uno según la naturaleza divina, en que nasce del Padre eternalmente, que solemos en nuestra lengua llamar Verbo o Palabra; otro según la humana naturaleza que es el que pronunciamos *Iesús*" (Christ, just as He has two natures, also has two proper names: one, according to the divine nature, in which He is born eternally of the Father, which in our language we usually call *Word*; another according to His human nature, which is the one we express as *Jesus*; pp. 615–16). The friar then proceeds to give a rather more Hebraic than Hellenic look at *Verbo*: "Y assí, en el primer nombre que dezimos *Palabra*, el original es *Dabar*" (And so, in the first name which we call *Word*, the original is *Dabar*; p. 616).

Then, in the interpretive manner so intrinsic to the Cabalistic sensitivity to language, he begins to analyze the letters and syllables of *Dabar*. He writes, "Porque *Dabar* no dize una cosa sola, sino una muchedumbre de cosas; y dízelas comoquiera y por doquiera que le miremos, o junto a todo él, o a sus partes cada una por sí, a sus sýllabas y a sus letras" (For *Dabar* does not express one single thing, but a multitude of things; and it expresses them however and in whatever way we may look at it, either at the whole of it together or at each one of its parts separately, at its syllables and letters; p. 616). As he notes, the *D* has the significance of the article *el* in Spanish. He briefly cites Saint Jerome's interpretation that the letter *B* "tiene significación de edificio" (has the meaning of "building") and that the *R* means "cabeza o principio" (head or beginning; pp. 617–18).[103] Indeed, Saint Jerome knew Hebrew, but in light of the Cabalistic elements used throughout *Nombres* and the continued description Fray Luis gives of *Dabar*, it is probable that his other sources on the name were Cabalistic. The letters *B* and *R* are highly significant in the word *Bereshit*—i.e., the name given to Genesis—since it translates "In the Beginning."[104] To the Cabalists, the letters have sacred meaning. The *B* is called by the divine name *Ehieh*, it is the *sefirah Keter* (Crown), and the *Zohar* refers to it as the

103. García, in his edition of the *Obras*, p. 736, suggests that Fray Luis's sources were the *Hebraici alphabeti interpretatis* and *Epistola 80 ad Paulum*.
104. Oesterley and Box, *A Short Survey*, pp. 65–66.

"Most Mysterious and Recondite King."[105] Similarly, the letter *R* is known as *Ehieh* or *Asher*, *Hokhmah*, and the "First Point; Wisdom; Father." A general reader of Fray Luis with but a rudimentary knowledge of Hebrew or Cabala would see that the references to *B* and *R* (plus *S* and *T* = *BeRe'ShiT*) in the context of the friar's argument would emphasize that Christ was One with God the Father even before Creation (*BeRe'ShiT*).

Luis de León manipulates the letters *B* and *R* even more Cabalistically when he says,

> Por manera que el nombre *Dabar*, en cada una de sus letras, significa alguna propiedad de las que Christo tiene. Y si juntamos las letras en sýllabas, con las sýllabas lo significan mejor, porque las que tiene son dos, *da* y *bar* que juntamente quiere dezir el *hijo*, o *este es el hijo* . . . Y aun si leemos al revés este nombre, nos dirá también alguna maravilla de Christo. Porque *bar*, vuelto y leído al contrario, es *rab*, y *rab* es muchedumbre y ayuntamiento o amontonamiento de muchas cosas excellentes en una, que es puntualmente lo que vemos en Christo, según que es Dios y según que es hombre. (pp. 620–21)

> (So that the name *Dabar*, in each one of its letters, represents some property possessed by Christ. And if we join the letters together in syllables, the syllables represent Him better because the two it has, *da* and *bar*, together mean "the Son," or "this is the Son" . . . . And even if we read this name backwards, it will also tell us some wonder concerning Christ. For *Bar*, turned around and read the other way, is *Rab*; and *Rab* is a multitude or accumulation of many excellent things in one, which is exactly what we see in Christ, insofar as He is God and Man.)

In effect, Fray Luis just used the technique of *temurah* to produce a Christian Cabalistic anagram.

Next, Fray Luis draws on the fact that the Hebrew *Dabar* not only signifies Logos or the Word, but it also refers to the actual words humans use. Thus the friar recalls the Cabalistic notion of the divine element in language to which he alluded in his general theory of names and in his treatment of YHVH: "*Dabar* significa también *la palabra que se forma en la boca*, que es imagen de lo que el ánimo esconde. Y Christo también es *Dabar*, assí, porque no solamente es imagen del Padre, escondida en el Padre y para solos sus ojos, sino es imagen suya para todos, e imagen que nos le representa a nosotros" (*Dabar* also denotes *the word formed in the mouth*, which is an image of what is hidden in the spirit. And Christ in this way is *Dabar*, because not only is He the image of the Father hidden in the Father and for His eyes alone, but He is the image of

Him for all and the image that represents Him to us; pp. 621–22).
In the same context, the friar continues to describe Christ with a
series of epithets that also describe *Hokhmah*, Wisdom, the Primordial Point of Light, and the Second Person of the Christian
Cabalistic Trinity. He says that Christ "es luz nascida de luz y
fuente de todas las luzes, y sabiduría de sabiduría nascida, y manan-
tial de todo el saber" (is the light that is born of light and the source
of all light, and wisdom born of wisdom, and the spring of all
knowledge; p. 622).

Having established the name *Verbo* or *Dabar*, Luis de León turns
his attention to the focal point of his whole work—the name *Jesús*.
As if to counteract any possible impression of overly Judaic uses of
Cabala in the preceding pages, the cautious friar writes, "Y no diré
del número de las letras que tiene este nombre, ni de la propiedad de
cada una dellas por sí, ni de la significación singular de cada una, ni
de lo que vale en razón de arithmética, ni del número que resulta de
todas, ni del poder, ni de la fuerça que tiene este número, que son
cosas que las consideran algunos y sacan misterios de ellas *que yo
no condeno*" (And I shall not speak of the number of letters this
name has, nor of the property of each one of them in itself, nor of
the individual meaning of each one, nor of their arithmetical value,
nor of the number resulting from all of them, nor of the power and
the might which this number has, for these are matters that some
pay attention to and draw mysteries from them *which I do not
condemn*; p. 623, my italics).[106] In effect, with this statement dis-
counting *gimatriyya*, Fray Luis has spread a smokescreen of sorts
because he immediately proceeds with a Christian Cabalistic discourse on the name *Jesús*. In this sense, the phrase "yo no condeno"
may be revealing his true sympathies.

Like Reuchlin in *De Verbo Mirifico*, Luis de León deals with
Verbo and *Jesús* as the culmination of a treatise on sacred names.
Like Reuchlin, Pico, and other Christian Cabalists, he outlines how
the name YHSVH is an expansion of YHVH and is therefore a new
revelation of God. Fray Luis explains that "el original deste nombre
Iesús, que es Iehosuah [IeHoSVaH], . . . tiene todas las letras de que
componen el nombre de Dios que llaman de quatro letras, y demás
dellas tiene otras dos [two *S*'s]" (the original of this name, which is
Jesus, which is *Jehosuah*, . . . contains all the letters of which the
name of God called the four-letter name is composed, and has

106. In *Les kabbalistes*, p. 137, Secret is correct to criticize Alain Guy's remark
(from *La pensée*, p. 750) that this passage from Fray Luis is "très pythagoricién."
However, with the exception of this comment by Secret, the French scholar has
largely ignored the use of Cabala by Fray Luis.

another two in addition to them; p. 623). Then, similar to Reuchlin and Alonso de Orozco, he explains that the name *Jesús* in Spanish with its two added *S* sounds makes the divine word pronounceable just as the Hidden God becomes manifest in the Incarnation. Fray Luis writes,

> Ya véys que en el nombre de *Iesús*, por razón de dos *letras que se le añaden*, tiene pronunciación clara y sonido formado y significación entendida; para que acontezca en el nombre lo mismo que passó en Christo, y para que sea, como dicho tengo, retrato el nombre del ser. Porque, por la misma manera, en la persona de Christo se junta la divinidad en el alma con la carne del hombre; y la *palabra divina*, que no se leýa, junta con estas dos letras, se lee, y sale a luz *lo escondido, hecho conversable y visible*, y es Cristo un Jesús, esto es, un ayuntamiento de lo divino y humano, de lo que no se pronuncia y de lo que pronunciarse puede, y es causa que se pronuncie lo que se junta con ello. (p. 624, my italics)

> (You can see that in the name of *Jesus*, by reason of the two *added letters*, it has a clear pronunciation and a well formed sound and an understandable meaning; so that there may take place in the name the same thing which came about in Christ and so that the name may be, as I have said, a portrait of the being. For the soul and flesh of man; and the *divine word*, which could not be read, when it is joined to these two letters, can be read, and what was hidden comes to light *in a form that can be spoken and seen*; and Christ becomes Jesus, that is, a combination of the divine and the human, of what can not be pronounced and what can be pronounced, and the cause of its being pronounced is what is joined to it.)

Thus, Fray Luis's Christian Cabalistic apologetic shows the Old Testament appropriately manifested in the New in a manner that is suitable to his readership in converso Spain.

Although Agrippa and Giorgi do not present the same proof as Reuchlin, Orozco, and Luis de León on the name of *Jesus*, in *De occulta philosophia* (3.12.380) and *De harmonia mundi* (2.4.4, 250v–251r; 2.6.8, 290r–291v), respectively, they both recognize that the name *Jesús* is the successor to the Tetragrammaton and that it contains all its "virtues." Fray Luis's conclusions on the name *Jesús* are especially similar to Giorgi's. The Venetian friar writes, "The virtue of all divine names is enclosed in the name Jesus."[107] Likewise the Augustinian of Salamanca writes, "los nombres que Christo tiene son todos necessarios para que se llame enteramente Iesús, porque, para ser lo que este nombre dize, es

---

107. ". . . virtus omnium nominum divinorum includeretur in nomine Iesu" (*De harmonia mundi*, 2.6.7, 288v).

menester que tenga Christo y que haga lo que significan todos los otros nombres. Y assí, el nombre de Jesús es propio nombre suyo entre todos" (the names that Christ has are all necessary for him to be called entirely Jesus, because, in order to be what this name says, Christ must needs have and do all the other names signify. And so the name of Jesus is His proper name above all others; p. 629).

Both writers focus on the name *Jesús* as "Salvation" or "Well-Being," and therefore as the keystone in their Christocentric world views. Fray Luis writes that "Iesús, pues, significa *salvación* o *salud* . . . . Y es grandíssima salud, porque la enfermedad es grandíssima" (Jesus, then, means *salvation* or *health* . . . . And the health is very great because the sickness is very great; pp. 624, 626). He then recalls all names applying to *Jesús* that he has treated in *Nombres* and many additional epithets as well. Over several pages the friar enumerates the ways in which Christ safeguards the well-being of every living creature and every aspect of the universe. He then summarizes:

> La salud es un bien que consiste *en proporción y en armonía* de cosas diferentes, y es una como *música concertada* que hazen entre sí los humores del cuerpo; y lo mismo es el officio que Christo haze . . . . Porque no solamente, *según la divinidad, es armonía y la proporción* de todas las cosas, más también, según la humanidad, es *la música y la buena correspondencia de todas las partes del mundo.* (p. 633, my italics)

> (Health is a benefit which consists *in the proportion and harmony* of different things, and it is like *concordant music* produced among the humors of the body; and this is the same office that Christ performs . . . . For not only *is He the harmony and proportion* of all things, in accordance with His divine nature, but also, according to His humanity, He is *the music and proper conformity of all parts of the world.*)

This quote reminds one of the essence of Giorgi's *De harmonia mundi*, somewhat evident in this citation: "Since in the Word all things are counted and balanced, and since Harmony depends on number and balanced weight, we can easily conclude that all things acquire their harmony through the Word Himself."[108]

Reuchlin had also elaborated on the epithet *Salvation* in relation to Christ. In *De arte cabalistica*, he recalled that the Hebrew name *Yeshuah* is what the Latins call *Salus* (1:621). More significantly, he wrote that "Cabala is, in effect, the symbolic reception of divine

---

108. "Cum in verbo omnia numerata, & ponderata sint, & harmonia a numero, pondereque dependeat, facile concludimus cuncta consequi suam harmoniam ab ipso verbo . . ." (*De harmonia mundi*, 2.1.11, 196r).

revelation, transmitted in order to permit the contemplation of God and of the separate forms, which ensures Well-being and Salvation."[109] Thus Reuchlin associates the concept of *Salus* with Cabala in a manner agreeable to Christian Cabalists when considering *Salus* as a name of Christ.

One of the last points Fray Luis makes on the name *Jesús* in closing off the dialogue of *Nombres* is a reference highly significant to Cabala. He writes that in Christ's two proper names, the Garden of Eden's Tree of Life and Tree of Knowledge are found in one. The friar writes that "en el estado del paraýso, en que puso Dios a nuestros primeros padres, tuvo señalados dos árboles, uno que llamó el saber, y otro que servía al bivir . . . . Assí, en este estado [Christo] en un supuesto mismo tiene puestas Dios aquestas dos maravillosíssimas plantas; una del saber, que es el Verbo, . . . y otra, del reparar y sanar, que es Iesús" (in the state of paradise in which God placed our first fathers, He singled out two trees, one of which He called the tree of knowledge, and another which ministered to life . . . so in this second state, [He] has placed in the same individual these two most marvellous plants: one of knowledge, which is the Word, . . . and the other, of reparation and healing, which is Jesus; p. 652). The identification of the two trees of life in the Person of Christ is also found in *De harmonia* (2.1.7, p. 368), but the *Zohar* and the Midrashim on which it draws provide a more complete explanation.[110] Cabala says that the *Shekhinah* is both trees: the Tree of Knowledge, identified with the Oral Law and the *sefirah Malkhut* (Kingdom); and the Tree of Life, identified with the Written Law and with the two *sefirot Tif'eret* and *Yesod* (Foundation). In Paradise, both trees were bound together in perfect harmony until Adam sinned. With the coming of the Messiah in the grand Jubilee, *Malkhut* and *Tif'eret*—as the two trees—will find union again. Thus, through Christian Cabala, Fray Luis provides a dramatic conclusion to *Nombres* in which he unites his apologetic and eschatological purposes. In stating that Christ is the Tree of Life and the Tree of Knowledge, Luis de León demonstrates—in a manner conversos might appreciate—that the final millennium, the final *shemitah*, is near and that the hidden meaning of the Torah is evident in Christ, whose Second Coming will disclose all the sacred secrets God had destined mankind to understand.

109. "Est enim Cabala divinae revelationis, ad salutiferam Dei & formarum separatarum contemplationem traditae, symbolica receptio . . ." (*De arte cabalistica*, 1:620).

110. Scholem, *Kabbalah*, pp. 112, 124, 166–67.

Conclusion

It may be argued that if Luis de León shows such similarity to Giorgi, Alonso de Orozco, Reuchlin, and other Christian Cabalists, it is because, as educated men, they are drawing upon the same basic Christian theology for their works. That they all rely on Christianity is of course true. But it is the similarity of using the same Christian themes along with Cabala that is more than mere coincidence. Like them, Fray Luis chooses to treat the subject of sacred names Cabalistically and to appreciate the Hebrew sense of letters and words as representative of a divine reality. Just as Hebrew is both a language and a theological manifestation, Christ's names are seen to have a dual function: they are bridges between his human and divine attributes. Through study and contemplation of these names, the Christian comes closer to understanding Christ's gift to mankind and His role within the Trinity. In this sense, Luis de León's *Nombres* resembles the prayer guides of Francisco de Osuna, Bernardino de Laredo, and others, although the Salamancan humanist also relies on Cabalistic symbolism to enrich his work and to make the names yet more significant on other levels. In a manner of speaking, then, the *Nombres* is a mystical tool like the prayer guides of its time. But its techniques of contemplation on the names of Christ call to mind Cabalistic methods of meditation on sacred names.

Fray Luis interweaves the titles of Christ with their parallel Cabalistic strands of meaning. The humanity of Christ is seen in the divine emanations of the *sefirot* with all its "sprouts," "faces," and "limbs" as well as all the sacred names and attributes associated with each *sefirah*. And always, there is the identification of Christ with the *Shekhinah*, the divine presence that will be most clearly manifested in the Second Coming. Thus, underlying all the *Nombres* is Fray Luis's apologetic and apocalyptic message to Christians who, like himself, may have been conversos for three or more generations but who might still harbor some sort of "Hebraic soul" or who might only subconsciously retain an awareness of popularized Cabalistic symbols. For them, Fray Luis reveals in his selection and Cabalistic treatment of names that Christ really is the Messiah, that Christianity is the fulfillment of the Old Law, and that the time is near for all His glory to be revealed.

5

cabalistic symbolism
in luis de león's original verse

Luis de León's uses of Christian Cabala in *De los nombres de Cristo* and in his Latin tractates are not isolated occurrences. The underlying and steadfast Cabalistic supports to his profound Christianity can be detected in his original verses as well as in *Nombres*. The treatment of Cabala in the friar's poetry, however, does not follow the same pattern found in his great prose exposition of Christ's names. The poetic medium does not tolerate the lengthy explanations Fray Luis would have needed as a more Christian camouflage for treating the Cabalistic significance of the Tetragrammaton or the name *Dabar*, for instance. Hebrew words or even excessive use of Judaic sources would have been much more apparent in verse and much more suspect therefore. Although the Salamancan humanist did not publish his poems, he knew from the experience he suffered with his Castilian translation of Canticles that keeping forbidden materials in private hands was no guarantee of secrecy and security.[1]

Even though there may be no straightforward Cabalistic anagrams or Hebrew names[2] in his verse, the friar uses the nature of the

---

1. Fray Luis's translation had been made at the request of his cousin, the nun Isabel Osorio. It was intended for her use alone, but a friar surreptitiously copied Luis de León's manuscript. Aubrey Bell reports that "copies multiplied rapidly and spread through Spain, penetrating even to Portugal and to Peru" (*Luis de León*, p. 146). That Fray Luis translated the Song of Songs was well known by the time he was charged by the Inquisition. The fact that he had made a translation of Scripture into the vernacular was listed as one of the causes for his arrest (see Chapter 4, note 9). Adolphe Coster writes that apparently Fray Luis had intended to publish his original poetry (*Luis de León*, p. 194). The poems contained, on the surface, little evidence of Cabalistic or Hebraic dependency that would warrant fears of Inquisitional disapproval. His verse would not be published until well after his death, by Francisco de Quevedo in 1631 (p. 201).

2. For examples of anagrams, names, and other devices in Spanish Hebrew poetry, see Millás Vallicrosa, *La poesía sagrada hebraico-española*, pp. 140–52, et passim.

genre for his Christian Cabalistic purposes. The poetic symbol provides the dressing in which the converso humanist can disguise a variety of Neoplatonic, Christian, and Cabalistic concepts. Indeed, Luisian scholars have continued to debate whether many of the friar's major poems are purely Christian, Christian yet metaphorically Neoplatonic, or fine examples of Renaissance humanistic Neoplatonism.[3] Despite the differences among critics, none of them doubts the sincerity of Luis de León's Christianity. Perhaps that is why they have neglected to examine the Cabalistic elements of the friar's Renaissance Neoplatonism. An investigation of the more widely syncretic aspects of Fray Luis's humanism could lead to a more profound understanding of the pagan-versus-Christian issues that have so long characterized the debate over his poetry. To see the friar as a syncretist—one using Cabala along with Christianity and pagan antiquity—is to reveal a devout Christian searching for more spiritual legitimacy. Thus, for Fray Luis to use pagan poetic symbols that are also Cabalistic metaphors is to strengthen the Christian essence of his poetry. Just as Fray Luis employs Cabala at the service of Christianity in *Nombres*, so too in the original poems. In fact, it has been said that the *Nombres* are a perpetual commentary on the friar's verse.[4]

Harmony of the Spheres

As this study will show, there are indeed many reminiscences of our discussion on *Nombres* in Fray Luis's verse. A prime example is the Augustinian humanist's preoccupation with harmony and accord within the individual, among all humans, and throughout the entire universe (*Nombres*, p. 749). But it was much more than a

3. Writers who have concentrated on Fray Luis's Christian sources are L. J. Woodward in "Fray Luis de León's 'Oda a Francisco Salinas'"; Richard Picerno in "Temas espirituales en la 'Vida retirada' y puntos de contacto entre esta obra y el 'Cántico espiritual'"; and Gemma Roberts in "Trasfondo cristiano en la oda 'Morada del cielo' de Fray Luis de León." Luisian scholars stressing the friar's Christian-pagan blend are Bell in *Luis de León* and in "Notes on Luis de León's Lyrics"; Dámaso Alonso in *Poesía española*; and the following articles by Alberto Huerta: "La composición de lugar y la oda al apartamiento"; "Katharsis en la 'Oda a Salinas'"; "El lugar de los astros en Fray Luis de León"; and "Música de ser: transcendente e inminente." Two authors who concentrate more on Fray Luis's revival of classical modes are Leo Spitzer in *Classical and Christian Ideas of World Harmony* and Francisco Rico in *El pequeño mundo del hombre*.

4. See Oreste Macrí, *La poesía de Fray Luis de León*, trans. Francisco del Pino Calzacorta (Madrid: Anaya, 1970), p. 30. Gemma Roberts, "Trasfondo cristiano," p. 62, also sees *Nombres* as the key to understanding the Christian meaning of Fray Luis's verse. See in addition Humberto Piñera, *El pensamiento español de los siglos XVI y XVII*, pp. 106–12.

musical metaphor for Fray Luis. His ode to a dear friend, the musician and musical theorist Francisco Salinas, manifests his belief in the divine harmony of the spheres in the Pythagorean and Neoplatonic manner.[5] Yet all the pagan classical elements of the poem also have Cabalistic parallels to further reinforce the Christianized classical tradition.

In the ode to Salinas ("El aire se serena"; "The Air Becomes Serene"), Luis de León describes the divinely ordered and harmonious nature of the universe by saying that the soul, along with Salinas's music,

> Traspasa el aire todo
> hasta llegar a la más alta esfera,
> y oye allí otro modo
> de no perecedera
> música, que es de la fuente y la primera.
> [Ve cómo el gran Maestro
> aquesta inmensa cítara aplicado,
> con movimiento diestro
> produce el son sagrado,
> con que este eterno templo es sustentado.]
> Y como está compuesta
> de números concordes, luego envía
> consonante respuesta;
> y entrambas a profía
> se mezcla una dulcísima armonía.[6] (vv. 16–30)

(passes through the whole atmosphere until it reaches the highest sphere, and there it hears another mode of imperishable music, which is the primary source of all musics. It sees how the great Musician, leaning over this immense harp, with dextrous movement produces the sacred sound which sustains this eternal temple. And since it is itself composed of harmonizing elements, it then sends forth a reply in tune; and as they vie together, a very sweet harmony is compounded.)

Similar references are found in the "Noche serena" ("Still Night") when, upon contemplating the night sky, Fray Luis writes:

> Quien mira el gran concierto
> de aquestos resplandores eternales,
> su movimiento cierto,

---

5. The works listed in note 3, by Alonso, Spitzer, Rico, and Huerta, treat the Neoplatonic and Pythagorean elements of the friar's thought on world harmony.
6. This and all further citations of Fray Luis's verse are from the edition of Oreste Macrí, *La poesía de Fray Luis de León* (Salamanca: Anaya, 1970). Whenever possible, the translations of Fray Luis's poems were based on the works included in Elias Rivers's *Renaissance and Baroque Poetry of Spain* (New York: Scribner's, 1966).

sus pasos desiguales,
y en proporción concorde tan iguales; (vv. 41–45)

(He who looks at the great concert of these eternal lights, their fixed
movements, their footsteps unequal and yet so matched in harmonious
proportion;)

The role of music and musical metaphors is highly significant in
Cabala and in Judaism in general. It is curious to note that Oreste
Macrí has listed musical interest as one of the Hispano-Hebraic or
converso traits manifested by Fray Luis.[7] Indeed, Cabalistic theories of music have been traced to the early Merkavah mystics. Their
hymns attached amazing power to the divine harmonies, and they
expressed the conviction that the entire cosmos was alive with
celestial song.[8] The twelfth-century Provençal Cabalists expanded
on the Merkavah views by adding, in the *Sefer ha-Bahir*, that sound
is a vital force of Creation and that the mysteries of the universe are
revealed to the adept through the seven voices. This may be a
reference to the seven celestial spheres of the lower seven *sefirot*.
To the Merkavah and *Bahir* traditions, the mystics of the
Zoharic era applied more musical speculation on the nature of
the Deity. They held that initially "nothing disturbed the blissful
union of the rhythms of divine existence in the one great melody of
God. Equally, nothing disturbed at first the steady contact of God
with the worlds of creation, in which His life pulsates, and particularly with the human world."[9] Every aspect of life was seen to
be touched by the divine harmonies echoing throughout the entire
universe. The angels, for instance, were said to have been created
when God breathed/sang into them, and for that reason they continue to sing his glory day and night among the spheres.[10] Isaac
Arama, a late-fifteenth-century Cabalist, wrote that the secret music was delivered to Israel together with the Torah.[11] He also held
that the Jews' special feeling for the divine harmonies was represented by the *shofar*, the ram's horn, which, when blown in the
accompaniment of song, was said to bring harmony between the
spheres of the upper region and the lower world. This is the sort of
popular Cabalistic belief that Luis de León might have known as a
member of a converso society. It complements the Cabalistic views
on music he could have known from the *Bahir* or the *Zohar*.

7. *La poesía*, p. 11.
8. Edward Hoffman, *The Way of Splendor*, p. 155.
9. Scholem, *Major Trends*, pp. 230–231.
10. Amnon Shiloah, "The Symbolism of Music in the Kabbalistic Tradition," p.
64.
11. Ibid., pp. 56–63.

For both Fray Luis and the Cabalists, music and theories of divine harmonies are closely tied to conceptions of the mystical experience. In the ode to Salinas, Luis de León recognizes the mystical power of his friend's music to make his soul rise and return through the spheres to his heavenly origin:

El aire se serena
y viste de hermosura y luz no usada,
Salinas, cuando suena
la música estremada
por vuestra sabia mano gobernada.
    A cuyo son divino
el alma, que en olvido está sumida,
torna a cobrar el tino
y memoria perdida
de su origen primera esclarecida. (vv. 1–10)

(The air becomes serene and puts on an unusual beauty and light, Salinas, when that exceptional music resounds which is governed by your skilled hand. At that divine sound the soul, buried in forgetfulness, recovers its good judgement and the lost memory of its primordial, illustrious source.)

Similarly, for the early Cabalists of the Merkavah-Heikhalot tradition, the recitation of their hymns brought about an ecstatic ascent through the gates of the seven heavenly dwelling places.[12] In this regard, it is pertinent to remember that the seven-staged mystical journey of Fray Luis's predecessor, Santa Teresa, also demonstrates similarities with the Merkavah and Heikhalot mystics.

The songs with which those early Cabalists induced their mystic ecstasy are considered to be of an "immense solemnity of style . . . unsurpassed in Hebrew hymnology."[13] In fact, the Merkavah mystics held that they shared the angels' songs.[14] This point is similar to Fray Luis's association of Salinas and his music with the "apolíneo sacro coro" ("Apollo's sacred choir"; v. 42). The Christianization of Apollo was an ongoing process when Fray Luis used the figure of speech.[15]

Given Fray Luis's penchant for Christian Cabala, however, it is

12. Scholem, *Major Trends*, pp. 57–59. See also Scholem's *Jewish Gnosticism, Merkabah Mysticism, and Talmudic Tradition*, p. 20.

13. Scholem, *Jewish Gnosticism*, p. 21.

14. Ithamar Gruenwald, *Apocalyptic and Merkabah Mysticism*, pp. 152–55.

15. On Fray Luis's role in the process, see Spitzer, *Classical and Christian Ideas of World Harmony*, pp. 112–14. In general, see Spitzer's work and Curtius's *European Literature* on the Christianization of Apollo, Orpheus, and the Muses; also see Jean Seznec, *The Survival of the Pagan Gods*, trans. Barbara Sessions (New York: Pantheon, 1953).

likely that he would welcome the additional sanctification of the pagan god by means of the Cabalistic conception of mystic harmony with the angelic choirs. Christian Cabalists were known to sanctify or safeguard the more pagan aspects of their syncretism with Hebrew psalms and with the identification of David with Orpheus.[16] This was the case with Pico in particular. For Lefèvre d'Etaples, his Psalter was "a safer place than a tract on magic . . . for allusions to the Cabalistic understanding of God's secret names."[17]

No discussion of Christian Cabala and universal harmony would be complete without mentioning Francesco Giorgi. As was shown in our discussion of Christ and harmony in *Nombres*, Giorgi agrees with Luis de León that Christ is both the symbol and the guarantor of universal accord. This Christological conclusion to *De harmonia mundi* is supported by the Venetian friar's extensive Neoplatonic and Pythagorean pronouncements on universal harmony, which he correlates with Cabala, Hermeticism, and Pseudo-Dionysian hierarchies.[18] Most importantly for Giorgi, it is Cabala that safeguards all the pagan *prisca theologia* of his syncretic world view and that provides proof of the truth of Christianity.[19]

The Mystical Ascent

Three of Fray Luis's major poems refer to the divine origins of the human soul in the Neoplatonic manner. But, as another Gnostic system, Cabala also describes the birth of the soul in the depth of the divine sphere, its descent through the spheres to earth, and its aspiration to return to heaven.[20] In the following references, Luis de León's verses on the soul's origin and longing to return could be interpreted Cabalistically as well as Neoplatonically. In fact, in the poet's theological view, the Cabalistic interpretation would be more acceptable. In the ode to Salinas, Fray Luis writes:

el alma, que en olvido está sumida,
torna a cobrar el tino
y memoria perdida
de su origen primera esclarecida (vv. 6–10)

16. See Frances Yates, *Giordano Bruno and the Hermetic Tradition*, p. 104; D. P. Walker, *Spiritual and Demonic Magic*, pp. 1–5, and his *The Ancient Theology*, pp. 22–24, 103.
17. Brian Copenhaver, "Lefèvre d'Etaples, Symphorien Champier, and the Sacred Names of God," p. 210.
18. In particular, see cantos 1 and 2 of *De harmonia mundi*.
19. Yates, *The Occult Philosophy in the Elizabethan Age*, pp. 29–30.
20. Scholem, *Major Trends*, pp. 239–41. Here Scholem is mainly speaking of the slightly pre-Zoharic work of Nahmanides (Moses ben Nahman).

(the soul, buried in forgetfulness, recovers its good judgement and the lost memory of its primordial, illustrious source)

In the "Noche serena," the longing to return to his heavenly home is made more poignant through contrasts with the terrestrial abode:

> Cuando contemplo el cielo
> de innumerables luces adornado,
> y miro hacia el suelo
> de noche rodeado,
> en sueño y en olvido sepultado,
>   El amor y la pena
> despiertan en mi pecho un ansia ardiente;
> despiden larga vena
>   los ojos hechos fuente (vv. 1–9)

(When I regard the heavens adorned with innumerable lights, and I look toward the earth, surrounded by night, buried in sleep and oblivion, love and grief awaken in my breast an ardent yearning; my eyes, transformed into a spring, pour out an abundant stream)

Another ode dedicated to a friend ("A Felipe Ruiz") reveals similar displeasure with earthly life and longing to return to his home in a heavenly sphere:

> ¿Cuándo será que pueda
> libre de esta prisión volar al cielo,
> Felipe, y en la rueda,
> que huye más del suelo,
> contemplar la verdad pura sin duelo? (vv. 1–5)

(When shall I be able, free from this prison, to fly to heaven, Felipe, and in the sphere which flees farthest from the earth to contemplate without sorrow the pure truth?)

As the poem to Felipe Ruiz ("¿Cuándo será?") continues, the poet enfolds a tableau of visions he might expect to see or of questions he would hope to have answered in the afterlife or through mystical experience. His expectations of greater awareness are concerned with all aspects of God's handiwork, the Creation:

> Veré las inmortales
> columnas, do la tierra está fundada;
> las lindes y señales,
> con que a la mar hinchada
> la Providencia tiene aprisionada;
>   por qué tiembla la tierra;
> por qué las hondas mares se embravecen,

do sale a mover guerra
el cierzo, y por qué crecen
las aguas del océano y descrecen;
   de dó manan las fuentes;
quién ceba y quién bastece de los ríos
las perpetuas corrientes;
de los helados fríos
veré las causas y de los estíos;
   las soberanas aguas
del aire en la región quién las sostiene;
de los rayos las fraguas;
dó los tesoros tiene
de nieve Dios, y el trueno dónde viene. (vv. 16–35)

(I will see the immortal columns upon which the earth is founded, the
limits and lines within which Providence keeps the swollen sea impris-
oned; why the earth quakes, why the deep seas become rough, whence
the north wind sallies to wage war, and why the waters of the ocean
rise and ebb; whence the springs flow; who feeds and who nourishes the
unceasing currents of the rivers; I will see the causes of the frozen winters
and of the summers; who sustains the upper waters in the region of the
air; where God keeps the forges of His thunderbolts, His treasuries of
snow, and where the thunder comes from.)

It is appropriate to dwell on these verses since, in their detail as
well as in their relationship to the whole of Fray Luis's "mystical"
poetry, they resemble Giorgi's *De harmonia mundi*. Both the celes-
tial-mystical poems of Luis de León and the great opus of Giorgi
focus on the divinely structured universe, its harmonious balance of
powers, and the spiritual role of man. Like Fray Luis, Giorgi enumerates the mysterious forces of nature that contribute to the divine scheme. He speaks of skies, clouds, rain, dew, drizzle, hail, and
snow[21] in a manner similar to Fray Luis on divinely guided Nature
in "¿Cuándo será?" (vv. 16–35). For both writers the beauty and
harmony of the Deity are reflected in varied levels of the mac-
rocosmos and the microcosmos. In Christian Cabalistic terms, the
parallel worlds of Infinity and of Creation are maintained in harmonious balance by Divine Will and through Christ's intercession.

Fray Luis's poems "¿Cuándo será?," the "Noche serena," and
the ode to Salinas are of the same spiritual and aesthetic fabric as
Giorgi's *De harmonia mundi*. Both authors hold a mystico-poetic
view of the universe, although neither is consistently thought of as a
mystic. In Fray Luis's case, it is chiefly the message of the three
poems discussed above that has sparked debate on his possibly

21. See *De harmonia mundi* 1.7.17–20, 142v-146r.

mystic status. Félix García finds Luisian verse to be truly mystical and the closest possible to the unification of poetics and mysticism.[22] In his comparisons of the friar's poems with Hispano-Hebraic verse, Millás Vallicrosa finds that they share a common mystic quality.[23] Rafael Lapesa does not deny the mystic longing of Luis de León, but he holds that the humanist was "demasiado intelectual para ser místico" (too intellectual to be a mystic).[24] In a more recent examination of Fray Luis's mysticism, Jean Krynen has attempted to delineate a "humanistic" mysticism, but his rather limited definition of Renaissance Neoplatonism does not take into account its Cabalistic and more widely syncretic aspects.[25]

Most pro-mystical Luisian scholars stop short of calling the friar a true mystic in the mold of Santa Teresa or San Juan de la Cruz. Despite all his mystical longing and mystical poetics, the humanist never describes his possible mystical experience with the intense and total release of his Carmelite contemporaries. Thus, his lack of personal reaction to mystical ecstasy keeps Fray Luis from being considered a Christian mystic. The friar's restraint in this matter does not forbid him, however, from being considered a Cabalistic mystic. Scholem tells us that Cabalists refrain from describing the intimate details of their experience and that they prefer to speak of *devekut* (spiritual communion) rather than the actual mystical union with God described by many Christian mystics.[26] Mystical accounts of the divine nuptial union are rare in Cabala although there are a few interpretations of Canticles as a conjugal dialogue. As a whole, *devekut* can be called an ethical system of

> continuous attachment or adhesion to God . . . which . . . almost takes the place of the previous ecstatic experience. Although *devekut* is definitely a contemplative value, it is not predicated upon special or abnormal modes of consciousness. Indeed, according to Moses ben Nahman—a generation before the Zohar—true *devekut* can be realized in the normal life of the individual within the community. It is therefore capable of being transformed into a social value, a point of great importance in the subsequent influence of Kabbalism on popular ethics.[27]

The description of Cabalistic mysticism as *devekut* is the sort of spirituality manifested by Christian Cabalists such as Reuchlin and

22. See García's introduction to Fray Luis's verse in the *Obras completas*, pp. 1388–1400.

23. "Probable influencia," pp. 284–85.

24. "Las odas de Fray Luis de León a Felipe Ruiz," 2:316.

25. "De la teología humanística a la mística de las luces."

26. *Kabbalah*, p. 160.

27. Scholem, *Major Trends*, p. 233.

Egidio da Viterbo. They were deeply concerned with social and political issues and their relationship to spiritual values. These aspects of *devekut* also seem to describe the combination of factors characterizing Fray Luis's life: a profound and sincere religious experience, an active and accomplished academic career, and an intense involvement in controversial issues of the era. The combination of interests is visible in the friar's poetry as well. Most of the Luisian poems with mystical aspects also display ethical concerns for the individual and society. In the "Noche serena," Fray Luis speaks of "aquesa lisonjera / vida" (this seductive life; vv. 34–35). It cannot be forgotten that the ode to Felipe Ruiz, and the opening lines "¿Cuándo será que pueda, / libre de esta prisión, volar al cielo?" (When shall I be able, free from this prison, to fly to heaven?), may have been inspired by the memory of his incarceration by the Inquisition.[28] The poem beginning "¡Qué descansada vida / la del que huye el mundanal ruïdo" (What a restful life, that of him who flees from worldly noise) is one of the friar's most famous works and is perhaps the one that best combines a sense of mystic longing with one of moral exasperation with society. In that poem, he criticizes excessive concerns for wealth, fame, and power and prefers his "secreto seguro, deleitoso" (secret refuge of delight; v. 22). Other poems show stronger concerns for individual and social morality, but they nearly always suggest that the righteous path leads to a truly superior spiritual life. For example, the poem "De la avaricia" ("On Avarice") ends with:

> ¿Qué vale el no tocado
> tesoro, si corrompe el dulce sueño;
> si estrecha el ñudo dado,
> si más enturbia el ceño,
> y deja en la riqueza pobre al dueño? (vv. 21–25)

> (What value does hoarded wealth have if it spoils gentle sleep, if it binds and enslaves, if it wrinkles the owner's brow and leaves him poor amidst his wealth?)

Thus, the sort of mysticism we see in Fray Luis's verse seems to match Cabala's conception of *devekut*. Luis de León may have absorbed some of the more socially oriented aspects of this Cabalistic mysticism as a converso descendant and as a member of a rather converso society of scholars at Salamanca or Alcalá. The Augustinian humanist may have been influenced by Cabalistic mysticism through his Hebraic studies or through reading other Christian

---

28. Manuel Durán, *Luis de León*, p. 74. Durán states that he is following Dámaso Alonso on this point.

Cabalists. Basing his idea on Luis de León's Latin works, Kottman writes that the friar seems to follow other Christian Cabalists—most notably Pico, Ricci, and Egidio—in identifying Platonic and Mosaic mysticism.[29] More importantly, Fray Luis holds that Platonic mysticism stems from the Mosaic (Cabalistic), to which it is morally inferior. We can therefore no longer consider Fray Luis's mysticism as simply Neoplatonic dressing for his verse or as dilettantish Christian mysticism. His mystic flights are sincere, but they are more restrained and Christian Cabalistic than Carmelite and revealing.

Symbols in the Spheres

Both Christian and Judaic Cabala are concerned with the mystical ascent of the soul through the heavenly spheres. In *kavanah* (mystical intention) the aspiring mystic focuses his prayer on the name of the spiritual realm through which his prayer is passing.[30] The name may be one of the mystical names of God or one of the *sefirot*. Christian Cabalists, like Pico, associated each celestial sphere with a *sefirah*.[31] With Giorgi, the system was a bit more Christian since he placed more emphasis on the *sefirot* and the angelic hierarchies.[32]

Luis de León mentions the heavenly spheres frequently in his poetry. In "Noche serena" he exhorts Diego Olarte and all mortals, saying, "¡Ay!, ¡levantad los ojos / a aquesta celestial eterna esfera!" (Alas! Raise your eyes to this eternal celestial sphere!; vv. 31–32). The ode to Salinas describes the soul rising with mystical music "a la más alta esfera" (v. 17). A more extensive description is found in the Luisian poem of mystic longing dedicated to Felipe Ruiz ("¿Cuándo será?"). The poet describes the vision he aspires to behold:

> Y de allí levantado,
> veré los movimientos celestiales,
> ansí el arrebatado
> como los naturales;
> las causas de los hados, las señales.
>   Quién rige las estrellas
> veré, y quién las enciende con hermosas

29. *Law and Apocalypse*, p. 106.
30. Scholem, *Kabbalah*, p. 177.
31. Yates, *Giordano Bruno*, p. 100.
32. Yates, *The Occult Philosophy*, pp. 32–33; Walker, *Spiritual and Demonic Magic*, pp. 112–15.

y eficaces centellas;
por qué estén las dos Osas
de bañarse en el mar siempre medrosas.
　　Veré este fuego eterno,
fuente de vida y luz, dó se mantiene
y por qué en el invierno
tan presuroso viene,
quién en las noches largas se detiene.
　　Veré, sin movimiento
en la más alta esfera, las moradas
del gozo y del contento,
de oro y luz labradas,
de espíritus dichosos habitadas. (vv. 51–70)

(And from there uplifted I shall see the movements of heavenly bodies, both the sudden comet and the natural movements, the causes and the signs of one's fate. I shall see who rules the stars and who lights them with beautiful and efficacious sparks; why the two Bears are always afraid to swim in the sea. I shall see where this eternal fire, the source of light and life, is maintained; and why in the winter it comes so rapidly and who delays so during the long nights. I shall see motionless in the highest sphere the mansions of joy and happiness, built of gold and light, inhabited by blessed spirits.)

The Luisian dream vision of the celestial spheres recalls Santa Teresa's *Moradas del castillo interior*. As we pointed out in Chapter 3, the Teresian mystical way through the seven *moradas* is strikingly similar to the ascent of the Merkavah-Heikhalot mystics through the seven heavenly mansions. Fray Luis's description of the "moradas / del gozo y del contento / de oro y luz labradas" is reminiscent of the Heikhalot descriptions of the beauties of heaven and the glories of God. The friar's presentation most resembles the Heikhalot account by refraining from expressing highly personal reactions. However, the Carmelite nun's mystical presentation is more similar to the Heikhalot vision in its overall, seven-part structure.[33]

With regard to this poem for Felipe Ruiz ("¿Cuándo será?"), it is appropriate to note Fray Luis's possible astrological references. The verse "las causas de los hados, las señales" especially brings to mind the general astrological beliefs of his era and the integration of astrology into the systems of many Christian Cabalists in par-

---

33. I am not implying any Teresian influence in "Noche serena." Both authors made independent use of this Cabalistic idea. Macrí, *La poesía*, p. 339, estimates that Fray Luis's verse was composed between 1577 and 1578. This is approximately the same period in which Santa Teresa wrote the *Moradas*, but they were probably not known to Fray Luis until after her death.

ticular. Some of Luis de León's modern critics seem uncomfortable when trying to explain the Augustinian humanist's interest in astrology.[34] Francisco Pacheco, Fray Luis's contemporary, writes that the friar was a great astrologer and practitioner of the Chaldean art *astrología judiciaria*.[35] Another contemporary historian, Luis de Cabrera y Córdoba, tells that the Augustinian was interested in a Navarrese self-appointed prophet who claimed to foretell the future with symbolic lines and letters in combination with Scriptural texts.[36] The use of letters and Bible quotations may, indeed, have been Cabalistic. It is unfortunate that we do not have more information on Fray Luis's astrological interests in Cabala.

As for astrological determinism, it is clear that, like other Christian Cabalists such as Giorgi, Luis de León denīes the absolute power of the stars over earthly affairs. He also firmly upholds the principle of free will within the larger framework of Divine Providence.[37]

Another aspect of occult philosophy mentioned in Luisian verse is the importance of numerology. The friar specifically refers to it only once, in the ode to Salinas when he writes of "números concordes" (v. 27). But the context of the reference—one of balance and harmony—appears frequently in his poems with musical references, as this study has pointed out. Numerical implications can therefore be read into most of the friar's treatments of musical accord. It is important to remember his statement in *Nombres* concerning *gimatriyya* that "yo no condeno" (I do not condemn; p. 741). Fray Luis would not have denied Giorgi or Agrippa the numerical speculation of which they were so fond. And Christian Cabalists like them would not assume that the Luisian reference to "números concordes" was referring only to Neoplatonic and Pythagorean interests in numbers.

Another point of contact with Christian Cabalists and an especially interesting element of Fray Luis's vision of the spheres is his reference to Saturn in the "Noche Serena":

---

34. See the discussions of James Fitzmaurice-Kelly, *Fray Luis de León; A Biographical Fragment*, pp. 84–85; Guy, *La pensée*, pp. 75, 282–83; and Coster, *Luis de León*, 1:254–55. Coster, however, is more at ease than the other two critics mentioned with regard to Fray Luis's interests in the occult.

35. Pacheco's *Libro de verdaderos retratos* (1599) is quoted in Bell, *Luis de León*, pp. 248–49.

36. Bell quotes Cabreras's *Historia de Felipe Segundo* (1619) in *Luis de León*, p. 249.

37. Lapesa, "Las odas de Fray Luis de León a Felipe Ruiz," p. 315, thinks that Fray Luis's comments on Job 38:32–33 clearly show that Divine Providence controls the stars. As His instruments, they have some power but not absolute control over man.

Rodéase en la cumbre
Saturno, padre de los siglos de oro;
tras él la muchedumbre
del reluciente coro
su luz va repartiendo y su tesoro. (vv. 56–60)

(At the summit Saturn revolves, the father of the Golden Ages; behind him the throng of the gleaming chorus distributes its light and treasure.)

This is not the usual vision of Saturn as cruel Kronos eating his children and showering men with dreaded melancholy.[38] Fray Luis's view is that of the Renaissance humanists who revived two notions of Saturn. One, the Neoplatonic, reserved for Saturn the highest place among planets and the highest and noblest qualities of soul and reason. The other, the Aristotelian, held that all great men were Saturnine or melancholic. Agrippa combined Cabala with the Renaissance Saturnine synthesis and emphasized the mystical powers of the melancholic scholar.[39] This Christian Cabalistic view raises the interesting question as to whether Fray Luis might have considered himself to be a melancholy scholar of the Renaissance-Cabalistic sort. He was thought to be a fine writer and an outspoken scholar, even in his own time. In the poem we have just examined, he valued Saturn above all other planetary powers. As we have shown throughout this study, he was a Christian Cabalist, and therefore he could have been aware of Saturn's correspondence to *Binah*.[40] This *sefirah* of knowledge and understanding is the Cabalistic equivalent of the Holy Ghost, the inspiration and enlightenment of Christians.

With regard to the element of melancholy in Fray Luis, we only need to turn to his *Exposición del libro de Job*[41] or to his poetry to encounter constant reminders. Luis de León's "Saturnine" poems often combine praise of peace and nature's quiet with a longing for solitude and intellectual or spiritual fulfillment. The poems of this sort are many, but the prime example is the "Vida retirada," which opens:

¡Qué descansada vida
la del que huye el mundanal ruïdo
y sigue la escondida

38. This account of Saturn's altered image in the Renaissance is drawn from Raymond Klibansky, Erwin Panofsky, and Fritz Saxl in *Saturn and Melancholy*.
39. Yates, *The Occult Philosophy*, pp. 55–56.
40. Yates, *Giordano Bruno*, p. 100.
41. See Macrí, *La poesía*, p. 74, on the similarities of the Job commentary to the friar's poetry.

senda, por donde han ido
los pocos sabios que en el mundo han sido! (vv. 1–5)

(What a restful life, that of him who flees from worldly noise and follows the hidden path down which have gone the few wise men who have existed in the world!)

It closes:

A la sombra tendido
de yedra y lauro eterno coronado,
puesto el atento oído
al son dulce, acordado
del plectro sabiamente meneado. (vv. 81–85)

(stretched out in the shade, wearing a crown of ivy and eternal laurel, listening attentively to the sweet, well-tuned sound of the strings skillfully plucked.)

A similar poem that more emphatically reveals the melancholic side of Fray Luis's character opens with the line "Huíd, contentos, de mi triste pecho" (Flee from my mournful breast, thoughts of happiness) and continues: "La noche aquí se vela, aquí se llora / el día miserable sin consuelo, / y vence al mal de ayer el mal de agora" (Here one watches the night in grief and cries unconsolably during the miserable day; each one worse than the preceding; vv. 13–15).

In light of this study on Christian Cabala in Fray Luis's work, the most interesting Saturnine reference is probably the one line of verse in which the poet directly mentions Saturn. Because Fray Luis refers to him as "Saturno, padre de los siglos de oro," he reminds the reader of the eschatological interests of Christian Cabala and of the friar's own particular apocalyptic predictions, which we have discussed in reference to the name *Padre del siglo futuro*. The *siglos de oro* are like the new *shemitot* or messianic ages treated in our examination of *Nombres*. It is notable that in Francesco Giorgi's *De harmonia mundi*, the Christian Cabalistic work with which *Nombres* shares so many common concerns, the same phrase also appears. Giorgi also writes of the original golden ages of Saturn, when Adam lived blissfully in the earthly paradise (1.1.1, 5v). Later, the Venetian friar reveals his apocalyptic concerns as he writes of "the peace, the remission of sins, and that superabundance which is called the Jubilee, after the square of the number seven: which is consistent with Saturn the seventh planet."[42]

---

42. The entire phrase reads: "A quo loco affluit requies, peccatorum remissio, & exuberantia illa, quae iubileus dicitur, post quadratum numeri septenarij: qui cum Saturno septimo planeta consentit" (*De harmonia mundi*, 1.4.5, 60r-60v). The translations from *De harmonia* in this chapter are mine.

Giorgi continues in *De harmonia mundi* to speak of the special
position of Saturn nearest the Thrones in heaven and of the gifts
bestowed upon the Saturnine (1.5.5, 61r). Of most Christian
Cabalistic import, however, are the comments on Saturn's Hebrew
connections. Giorgi writes of "Saturn, which the Hebrews call
שבתי *Shabbathai*, which can be translated as my relaxation or my
resting place."[43] He says that the Hebrews ". . . say that they
received the law from the place or the measure of the Divinity [the
divine *sefirah*] which is called *Binah*, and to which Saturn corresponds."[44] Due to the supposedly Saturnine connections through
which the Law was given to the Chosen People, they are said to
follow the Saturnine religion that Moses is reputed to have established (1.4.5, 61r). Giorgi does not hesitate to use a Saturnine explanation in order to explain the treatment accorded the Jews
historically:

> And since Saturn endeavors to make his Saturnine ones imprinted with
> the form of God, full of indignation, he justly oppresses and punishes
> those who with wicked customs, more by deeds than words, slander his
> good influence, as we see confirmed frequently in the Hebrews who,
> compared with others, have received incomparably the most divine
> abundance of the true Saturn.[45]

Luis de León's phrase "Saturno, padre de los siglos de oro" is not
the only Luisian verse harboring eschatological meaning. As we
pointed out in Chapter 4, Fray Luis's Latin works reveal special
interest in the role of Spain in the era of wars with the Turk and the
discovery of the Americas. The friar felt that Spain—and perhaps
the Spanish conversos in particular—would play a major part in the
tumultuous times prior to the Second Coming. It is important to
remember this Luisian nationalism in examining poems such as
"La profecía del Tajo." The mournful exclamation "¡oh cara pa-
tria!" (oh beloved fatherland!; v. 80) can refer to more than the fall
of Spain to the Islamic forces in the year 711. Fray Luis's nationalistic allusions are more prominent in the poem "A Santiago." The
friar's reverence for the saint and respect for his homeland are
closely associated. Fray Luis's conception of the return of San-

43. ". . . denominatum a Saturno, qui Hebraice שבת Sabbatai, quod requies
meae, aut sedilia mea potest interpretari" (*De harmonia mundi*, 1.4.5, 60r).
44. ". . . cum ipsi dicant legem accepisse de loco, aut mensura divinitatis: quae
bina dicitur: cui respondet Saturnus. . ." (*De harmonia mundi*, 1.4.5, 60r).
45. "Et cum Saturnus Saturnios suos Deiformes facere studeat: eos qui pravis
moribus, factis magis, quam verbis influxum eius bonum calumniantur, indigna-
bundus merito deprimit, & castigat: ut in Hebraeis pluries comprobatum cernimus:
Qui affluentias divinissimas veri Saturni, prae caeteris incomparabiliter sus-
ceperunt" (*De harmonia mundi*, 1.4.5, 60v-61r).

tiago's body to the most western edge of the ancient world mingles
religious and nationalistic overtones:

> A España, a quien amaste
> (que siempre al buen principio el fin responde),
> tu cuerpo le enviaste
> para dar luz adonde
> el sol su resplandor cubre y asconde. (vv. 46–50)

(And since a fair ending corresponds to a good beginning, you sent to
Spain your body to bring another light to where the sun dims its splendor and sets.)

Fray Luis's normal opposition to the violence and bloodshed of
war contrasts with his praise of Santiago and implicit benediction
of Spanish foreign policy. Spain's sacred national destiny—associated as it was with Santiago—justified the holy wars against the
Moors and their contemporary successors, the Turks:

> ¡Oh gloria, oh gran prez nuestra,
> escudo fiel, oh celestial guerrero!
> vencido ya se muestra
> el Africano fiero
> por ti, tan orgulloso de primero; (vv. 135–40)

(Oh glory! Oh our great honor! Faithful shield! Oh heavenly warrior!
The fierce African, so proud at first, now conquered by you is revealed;)

The national destiny of Spain, supported by Fray Luis's Christian
Cabalistic views and symbolized by Santiago, is not unlike Egidio
da Viterbo's dreams of world harmony and order through the messianic leadership of Carlos V.[46] The positions of both Christian
Cabalists were opposed by Guillaume Postel's parallel aspirations
for French hegemony. In a final Luisian characterization of Santiago, Spanish predominance against all possible rivals is symbolized. Superficially the friar is referring to the journey of pilgrims
from many lands to Santiago de Compostela. However, given Luis
de León's Christian Cabalistic view of Spain's role and his reverent
association of Santiago with Spain, these verses can be interpreted
as a recognition of Spain's sacred national destiny:

> El áspero camino
> vence con devoción, y al fin te adora
> el Franco, el peregrino
> que Libia descolora,
> el que en Poniente, el que en Levante mora. (vv. 155–60)

---

46. See Chapter 1 on Egidio da Viterbo and Guillaume Postel.

(The Franks, others discolored by the Libyan sun, some from the West and others from the East, with devotion the pilgrims endure the difficult journey to adore you finally.)

In addition to Saturn and the other syncretic images Fray Luis places in his celestial and mystical presentations, there remains another significant symbol to examine: the sacred chariot. In "¿Cuándo será?," the poem to Felipe Ruiz, the Augustinian friar describes the wonders of life he hopes will be revealed to him in the afterlife or through a mystical experience. Among them is the chariot/sun:

> y entre las nubes mueve
> su carro Dios ligero y reluciente;
> horrible son conmueve,
> relumbra fuego ardiente,
> treme la tierra, humíllase la gente. (vv. 41–45)

(And among the clouds God drives his chariot, swift and gleaming; a terrible sound frightens us, blazing fires flash, the earth trembles, and the people fall to their knees.)

It is a truly syncretic image uniting Hellenic, Hebraic, and Cabalistic significancies. In the myths of Phoebus-Apollo and of Helios driving the chariot of the sun across the sky, the Renaissance humanists found a poetic image of providential regulation of the solar function. Biblical tradition also supported the vision of a divine refulgent chariot in the heavens through Ezekiel's account (1:4–21). As we noted in Chapter 3 on Santa Teresa, early Cabalists concentrated on throne or chariot mysticism by expanding on Ezekiel's vision. It was these Merkavah mystics who wrote the solemn hymns of praise related to their sacred vision of the *Shekhinah* guiding the mysterious chariot of light. Later Cabalists continued the Merkavah tradition and sang the hymns to guide their mystical prayers through the celestial spheres to the chariot/throne. Mention of the chariot is also frequent in the *Zohar*; the following is an example of how chariot mysticism became thoroughly integrated into scriptural tradition as treated by the Zoharic Cabalists: "when the Holy One moves towards the chariots and the hosts to give nourishment to all those supernal beings—as it is written, 'She (the *Shekhinah*) riseth while it is yet night and giveth food to her household and a portion to her maidens' (Prov. XXXI, 15)—all are filled with joy and song. They begin their hymning with the words: 'God be merciful unto us and bless us and cause *His face to shine upon us*'" (3.67b, p. 24; my italics).

All of these Hellenic, Hebraic, and Cabalistic traditions participate in the imagery of Fray Luis's "Mueve su carro Dios." Moreover, we should point out the similar treatment of this subject by
another Christian Cabalist, Francesco Giorgi. In *De harmonia
mundi*, the Venetian friar also subscribes to the unified tradition by
referring to the powers of God's chariot of light and grace (1.8.5,
168v-169r).

Of Light and Night

The discussion of God's brilliant chariot is an appropriate introduction to our examination of the role of light in Cabala and in Luis
de León's verse. Light imagery is one of the most common elements
of poetry and mysticism, and it is particularly important to the
Gnostic roots of both Neoplatonism and Cabala.[47] Cabalistic references to light have more profound meaning as a sacred mystery
than do the more purely metaphorical uses of light in the Neoplatonic manner of many Renaissance poets.

Light symbolism is important in all Cabalistic systems, being
most frequently used with regard to *Ein-Sof*.[48] The *sefirot* as the
manifestations of the Hidden God relate to each other in terms of
light, with every *sefirah* reflecting another and transferring light
from the upper to the lower *sefirot*. In turn, each *sefirah* reflects
light on the lower worlds and receives light from them. From his
position in the lower world, man strives to communicate with the
Deity through concentrating on the supernal lights of the divine
world (the *sefirot*) and of the spiritual worlds in general.[49] Only
through this process of meditation and of considering the *sefirot* as
intellectual lights can they be perceived by man. Thus, in general,
every Cabalistic description of the upper world usually contains
some aspect of light imagery. It is no accident that the title of the
major Cabalistic work is *Sefer ha-Zohar*, i.e., *Book of Splendor*
(Reflected Light), and that one of the most-read Cabalistic treatises
of the Renaissance was the *Portae lucis*, the Latin version of
Gikatilla's *Sha'arei Orah*, *Gates of Light*. The Christian Cabalists
of the Renaissance continued to emphasize the light symbolism
they had encountered in the *Zohar* and the *Sha'arei Orah*. Giorgi,
for example, described at length how all light—physical or metaphorical—is divine in origin (3.8.3–7, 433r–436r).

With the Cabalistic significance of light in mind, we turn to Fray

47. Scholem, *Kabbalah*, p. 126.
48. Ibid., pp. 90–115; Scholem, *Major Trends*, pp. 206–8.
49. Scholem, *Kabbalah*, pp. 369–70.

Luis's verse. As one might expect, light references are most prominent in his "mystical" poetry. In the Ruiz poem, "¿Cuándo será?,"
the friar longs for the enlightenment his soul will find in his heavenly home:

> Allí, a mi vida junto,
> en luz resplandeciente convertido,
> veré distinto y junto
> lo que es y lo que ha sido,
> y su principio propio y ascondido. (vv. 6–10)

(There, along with my own life, I shall see, converted into resplendent
light, separate yet together, that which is and that which has been, along
with its own source of being.)

In the poem "Inspira nuevo canto" ("Inspire a New Song"),
written to celebrate the birth of the Marqués de Alcañices's daughter, Fray Luis treats the descent of the soul from its divine origin.
The poem is filled with light to convey the beauty and joy surrounding the new soul, the new spark of divine light. The infant's bright
soul brings new light to all on earth as God's sun brings new light of
day: "que con la luz nacida / podrá ser nuestra esfera esclarecida"
(our earthly sphere can be brightened by the newborn light; vv. 14–
15). Even the child's physical aspects are described with light
imagery:

> los tus dos ojos sean
> dos luces celestiales,
> que guíen al bien sumo a los mortales.
>   El cuerpo delicado
> como cristal lucido y transparente, (vv. 53–57)

(May her two eyes be two immortal lights, that guide mortals to the
Supreme Good. The delicate body like brilliant and transparent glass,)

The poem called "Noche serena" shows a profoundly Cabalistic
treatment of light against the darkened heavens. Upon contemplating the night sky, the poet makes pronouncements that could be
compared to a Cabalistic meditation on the lights of the heavenly
palaces of the Heikhalot:

> Morada de grandeza,
> templo de claridad y hermosura,
> . . . .
>   Aquí vive el contento,
> aquí reina la paz; aquí, asentado
> en rico y alto asiento
> está el Amor sagrado,
> de honras y deleites rodeado;

> inmensa hermosura
> aquí se muestra toda, y resplandece
> clarísima luz pura,
> que jamás anochese;
> eterna primavera aquí florece. (vv. 11–12, 66–75)

(Mansion of grandeur, temple of brightness and beauty, . . . Here lives happiness, here reigns peace; here, seated on a rich and lofty seat, is sacred Love, surrounded by glory and delight. Immense beauty is here fully revealed, and there gleams the brightest purest light, which never turns to night; eternal springtime flowers here.)

In the same poem Fray Luis also speaks of lights of the planetary spheres:

> La luna cómo mueve
> la plateada rueda, y va en pos della
> la Luz do el saber llueve,
> y la graciosa Estrella
> de amor la sigue reluciente y bella; (vv. 46–50)

(How the moon moves its silver sphere, and behind her follows the light where wisdom pours, and the graceful star of love, follows it gleaming and beautiful;)

In the following strophes of the poem, the poet speaks of Mars, Jupiter, and Saturn as well. When we recall that the spheres all had Sefirotic equivalencies, the Cabalistic connections of these stanzas become more clear. Any of Fray Luis's colleagues who knew Cabala could have associated his planetary references with those of Agrippa. In *De occulta philosophia*, the Nettesheimer provided a detailed outline of the sacred names and numbers associated with each planet's sphere.[50]

One of the most interesting uses of Cabala's light symbolism in Fray Luis's poems is found in the ode to Salinas. Our Cabalistic poet opens with the verses:

> El aire se serena
> y viste de hermosura y luz no usada,
> Salinas, cuando suena
> la música extremada

The "luz no usada" of the Salinas poem is the same sacred light that the friar describes as "luz no corrompida" in the ode "Al apartamiento" (v. 35). Divine light is a very significant aspect of Cabala, but it is especially so in the phrase "viste de luz no usada,

---

50. Agrippa, *Three Books of Occult Philosophy*, 2.22, p. 243; 3.24, p. 415.

Salinas."[51] To be *clothed in light* is the Cabalistic point of interest. Even with the Merkavah initiates, those earliest Cabalistic mystics, God is said to clothe Himself in a garment (or skin or body) of light.[52] The corresponding secret name for this divine action is *Zoharariel YHVH*. His cosmic garment is said to be filled with repetitions of the Tetragrammaton. It is called "cosmic" because the light issuing from it fills the universe and all Creation. Merkavah hymns praise this vision of God, saying, "Resplendent king, robed in splendor / Glorified with embroideries of songs."[53] These lyrics concerning sacred song and the vision of splendor are similar to the combination in Fray Luis's poem: "y viste de hermosura y luz no usada, / Salinas, cuando suena / la música extremada" (vv. 2–4).

That a human soul should also wear a garment of light is a concept developed after the Merkavah era when the theories of the *sefirot* evolved. The *sefirot* itself has been considered as a garment or skin of light that acts as a shield to enable man to look at lights that would otherwise blind him.[54] Thus, the mystic is thought to look at a series of garments of light while moving up the mystical ladder. In addition, all souls are believed to wear garments of light they received during their formation in the Sefirotic world—the world of divine garments of light. When united with the *sefirot*, souls wear pure celestial garments, but when on earth they must wear more earthly—yet still divine—garments. It is possible that Fray Luis had the Cabalistic idea of garments of light in mind, not only for the Salinas poem, but also in the shimmering image of the infant's soul descending from heaven in "Inspira nuevo canto."

With these concepts in mind, it is not difficult to see how a humanist trained in Hebrew and the Christian Cabala would allude to the celestial garment of splendorous light worn by a dear friend, much admired for the mystical qualities of his music, or would speak of the pure glow of the newborn child's soul. The *Zohar* in particular frequently mentions the various aspects of garments of

51. Woodward has noticed the resemblance of this phrase to the *Zohar*: "this is a tempting line of speculation and, I think, a profitable one" ("Fray Luis de León's 'Oda a Francisco Salinas,'" p. 73). He hesitated to further explore the relationship of the Luisian verse to the *Zohar*, citing the difficulties of Hebrew as the restraining factor. Yet, it seems that Woodward saw the reference to a garment of skin of light as merely "the kind of linguistic play Fray Luis delights in." A closer examination of the possible Cabalistic influences on Fray Luis shows us that the interrelationship of the linguistic interests of Cabala and Fray Luis's works is deep indeed, as we have shown in the previous chapter.

52. Scholem, *Jewish Gnosticism*, pp. 57–62.

53. Ibid., p. 26.

54. Scholem, *Kabbalah*, p. 104.

light. A few examples of which Fray Luis may have been aware are the mystical garment in general (1.66a, 216–17); brilliant garments of the divine names (3.39b, 122); and garments appropriate to the upper and lower worlds (4.299b, 281).

Cabalistic ideas concerning night are closely related to those on light, music, and prayer or mystical ascent—all favorite themes of Fray Luis. It is the darkened sky of night, of course, that makes the light of celestial bodies perceptible to the human eye. Fray Luis's most lyrical treatment of the night sky is found in the poem to Diego Olarte, often called "Noche serena." The whole poem centers on the mystical longing experienced by the poet upon contemplation of the starry night sky. It begins:

> Cuando contemplo el cielo
> de innumerables luces adornado,
> y miro hacia el suelo
> de noche rodeado,

The night is an especially holy and mystical time for Cabalists, since night prayers are held to be the most perfect. The *Zohar* tells us:

> at midnight all the truly righteous arise to read the Torah and to sing psalms, and we have learnt the Holy One, blessed be He, and all the righteous in the [celestial] Garden of Eden listen to their voices, and in consequence a certain grace is imparted to them by day; so it is written, "the Lord will command his grace in the day-time, and in the night his song shall be with me." (Ps. XLII, 9). Hence it is that the praises which are sung at night constitute the most perfect praise. (1.82b, 275)

Night is also the time when the songs/prayers of men are most sanctified by the simultaneous singing of the angels in the upper world (2.231a, 339). At midnight especially the "souls of the righteous ascend to the bliss above" and "then there is a holy stirring in the world" (2.242a, 370). Specifically, it is the *Neshamah*, the highest portion of man's three-part soul, which can partake of the mystical and can leave his body at night (2.169b, 150). These are all constituent elements of the "background" of night sky against which the elaborate plot of Zoharic light symbolism is contrasted.

One other Luisian poem uses light symbolism with Cabalistic implications. The work that is called "Morada del cielo" or "De la vida del cielo" begins:

> Alma región luciente,
> prado de bienandanza, que ni al hielo

ni con el rayo ardiente
fallece, fértil suelo,
producidor eterno de consuelo;

(Loving region of light, meadow of blessedness, which neither under ice
nor under burning thunderbolts fails; fertile soil eternally producing
consolation;)

While the terms "alma región luciente" are usually taken to mean
"sweet" or "loving region of light" in reference to a heavenly dwelling place, other elements of the poem may indicate that Fray Luis is
probably referring to the soul as well as heaven. In "Alma región
luciente" the poet speaks of the sweet peace of heaven coming as
"immortal dulzor al alma" (immortal sweetness to the soul; v. 11),
and there is also in that poem the sense of the soul as a microcosm of
the shining heavenly home, as the *morada* that longs to return to,
and unite with, the "morada del cielo."

Fray Luis's "Alma región luciente" also resembles Reuchlin's
conception of the soul of the worthy Cabalistic mystic. In *De arte
cabalistica*, he speaks of the enlightenment of the mystic's soul
thus:

The happy Cabalist through the Cabala, that is, the path of tradition and
belief, breaks through the darkness and springs forth into the brightness,
where he reaches the ordinary light (*lumen*), and from the light moves
into the essential light (*lux*) which enlightens and through as much of the
lux as human nature can grasp, he understands the true source of light
(*luminare*). . . . The mind itself of the Cabalist . . . is transported to
supercelestial and invisible things transcending all human sense, and
then . . . like a certain inhabitant of a supercelestial dwelling place . . . he
visits the soul of the Messiah.[55]

Like Fray Luis, Reuchlin climaxes his characterization of the
sacred dwelling place by emphasizing the role of Christ. For

55. The entire passage from *De arte cabalistica* (1:640–41) reads: ". . . felix
Cabalista per Cabalam: id est, recepti & crediti semitam tenebras erumpit, & pros-
ilit in splendorem, quo attingit lumen, & sic a lumine migrat in lucem, & per lucem
quantum humana potest capere natura, illud verum luminare comprehendit sub
modo entis, non autem non entis, nisi fiat hoc per omnium abstractionem, quaecun-
que non sunt principium absolute primum. Cumque frequenter hac via per ineffabile
gaudium & alacritatem spiritus ipsa mens Cabalistae intra profundae taciturnitatis
secretum humilia deferens atque terrena, ad supercoelestia & invisibilia transfertur
omnem transcendentia humanum sensum, tunc & si adhuc mortali in cute hospi-
tatus, tamen socius fit angelorum, perinde atque domicilii supercoelestis quidam
inquilinus, cuius tam crebra conversatio in coelis esse cognoscatur, & tum quando-
que cum illis tanquam viarum suarum comitibus ad altiora spaciatur, animamque
Messihae visitat."

Reuchlin, the mystic's pleasures are found in attending to the soul of the Messiah. For Luis de León, heavenly life is made most delightful by the presence of Christ, the tender Shepherd. In both authors' works, Christian Cabalistic light symbolism plays a role. The German humanist turns the mystical principles and the light symbolism of Judaic Cabala into a unitive mystical experience of the soul with Christ. The same general pattern occurs in Fray Luis's "Morada del cielo." The Augustinian humanist moves from the vision of the enlightened soul—the "alma región luciente"—to Christ, the source of light.

Significantly, in the same poem, "Alma región luciente," the friar uses images of mystic union encountered elsewhere in his works. Christ is the "buen Pastor" (good Shepherd; v. 10) who carefully watches over his grazing sheep with the "inmortal dulzor" (immortal sweetness) of his "rabel sonoro" (sonorous rebec; vv. 11, 27). Here we again encounter the pastoral imagery so prominent in *Nombres* and so reminiscent of similar images from Giorgi's *De harmonia mundi*, Cabala's *Ra'aya Meheimna*, and biblical tradition. Fray Luis complements the pastoral imagery with other allusions to Christ found in *Nombres*. The shepherd is described as the "dulce Esposo" (sweet Bridegroom; v. 370), a symbol sometimes used by Cabalists for the mystical experience. There is another reference drawn from Canticles as well: Fray Luis describes the *Esposo* or *Pastor* "De púrpura y de nieve / florida la cabeza, coronado" (with His head crowned in purple and shining; vv. 6–7). This is the same verse from the Song of Songs Kottman has identified as being Cabalistically treated in the friar's Latin tractates and echoed in *Nombres*.[56] Thus, in the poem "Alma región luciente" Fray Luis again combines varied Cabalistic elements that parallel and support his Christianity.

Conclusion

We have seen that Fray Luis's poems employ a variety of syncretic symbols that can share Christian, Cabalistic, and Neoplatonic meaning. To a certain extent, the Neoplatonic guise—because of its frequent appearance in Renaissance literature—serves as a cover for the possibly unacceptable Cabalistic interpretation. To the Inquisitors, Luis de León's syncretic symbols could appear as the typical trappings of the era. But to those informed of Cabala as

56. See Chapter 4 above, notes 93 and 94; see especially Kottman's *Law and Apocalypse*, appendix 2.

scholars or as converso descendants, Fray Luis's poetry could be appreciated on another level. The references to the mystic's longing to return, and the notion of a harmonious universe of opposing forces in concert, could also be examined from different points of view. The same is true of the celestial spheres, the appearance of Saturn, and the role of light in Fray Luis's poetry.

Certain phrases, however, would provide more inspiration for Cabalistic comparisons. The verse "viste de luz no usada" is a powerful example. But, beyond the specifics, it is also the overall impression of Luis de León's poems that can be linked to the Cabalistic tradition. Millás Vallicrosa's description of Abulafia's Cabalistic poetry could even be applied to the friar's verses: "canta la gloria de Dios reflejada en la gradación de los mundos que de Él han derivado la existencia, en el misterio que reside en la llama ígnea con la cual centellean las esferas que nacieron a la palabra por él pronunciada, mientras con armonía, y fragancia exhalan, como un eco, aquella divina voz" (he sings God's glory reflected in the gradations of worlds which have derived their existence from Him. It is the glory of God reflected in the mystery that dwells in the blazing flames of the glimmering spheres that were born when He pronounced the word; and those stars exhale a fragrance in harmony like an echo of that divine voice).[57] Mystery, mystical light, divine will, and harmony—these aspects of Cabalistic poetry are also Fray Luis's. Luisian verse, like that of the Spanish Cabalists, is mainly concerned with mystical issues or mystic colorations. It is, as Millás has said of Cabalistic poetry in general, largely involved with the contemplation of God in His various manifestations and with the origin of being.[58] Like the Cabalistic poets, Fray Luis focuses on the Divine rather than on personal reactions to an actual union with the Divine such as we find in the works of Santa Teresa or San Juan de la Cruz. Fray Luis's mysticism is a blending of philosophy and poetry, somewhat like that of the Spanish Hebrew poet Solomon Ibn Gabirol (d. 1058).

For all the similarities Luis de León's poetry bears to Cabala, it is still very Christian Cabala. Again, as in *Nombres*, the Christian Cabala of his verse has many points of contact with Francesco Giorgi. Fray Luis may or may not have known *De harmonia mundi*, but it is not difficult to see how two humanists of similar training and temperament could produce such complementary Christian Cabalistic works. The areas in which Giorgi differed from Pico or

57. *La poesía sagrada*, pp. 143–44.
58. Ibid., p. 140.

Agrippa are the ones of correspondence to Luis de León. Neither the Venetian nor the Salamancan friar was dangerously infatuated with Cabalistic magic. In fact, Giorgi's flirtations with angelic magic have been called "too Christian" and "too metaphorical" to be considered in the same class with Agrippa and others.[59] But, it is that same combination of Christianity, Cabala, and a poetic outlook that we find in Luis de León's verses and in the *Nombres*.

59. Walker, *Spiritual and Demonic Magic*, p. 112. See also Chapter 1 above.

6

the christian cabala of san juan
de la cruz and of the mystical union

San Juan de la Cruz, like his slightly older contempo-raries Santa Teresa and Luis de León, was proba-bly of converso stock.[1] His situation is especially similar to Santa Teresa's in that his relatives' occupations were those normally practiced by Jewish converts to Christianity, just as they had been practiced by their Jewish ances-tors. For instance, his uncle was a physician, a profession almost universally controlled by conversos, as it had been by Jews before 1492. San Juan's paternal family, the Yepeses, were silk mer-chants—another largely New Christian profession. The Yepeses were mainly Toledans, and there is strong evidence that San Juan's family and that of Santa Teresa were well acquainted. A Yepes family member had been the *padrino* for a Cepeda child. Also, as was the case with some members of Santa Teresa's family, several Yepeses became clerics—a vocational choice frequently made by conversos seeking acceptance within Christian society.

Like the Carmelite Mother, San Juan avoids talking about his lineage. His silence about his family may have been more than a customary sign of humility and commitment upon his entrance into the Order of Carmel. San Juan is said to have remarked that he was not an "hijo de un labrador" (son of a farm worker, i.e., not an Old Christian) but the son of a "pobre tejedor" (poor weaver, i.e., of a New Christian family). Another family mystery concerns the rea-sons for which the Yepeses disinherited San Juan's father, Gonzalo; supposedly it was for marrying a weaver's daughter, Catalina Álv-arez, but since a mixed-class marriage would not have been a likely reason for banning Gonzalo Yepes, there is speculation about the supposed "mácula" or blemish on the Álvarez family name. Gómez-Menor Fuentes has hypothesized that San Juan's maternal

1. José Gómez-Menor Fuentes has established the best case for San Juan's sus-pected ancestry in *El linaje familiar de Santa Teresa y San Juan d la Cruz*, pp. 54–71. The discussion on San Juan's family is mainly drawn from this study.

155

grandfather may have been burned at the stake for Judaizing. He has also conjectured that the Álvarez family may have had *morisco* blood. Both theories add new variations to speculation about the possible Judaic and Moslem influences in the saint's mystical imagery.[2]

As has been shown in Chapter 3, sincere Judaizing persisted in converso families well into the seventeenth century. But even in the case of devout New Christians, social historians have found remnants of a Judaic heritage coming to the surface. This sort of subconscious knowledge of Jewish Cabala may have inspired some of the mystical imagery of Santa Teresa. The same possibility for a Cabalistic influence exists in the case of San Juan's mystical experience. Unlike his Carmelite predecessor, San Juan's knowledge of Latin could have given him greater access to Christian Cabalistic literature, just as it enabled him to be highly familiar with Scripture. However, since he is not known to have read Hebrew, he probably would not have been able to explore some of the linguistic applications of Cabala that we found in Fray Luis de León.

San Juan was raised in a converso society, and he may have absorbed elements of Cabalistic symbolism at the folk level. It is interesting to note that he lived for a time in Arévalo and spent most of his youth within a twenty-mile radius of the town.[3] That area had been a stronghold of Zoharic Cabala, the movement that popularized Cabalistic symbolism. The author of the *Zohar*, Moses de León, had spent the last part of his life in Arévalo.[4] It is possible that some elements of the *Zohar* and other Cabalistic customs were maintained among the New Christians of the region in which San Juan was nurtured. The same area had also been home to *moriscos*, and it is possible that folk customs from the Cabalistic and Sufi traditions intermingled in that environment. San Juan may have been exposed to some complementary aspects of the two mystical systems as part of the folk heritage of his childhood.

Evidence of the old Judaic traditions could be found in other communities where San Juan later lived. When the reform move-

2. Gómez-Menor Fuentes cites several contemporary references to the "mácula" on the Álvarez name as a cause for the Yepeses' disapproval of the marriage. Although he has discovered no sound explanation, his hypotheses on the family's probable converso background—Jewish or Moslem—are based on a thorough examination of references to the family and the social and cultural history of the community. The mixed Jewish and Moslem heritage may have some bearing on our discussion in this chapter of the intermingling of Cabalistic and Sufi elements in San Juan's work.

3. Bernard Gicovate, *San Juan de la Cruz*, pp. 32–33.

4. Ariel Bension, *The "Zohar" in Moslem and Christian Spain*, p. 79.

ment of Carmelite monks was young, San Juan lived in Ávila in a house built on the site of a Jewish cemetery. It is a curious coincidence that the great Zoharic Cabalist Moses de León had been buried in that very cemetery.[5]

San Juan de la Cruz, Christian Apologist

All three writers on whom this study focuses demonstrate an educational intent.[6] Fray Luis's purpose, particularly in the *Nombres*, also illustrates an apologetic concern that may have been directed at New Christian readers. San Juan, like Santa Teresa, writes for the Carmelite community or other religious followers to whom his works might have been passed. In the *Subida del Monte Carmelo*, San Juan states that he writes for "los primitivos del Monte Carmelo, frailes y monjas, por habérmelo ellos pedido" (both friars and nuns of the Order of Mount Carmel of the primitive observance, since they have asked me to do so).[7] But in the same section of the *Subida*, he also states that "procuraremos decir algo, para que cada alma que esto leyere en alguna manera eche de ver el camino que le conviene llevar" (we will endeavor to say something, so that everyone who reads this may be able to see something of the road that he ought to follow; *Prólogo*, 7). San Juan wished to reach all, laymen and religious alike, who were truly interested in coming closer to God.[8]

San Juan's pedagogical purpose is clear throughout all his works. An indication that his intent may be apologetic is suggested by his choice of sources. His primary source was Scripture—especially the Old Testament, which is referred to nearly twice as often as the New Testament.[9] Old and New Testament quotations are blended

5. Gerald Brenan, *Saint John of the Cross*, p. 25.
6. Critics have frequently called attention to San Juan's role as a teacher and mystic master. See John J. McMahon, *The Divine Union in the "Subida del Monte Carmelo" and the "Noche oscura" of Saint John of the Cross*, pp. 4–6; E. Allison Peers, *Spirit of Flame*, pp. 148–51; and Brenan, *Saint John of the Cross*, p. 53.
7. *Subida*, "Prólogo," 7, p. 457. The edition used for this and all further references to San Juan's works is *Vida y obras de San Juan de la Cruz*, eds. Crisógono de Jesús, Matías del Niño Jesús, and Lucinio Ruano, 8th ed. (Madrid: Biblioteca de Autores Cristianos, 1974). Most of the English translations of San Juan's works were based on E. Allison Peers's *The Complete Works of Saint John of the Cross, Doctor of the Church* (London: Burns Oates, 1943), 3 vols.
8. Critics who stress this point are Georges Morel, *Le sens de l'existence selon Saint Jean de la Croix*, 1:226, 2:343–44; and an anonymous Benedictine of Stanbrook Abbey, *Mediaeval Mystic Tradition and Saint John of the Cross*, p. 145.
9. See the listing provided in Jean Vilnet's *Bible et mystique chez Saint Jean de la Croix*, pp. 241–48. See also comments by Alberto Colunga, "San Juan de la Cruz, intérprete de la Santa Escritura," pp. 260–72; and José Camón Aznar, *Arte y pensamiento en San Juan de la Cruz*, p. 138.

to show that the mystic tradition of the Hebrew prophet is continued in Christianity. This is especially evident in the explanation of the *Cántico espiritual*. In that work, his mystical interpretation of the mysteries of the Song of Songs is elaborated by varied interwoven references to the Old and New Testament. The tendency is visible from the first line of San Juan's "Canciones entre el alma y el Esposo," which the friar explains with quotes from Isaiah, Job, and the Gospel of Saint John (*Cántico* 1.3).

Scholars have been fascinated by San Juan's use of biblical sources to suit his needs and his apparent reliance on his own deep understanding and memory of Scripture rather than on texts.[10] In particular, San Juan seems—more than other Christian mystics—to speak frequently of the relationship of Old Testament prophecies to Christianity.[11] Because of the special blending of the Old and New in San Juan's works, their content could have been especially appreciated by readers of New Christian descent. In showing the mystic path to the Carmelites and other potential readers, he tried to make clear that the way of the devout was a continuation of Judeo-Christian orthodoxy.

With regard to Scripture and converso attitudes, the history and traditions of the Carmelites warrant closer examination. The Carmelite Rule is said to have an inordinate number of Old Testament citations when one considers its brevity and compares it with similar documents from other orders.[12] In fact, the model for the Order of Carmel's spirituality is the prophet Elijah.[13] His reputation as a prophet and mystic was so great that legend considered him to be an early founder of the Carmelites.[14] The legend is that Enoch had founded the order on Mount Carmel, but Elijah had renewed it and recognized a prefiguration of the Virgin in the cloud over the

10. Morel, *Le sens de l'existence*, 1:203–5; Colunga, "San Juan de la Cruz," pp. 275–76. See also José Nieto, *Mystic, Rebel, Saint: A Study of Saint John of the Cross*, pp. 54–55.

11. Camón Aznar, *Arte y pensamiento*, p. 138; see also Edward Ingram Watkin, *The Philosophy of Mysticism*, p. 365.

12. Pietro della Madre di Dio, "Le fonti bibliche della Regola Carmelitana," pp. 65, 70–92.

13. François de St. Marie, ed. and trans., *Les plus vieux textes du Carmel*, 2d ed. (Paris: Editions du Seuil, 1945), pp. 13–18; Anastasio del Santo Rosario, "L'eremitismo della Regola Carmelitana," *Ephemerides Carmeliticae* 2 (1948): 245–46, 250; and Alberto M. Martino, "Il commento della Regola nel Carmelo antico," pp. 104–16. On the prophet's ties to the Carmelites, see also two studies in *Études Carmélitaines* 35 (1956): Pascal Kallenberg, "Le culte liturgique d'Elie dans l'Ordre du Carmel," 134–50; and Elisée de la Nativité, "Les carmes imitateurs d'Elie," 82–116.

14. Brenan, *Saint John of the Cross*, p. 10; and Yvonne Pellé-Douël, *San Juan de la Cruz y la noche mística*, trans. Luis Hernández Alfonso, pp. 103–4.

Mount. She was said to have thus been in contact with the prophets, the Essenes, and the apostles who dwelt there. Legends like this show the reverence the Church Fathers felt for Elijah.[15] The prophet was seen as a prefiguration of Christ and of Christian mysticism. San Juan was probably aware of that apologetic tradition and of Elijah's legendary attachment to the Carmelites. In the *Subida*, San Juan describes the similarities among the visions of Saint Paul, Moses, and "nuestro padre Elías" (2.24.3).

The Christian Cabalists of San Juan's epoch had also been interested in Elijah as a great mystic, and some, like Fray Luis, attempted to calculate the end of the world by interpreting Elijah's prophecies.[16] There was a strong Cabalistic tradition of reverence for Elijah that Christian Cabala could follow. The prophet's ascent into heaven was a model for the Merkavah mystics.[17] There are numerous references to Elijah's mystic experience and its relationship to Judaic spirituality in the *Zohar*.[18] The prophet Elijah was a traditional yardstick of orthodoxy when interpreting the value of Jewish mystical experience. Scholem writes that Cabalists called themselves "receivers of a 'revelation of the Prophet Elijah.'"[19] Any Cabalistic mystical doctrines that could be reconciled with the Elijah standard were considered acceptable. He was held to be the vigilant custodian of the Jewish religious ideal and the messianic guardian or guarantor of the tradition.

We should not underestimate the significance of Elijah to the Carmelite Order and to Saints Juan and Teresa in particular. As conversos, they could have been aware of the Elijah tradition in Judaism and in Cabala as well. They were probably aware of the Elijah legend in the Order of Carmel and of the traditionally eclectic nature of their order's theology and spirituality.[20] It is possible that they saw their own reform of the Carmelite order and its restoration to the Old Rule as somehow being closer to the spiritual traditions of Elijah and all the prophets. It is possible that they saw the Discalced Carmelites as the order that most legitimately wed the Old Law to the New in the general sense and that best combined the old mystic heritage with the Christian. The Church Fathers, Judaic Cabalists, and Christian Cabalists had seen Elijah as an

15. Sainte Marie, *Les plus vieux textes du Carmel*, pp. 29–53.

16. See Chapter 4 above.

17. Ithamar Gruenwald, *Apocalyptic and Merkabah Mysticism*, pp. 93, 119, 202.

18. For examples see the *Zohar* 1.93a-b; 2.209a; 4.197a, 198b, 199a, 201b; 5.59a, 221a.

19. *On the Kabbalah and Its Symbolism*, p. 20.

20. The anonymous Benedictine of Stanbrook speaks of the order's eclectic nature (*Mediaeval Mystic Tradition*, p. 145).

authentic link between theosophical systems sharing similar elements. San Juan and Santa Teresa may have sensed the authentic link between the spirituality of Jews and Christians that the prophet symbolized. In other words, it is possible that the Carmelite founders, two great saints of New Christian descent, may have seen themselves as continuers of an apologetic tradition in Christianity and particularly in sixteenth-century Spain.

We have already seen how another great converso figure of the era, Luis de León, used Christian Cabala to bridge the Hebraic and Christian traditions. San Juan's works also have an apologetic content with Cabalistic colorations. His approach, however, is probably more reminiscent of Santa Teresa's Christian Cabalistic imagery than the Cabalistic exegesis of names in Fray Luis's *Nombres*. Like Santa Teresa, San Juan employs the nut analogy, which had been used by Jewish mystics since the thirteenth century.[21] Santa Teresa echoes the Zoharic idea that all things holy must be acquired with difficulty, as one must do when opening the shell and the layers surrounding the meat of a nut. Cabalists had also applied the image of different layers in a nut to the different levels on which the sacred Torah could be understood and to the changing manners in which that Testament could be interpreted in different epochs or *shemitah*.[22] San Juan employs the analogy of layers for a Christian interpretation when he intimates that the "Old Testament is a rind, husk . . . and so is its literal fulfillment."[23] The Carmelite friar wants to show that the revelations of the Torah must be understood through Christianity. He writes, for example, that

> importa tanto esto de allegarse los ojos cerrados a las profecías pasadas en cualquiera nueva revelación, que, con haber el apóstol San Pedro visto la gloria del Hijo de Dios en alguna manera en el monte Tabor, con

21. San Juan and Santa Teresa apply the nut imagery in a mystical manner not used by Luis de León. Like Santa Teresa, San Juan compares the grades of a mystic's journey to the opening of concentric layers that surround the sacred dwelling place of God in the soul. He writes that "cuantos grados de amor de Dios el alma puede tener, tantos centros puede tener en Dios uno más adentro que otro, porque el amor más fuerte es más unitivo. Y de esta manera podemos entender las muchas mansiones . . ." (*¡Oh llama de amor viva!*, 1.13). San Juan goes on to describe the Judeo-Christian concept of the heavenly palaces of God. Cabala, from the time of the Merkavah, had attached special meaning to the mystic's journey through the palaces. In thirteenth-century Spain, Moses de León had also spoken of the circles of courts and camps surrounding the heavenly dwelling place. These were likened to the many rooms of the Temple that encircled the Tabernacle (*Zohar*, 5.161b).

22. Scholem, *On the Kabbalah*, p. 54, and "The Meaning of the Torah in Jewish Mysticism II," pp. 87–88.

23. This is San Juan's approach as characterized by Watkin, *The Philosophy of Mysticism*, p. 366.

todo, dijo . . . "Aunque es verdad la visión que vimos de Cristo en el
monte, más firme y cierta es la palabra de la profecía que nos es revelada,
a la cual arrimando vuestra alma hacéis bien." (*Subida*, 2.27.5)

(it is equally necessary to consider any new revelation with one's eyes
closed, and holding fast the prophecies of old; for the apostle Saint Peter,
though he had seen the glory of the Son of God in some manner on
Mount Tabor, wrote . . . "Although the vision we have seen of Christ on
the mount is true, the word of prophecy that is revealed to us is firmer
and surer, and, if you depend on it you do well.")

As San Juan continues to compare the Christian mystic experience
to the mystical or prophetic experiences of the great figures of the
Old Testament, he seems to be attempting to establish the legitimacy of his own mystic way or to make it comprehensible to
others, especially to New Christians.

San Juan's apologetic approach may help us understand one of
his more puzzling poetic works, a series of nine *romances* or ballads
united by a continuing rhyme and by themes on the Trinity and the
Incarnation (*Poesías*, 392–400). Most scholars have found the *romances* artistically inferior to San Juan's major poems.[24] They are
considered monotonous or poetically unimaginative and are dismissed as "doctrinal," "metaphysical," and more interesting for
"the light they throw on San Juan's ideas."[25] Thus the *romances*
have remained neglected and misunderstood when compared to the
better-known and more mystical works of the saint.

The first *romance*, "Romance sobre el evangelio *In principio erat
Verbum*," sets the tone for the entire series of *romances* and is, in
many ways, the most attractive of the nine. San Juan's description
of God and of the Incarnation in the first *romance* can be considered apologetic because his Christian Cabalistic approach could
have been appealing to conversos. The Cabalistic elements he employs are among the best known and most popularized and are the
very sort of traditions that were likely to have been absorbed into
the general culture and maintained—to some degree—at the folk
level even after conversion to Christianity. San Juan, in the manner
of other Christian Cabalists, could apply Cabalistic elements to
similar Christian beliefs in order to make Christianity more appealing to conversos.

This approach is particularly evident in San Juan's elaboration

---

24. Peers, *Spirit of Flame*, p. 46; Watkin, *The Philosophy of Mysticism*, p. 389.
Jean Baruzi even doubts the authenticity of the verses. See his *Saint Jean de la Croix
et le problème de l'expérience mystique*, p. 54.
25. Brenan, *Saint John of the Cross*, p. 128.

on the sexual nature of the relationship among the Persons of the Godhead:

> Como amado en el amante
> uno en otro residía,
> y aquese amor que los une
> en lo mismo convenía
> con el uno y con el otro
> en igualdad y valía.
> . . . .
> Por lo cual era infinito
> el amor que las unía,
> porque un solo amor tres tienen,
> que su esencia se decía;
> que el amor, cuanto más uno,
> tanto más amor hacía. (vv. 21–26, 41–46)

> (As the Beloved in the lover, each one resided in the other, and that love which united them was the same to each one. One and the other were the same in equality and worth: There were Three Persons and one Beloved among all three. . . . Therefore the love that united them was infinite, for the three had only one love, which is said to be their essence; and this love, the more it was one, the more it grew.)

The sense of a love relationship within the Godhead as San Juan has treated it appears to be somewhat rare in Spanish religious poetry,[26] but its parallel is rather common in Cabalistic speculation on the nature of the Deity. Scholem writes that while Cabala resists sexual comparisons in describing the relationship between God and man, there is

> no such hesitation when it comes to describing the relation of God to Himself. . . . The mystery of sex, as it appears to the Kabbalist, has a terribly deep significance. This mystery of human existence is for him nothing but a symbol of the love between the divine "I" and the divine "you," the Holy One, blessed be He and His Shekhinah. The . . . "sacred union" of the King and the Queen, the Celestial Bridegroom and the Celestial Bride, to name a few of the symbols, is a central fact in the whole chain of divine manifestations in the hidden world.[27]

26. In perusing collections of Spanish religious verse by San Juan's predecessors or contemporaries, I have not encountered a similar Trinitarian love analogy. The more doctrinal form of the saint's approach is found, however, in patristic commentaries—principally those of Augustine and Aquinas. San Juan's treatment may have more in common with Ramón Lull's application of the same amorous analogy of the Trinity. The Carmelite saint, like the Mallorcan martyr, adapted the doctrinal Trinitarian proof, making it more understandable and convincing for those who could not or did not read Latin. It is possible that San Juan, like Lull, used the Trinitarian love analogy apologetically.

27. *Major Trends*, p. 227.

Scholem continues to describe other sexual images and their variations, which are abundant in Cabala. They include the primeval
seed of Creation or the point of light from which the *sefirot* spring
forth and light up the sacred Palace or tomb. As we saw in Chapter
3, this Zoharic image resembles Santa Teresa's description of light
in the palace of the soul.

Scholem notes that of all the sexual symbolism in Spanish
Cabala, the eroticism is most uncompromising in the *Zohar*.[28]
Since Zoharic Cabala was most closely tied to the mass appreciation of Jewish mystical imagery, a few selections from the *Zohar*
will illustrate the ideas of divine sexuality that might have persisted
in the sixteenth-century converso population. One of the variations
of the divine love theme says that "the Female spread out from her
place and adhered to the Male side, until he moved away from his
side, and she came to unite with him face to face. And when they
united, they appeared as veritably one body."[29] This is reminiscent
of San Juan's more Christianized verses in the *romance*, which
reduce the Cabalistic elements to a more figurative and suggestive
level: "Como amado en el amante / uno en otro residía" (vv. 21–
22).

The *Zohar* also describes the love relationships among the *sefirot*
as divine light mysteriously refracting itself. The light imagery helps
to maintain essential monotheism in peaceful coexistence with the
belief in the ten Sefirotic emanations of the divine. The *Zohar* says
that "therefore the whole is linked together and it illumines both
one and the other" (1.16b). This quote is reminiscent of the verses
from San Juan's *romance*: "Eres lumbre de mi lumbre / Eres mi
sabiduría" (You are the light of my light / You are my wisdom; vv.
67–68). Even San Juan's reference to "lumbre" (light) along with
"sabiduría" (wisdom) reminds the Cabalist of the spreading of
light from *Hokhmah* (Wisdom) throughout the *sefirot*. This combination is also convenient for Christian Cabalists since Jesus is
also known as the Light and the Wisdom to Christians.[30]

After the expression of love between the *Padre* and *Hijo* in San
Juan's *romance*, the poet describes how God the Father wishes to
give His Son "Una esposa que te ame" (A wife to love you; v. 77).

---

28. Ibid., p. 228.

29. Marvin H. Pope, trans. and commentator, *Song of Songs*, in *The Anchor
Bible*, p. 164. The author cites the *Zohar*, 3.296a. This selection was omitted from
the Sperling and Simon edition of the *Zohar* (1949), which is used elsewhere in this
study for Zoharic quotations.

30. See Leopold Sabourin, *The Names and Titles of Jesus*, trans. Maurice Carroll,
p. 315.

Then San Juan writes of the world God would create for Himself and mankind, i.e., the *esposa*:

> —Hágase, pues—dixo el Padre—
> que tu amor lo merecía.
> Y en este dicho que dixo,
> el mundo criado había; (vv. 99–102)

> ("Let it be done, then," said the Father, "for your love has deserved it."
> And the moment that He pronounced this the world was created;)

Man is thus seen as the focus of all Creation, and the very idea of creating Man is seen to precede the idea of creating the world. This is similar to the ancient Cabalistic idea of Adam Qadmon, the primordial human being through whom the whole world was created (see Figure 1).[31]

Another, more Zoharic, Cabalistic view of Creation continues to describe how *Hokhmah* (Wisdom) created *Binah* (Palace) in the upper world and made a parallel or earthly palace in the creation of the lower world.[32] In a similar manner, San Juan describes how God created the two levels:

> palacio para la esposa,
> hecho en gran sabiduría;
> el cual en dos aposentos
> alto y bajo, dividía.
> El bajo de diferencias
> infinitas componía;
> mas el alto hermoseaba
> de admirable pedrería, (vv. 103–10)

> (a *palace* for the Bride, made with great *wisdom,* and divided into two *mansions, one above* and *one below.* The lower one was composed of infinite differences, but the upper one he beautified with wondrous gems,)

Even the friar's mention of the beautiful "pedrería" in the heavens is reminiscent of the ancient Jewish mystical fascination with Ezekiel's vision of the heavens and the divine throne of sapphire or crystal.[33]

Within this concept of the levels of Creation as emanations that parallel the operations within the Divinity, San Juan treats the Incarnation. Like Fray Luis, the Carmelite treats the coming of the *Verbum* more as an act of divine will than as a reaction to Adam's

---

31. Scholem, *Major Trends,* p. 215; *On the Kabbalah,* pp. 112–15; and *Kabbalah,* pp. 116–17.
32. Scholem, *On the Kabbalah,* pp. 117–18.
33. Gruenwald, *Apocalyptic and Merkabah Mysticism,* pp. 33, 35.

sin and to the subsequent need for redemption. There is, in fact, no mention of the fall of mankind in San Juan's *romance*. For both San Juan and Fray Luis, the Incarnation is seen as part of the continuing process of Creation. Their Christian treatment of the Creation-Incarnation complements the Cabalistic sense of Creation as the lower world's correspondence with the upper world. In Christian Cabalistic terms, it could be said that Christ's existence in heaven was paralleled or completed by His actions as Redeemer on Earth. San Juan's version of the Incarnation in the *romance* could serve the same Christian apologetic purpose that Luis de León's variation did in *Nombres*.

José Nieto has noticed in San Juan's mystical works a "realized eschatology," meaning that the apocalyptic promises are fulfilled through mystical experience now that the Incarnation and Resurrection are historical fact.[34] Although Nieto does not discuss it, the element of "realized eschatology" would have had special meaning to San Juan's fellow conversos. In the sixteenth century, Jewish and Christian Cabalists alike were interested in eschatological speculation that revived elements of Judaic messianism. Fray Luis and his Augustinian predecessor Egidio da Viterbo are two notable examples discussed in previous chapters of this study. And, as was indicated in Chapter 3, many conclusions drawn by social and cultural historians show that messianic speculation persisted in Spanish conversos. San Juan may have been cognizant of vestiges of Judaic messianism persisting within the apocalyptic speculations of his own era. In this context, his treatment of the Incarnation as the beginning of the prophesied end serves an apologetic function. Of Christ's coming, he writes:

> y con ellos moraría;
> y que Dios sería hombre
> y que el hombre Dios sería,
> y trataría con ellos
> . . . .
> hasta que se consumase
> este siglo que corría
> cuando se gozarán juntos
> en eterna melodía; (vv. 138–41, 145–48)

(And He would dwell with them; and God would be man and man would be God, and he would mingle and eat and drink with them . . . . He Himself would remain with them until this period of time would be consummated when they will joyfully join together in eternal harmony;)

34. *Mystic, Rebel, Saint*, pp. 90–91.

The last two lines in reference to redemption through the love union of Christ and the Church are a Christian version of the Cabalistic interpretation of Canticles. As Scholem has written, "The reunion of God and His *Shekhinah* constitutes the meaning of redemption."[35] Or, as a more conservative tradition of Cabala has it, God is united with the Community of Israel.[36]

Other verses of San Juan's *romance* also illustrate the apologetic nature of the poem. Like Fray Luis, San Juan wants to show that the Old Law has been improved by the New:

> Ya que el tiempo era llegado
> en que hacerse convenía
> el rescate de la esposa
> que en duro yugo servía,
> debajo de aquella ley
> que Moisés dado le había, (vv. 221–26)

(Now that the time had come when it was suitable to rescue the Bride who was serving under the hard yoke of that law that Moses had given her,)

Thus, for San Juan, Christ came to rescue His *esposa* from Moses. In saying this, San Juan maintains the Cabalistic imagery of divine love flowing into the lower world. He also continues Cabala's sexual sense of the divine.

As San Juan describes the Annunciation of the Incarnation to the Virgin Mary, he uses another familiar Cabalistic concept that complements a similar Christian one. The human body is considered a garment:[37] "el misterio se hacía; / en la cual la Trinidad / de carne al Verbo vestía" (the mystery took place in her [the Virgin Mary] as the Trinity clothed the Word with flesh; vv. 273–75). One of the earliest discussions of heavenly garments versus earthly ones in the Cabalistic tradition is found in Merkavah literature. In an elaborated Merkavah commentary on Isaiah's ascension into heaven, there is a description of metaphorical garments he observed during

---

35. *On the Kabbalah*, p. 108.

36. Ibid., p. 106.

37. In Luis de León's poem "Oda al apartamiento," the friar refers to his "corporeal velo" (v. 32). Some of San Juan's younger contemporaries use the garment concept to refer to the Incarnation in their religious lyrics. Diego Cortés writes of the "Verbo . . . / vestido de carne"; Ledesma tells Christ, "te pusiste mi vestido"; and Alonso de Bonilla speaks of the Redeemer as "vestido de nuestro barro." (See *Biblioteca de Autores Españoles*, 35, nos. 511, 520, and 588, respectively.) The garment analogy for the Incarnation may be a traditional Christian one. However, it would be useful to learn whether it is especially common in Spanish religious lyrics and, if so, whether Spanish Cabalistic symbolism was influential in the application of the analogy.

his visit to the upper regions. It is said that he saw the righteous "stript of the garments of the flesh" and wearing heavenly attire.[38] In Spanish Cabala, there are descriptions of the soul's use of the human body as a garment worn during one's stay on earth. The *Zohar* says that the souls "enter into the bodies of the holy seed of Israel wearing this garment to be served therewith in this world. When these garments draw to themselves the good things of this world, these holy souls regale themselves with the aroma which they gather from the garments" (3.98b). The notion of garments—both earthly and celestial—is fairly common in Cabala, and it will be discussed again with reference to San Juan's *Cántico espiritual*.

After considering the Cabalistic elements of San Juan's set of nine *romances*, we can see new meaning in the series as an apologetic Christian work. The friar's treatment of the Trinity, the Incarnation, Creation, and Redemption is complemented by the Cabalistic perspectives discernible in the poem. Although the *romances* may lack the artistry of his better-known, more mystical poems, they employ Christian Cabalistic themes and images that may be found elsewhere in San Juan's works. In light of his mystical works—the *Cántico espiritual* in particular—the *romances* can be seen as another variation on the theme of divine love and as another interpretation of the Song of Songs.

The Spiritual Marriage

Among the descriptions of the mystical union, the imagery of the spiritual marriage is perhaps the most sensitive for Christians. It is assumed that the concept developed from expositions on Canticles. San Juan's version of the Song of Songs is found in "Canciones entre el alma y el Esposo" ("Songs between the Soul and the Bridegroom") and in his commentary on that poem, the *Cántico espiritual*. When comparing the Carmelite's commentary with those of his predecessors, it is difficult to find any particular model.[39] Saint Bernard's eighty-six sermons on the Song of Songs do not exude the passionate essence of San Juan's "Canciones," nor do they provide the detailed description of the mystic way found in *Cántico*. Fray Luis's *Exposition* on Canticles or his Spanish version of the Song of Songs may have been known to San Juan,[40] but the

---

38. Gruenwald, *Apocalyptic and Merkabah Mysticism*, p. 61.

39. For a survey of Christian commentaries and of other works based on Canticles, see Brenan, *Saint John of the Cross*, p. 109; and Ángel Custodio Vega, *Cumbres místicas*, pp. 144–49.

40. Francisco García Lorca, *De Fray Luis a San Juan*.

Carmelite's approach is more an original paraphrase than a translation or commentary. Both converso friars do share, however, an appreciation for the sensuality and the exotic richness of the Song of Songs. It is possible that they found in the essence of the songs an appropriate apologetic medium. Saint Bernard, for example, deemed his own mystical exposition on Canticles a suitable means of discussing the need to convert the Jews and the necessary transition from the Old Law to the New.[41]

Finding no specific Christian model for San Juan's version of Canticles, scholars have attempted to describe the unique essence of his work. Colin Thompson has provided some of the most insightful comments on the friar's originality.[42] He finds that none of the medieval Christian poems or commentaries on Canticles have the lyrical beauty or structural perfection of San Juan's "Canciones." Yet Thompson seems puzzled by the poet's deviations from classical and Renaissance poetics. He points to the friar's accumulation of symbols from varied biblical sources and his combination of a bewildering assortment of tenses. In addition, the *Cántico espiritual* makes no clear distinction between the hidden mystical doctrines of Scripture and the hidden meanings of San Juan's own words. In effect, the friar's poetry can be said to have a rather Hebraic flavor.

In recent studies, Luce López Baralt has examined more closely San Juan's allusive poetic style and his tendency to "Hebraicize" the language and structure of his work—particularly in the "Canciones entre el alma y el Esposo."[43] As in the Song of Songs, the friar's "Canciones" display temporal zigzags and the elimination of the verbs *ser* and *estar*. Such elements of San Juan's works—considered incoherent by many critics—have been reexamined by López Baralt, who relates them to Hebrew—or more generally, Semitic—concepts of the arbitrariness of language. She illustrates how the friar's use of simultaneous meanings and transformations of a single word differ from commentaries on Canticles written by his Spanish contemporaries. The richness of San Juan's "plurivalent" language is particularly fitting to describe the love union of the "Canciones" and the interior vision of his mystical experience.

Since San Juan is not known to have read Hebrew—and even less probably Arabic—the evidence of a Semitic quality in the Carmelite's language and imagery is intriguing. We must consider the

41. Saint Bernard de Clairvaux, *Oeuvres mystiques*, trans. Albert Béguin, sermon 14, pp. 187–94; sermon 30, pp. 364–67.

42. *The Poet and the Mystic.*

43. *San Juan de la Cruz y el Islam*, pp. 33–53, in particular.

possibility that San Juan was influenced by Carmelite brothers more knowledgeable of either language or by traditions maintained with the converso culture. As this study has shown, Zoharic Cabala was in continuous use by Spanish Christian Cabalists into San Juan's era, and the *Zohar*'s message of piety could have survived at the folk level in Spain as well. It is significant that the conglomerations of symbols, variety of tenses, and unexpected combinations of biblical quotations that distinguish much of San Juan's work are common features of the Zoharic style. Daniel Chanan Matt has noted that the *Zohar*'s style is characterized by "deliberately confusing vocabulary and chaotic activity."[44] He also reminds us that passages from the *Zohar* were chanted by the faithful, and, as a Cabalist described, the language was held to be good for the soul even if one did not understand it.[45] The similarities between the Zoharic language and San Juan's verbal incoherence strengthen the theory that the Carmelite may have been familiar with aspects of Cabala.

In light of what might be called a Zoharic style in San Juan's version of the Song of Songs, we should examine the special fondness Judaic Cabalists held for that book. Along with the Pentateuch, the Five Scrolls, the Book of Ruth, Psalms, and Ecclesiastes, the Song of Songs is one of the biblical works most frequently commented on in Cabalistic literature.[46] From the time of the *Bahir*, one of the earliest Cabalistic texts, the Song of Songs was held to be especially holy for its treatment of the splendor of the female and male, i.e., its symbolism of divine love relations in the upper and lower worlds.[47] The physical descriptions of the lovers in Canticles gave rise to Cabala's *Shiur Qomah*, in which there are speculations on the mystical significance of the corporeal appearance of God.[48] Also in that work, the Song of Songs is said to be the holiest book and the very one recited by Moses on Mount Sinai. Scholem tells us that through Cabalistic commentaries on Canticles, the idea of the *Shekhinah* as the feminine element of God was revived.[49] In addition, all the interpretations of the Bride of Canticles as the Community of Israel were transferred to the

44. *Zohar: The Book of Enlightenment*, p. 298.

45. Ibid., p. 193, n. 3. Matt cites an eighteenth-century Cabalistic scholar, Moses Hayyin Luzzatto, as quoted in Isaiah Tishby, *Mishuat ha-Zohar* 1:44 (Introduction).

46. Scholem, *On the Kabbalah*, p. 33.

47. *Book Bahir*, trans. Joachim Neugroschel, in *The Secret Garden*, ed. David Meltzer, p. 86.

48. Gruenwald, *Apocalyptic and Merkabah Mysticism*, pp. 94–95.

49. *On the Kabbalah*, p. 106.

Shekhinah. That may have resulted in some confusion as to whether the Song of Songs was an allegory of the love relationship within the Godhead or between God and His people. Although Cabala may try to maintain the traditional Judaic interpretation of the Bride and Bridegroom as a symbol of the covenant, many Cabalistic notions support a view more harmonious with Christian exegesis of Canticles.

As in Christianity, there are Cabalistic tendencies to speak of individual human souls united in a spiritual marriage with God. The individuals involved are all Old Testament prophets, i.e., the pre-Christian version of mystics. Moses, Jacob, Abraham, and others have been described as being in union with the Divine Presence, the *Shekhinah*. The imagery is most sensual in the case of Moses, who is said to have had intercourse with the *Shekhinah*.[50] In both the *Bahir* and the *Zohar*, the human soul is sometimes referred to as the *Shekhinah*.[51] With one small step, a Christian Cabalist could easily substitute the individual soul for the *Shekhinah* as the Bride of Canticles. The Christian Cabalist could thus apply all the divine mysteries and images associated with the *Shekhinah* to the soul in union with the Godhead.

Recalling the special attachment of Cabala to the Song of Songs, we should reexamine Santa Teresa's vocabulary of spiritual marriage and San Juan's version of the love motif from Canticles. Could the Christian mystics have applied Cabalistic symbolism to Old Testament imagery? In San Juan's *Cántico* and "Canciones" and in Santa Teresa's *Moradas*, the spiritual union is consummated in a deep and hidden place after the mystic has struggled through each grade of spiritual development along the mystical way. For San Juan it is the "interior bodega" (inner wine cellar/chamber; can. 26), a term that combines the Song of Song's references to love, secret places, and the fruit of the vine with allusions to the mystic's inward journey. In his explanation of that *canción*, he speaks of the place as "la más interior. De donde se sigue que hay otras no tan interiores que son los grados de amor por do se sube hasta este último; podemos decir que estos grados o bodegas de amor son siete" (the most interior. From this it follows that there are others less interior which are the degrees of love whereby the soul rises to this, the last of all. We may say that these degrees or chambers of love are seven; can. 26, 3). This is very similar to Santa Teresa's seven *moradas* of the *palacio interior*. Both Carmelites' descriptions are reminiscent of the Zoharic mystic's journey into the seven

---

50. Scholem, *Major Trends*, pp. 226–27.
51. Scholem, *On the Kabbalah*, p. 106.

Sefirotic levels of spiritual and psychological discovery—seven levels within the self that correspond to the seven lower divine emanations. Like San Juan and Santa Teresa, the *Zohar* (5.267b) shows that the pure essence of love is synonymous with that most inner chamber or palace of the Divine One that the mystic aspires to enter through the self. For the Carmelites and the Zoharic mystic the inward journey is associated with verses from the Song of Songs. In Cabala a phrase from the Song, "Let him kiss me with the kisses of his mouth" (1:2; in *Zohar*, 4.146b), could even be used as a mystical prayer.

In addition to the similar use of the chamber-of-love symbolism, San Juan's and Santa Teresa's treatment of the spiritual marriage imagery resembles Cabala's in the emphasis placed on the "secrets" to be revealed. The sense of secrecy and the idea of fulfillment in the heavenly love chambers are linked in the *Zohar*. We read that "this is a secret entrusted to the keeping of the wise alone, and here is the substance thereof. In the midst of a mighty rock, a most recondite firmament, there is set a Palace which is called the Palace of Love. This is a region wherein the treasures of the King are stored, and all his love-kisses are there. All souls of the Holy One enter into that Palace" (3.97a).

We should recall that this secret place in the divine *sefirot* and in the self can be discovered only by the pious, particularly those who pursue the mystic way. The secrecy of the Cabalistic mystical experience is also illustrated by Solomon Ibn Gabirol's *Keter Malkhut* when he speaks of the divine names and the emanations of the *sefirot*. In that work he tells Adonai that "secrets are yours which thought and reason cannot hold" and that "who comes towards your secret finds eternal delight."[52] Secretism had been especially associated with the early Cabala when it was considered an occult tradition to be revealed only to a select few. For instance, the *Sefer Yezirah*—a very obscure and secretive book as a whole—mentions the secret knowledge and symbolism contained in the letters of the sacred alphabet.[53]

Both San Juan and Santa Teresa frequently refer to the "secretos" revealed through the mystical union. Their use of the term is much more frequent than in the works of Northern mystics who are sometimes suggested as possible influences on the Carmelite mystics or their Spanish predecessors. In fact, from a superficial study, references to secrets rarely appear in Saint Bernard, Eckhart, Tau-

52. *Keter Malkhut*, trans. Harris Lenowitz, in *The Secret Garden*, ed. Meltzer, pp. 100, 102.
53. *Sefer Yetzirah*, trans. and ed. Knut Stenring.

ler, or Ruysbroeck.[54] The abundant references to secrets in San Juan and Santa Teresa are frequently reminiscent of the Song of Songs. The Carmelite Mother exclaims in her *Meditaciones sobre los Cantares*, "¡Qué secretos tan grandes hay en estas palabras [de los Cantares]!" (Such great secrets there are in these words [of the Songs]!).[55] Her most frequent and most mystical treatment of secrecy is found in the *Moradas* when she discusses the secret knowledge the soul receives in the inner palace. She writes, for example, that "son muy ocultos los secretos de Dios" (God's secrets are very hidden; *M* 3.2.11) and that "en el centro de estas moradas . . . es adonde pasan las cosas de mucho secreto entre Dios y el alma" (in the center of these mansions . . . is where things of great secrecy take place between God and the soul; *M* 1.1.3).

Elements of San Juan's works are also reminiscent of Cabala's emphasis on the secrecy of the Palace of Love or of the secrecy found in the Song of Songs. In the *Cántico*, he speaks of the "bodega secreta" (secret wine cellar; can. 26, 7), of the "ciencia secreta de Dios" (secret science of God; can. 27, 5), and of "sabiduría y secretos" (wisdom and secrets; can. 27, 3). In *Dichos de luz y amor* (*Points of Love*), he exclaims, "Mire aquel infinito saber y aquel secreto escondido, ¡qué paz, qué amor!" (Behold that infinite knowledge and that hidden secret. What peace, what love!; no. 138, p. 425). San Juan describes in *Subida del Monte Carmelo* how "el espiritu del discípulo conforme al de su padre espiritual oculta y secretamente" (the spirit of the disciple conforms to that of his spiritual father in a hidden and secret way; 2.18.5). Similarly, in his commentary *Noche oscura*, he declares that "este camino de ir a Dios es tan secreto y oculto para el sentido del alma como lo es para el del cuerpo que se lleva por la mar cuyas sendas y pisadas no se conocen" (this road whereby the soul journeys to God is as secret and as hidden from the senses of the soul as the one who walks by the sea whose paths and footprints are not known, is hidden from the senses of the body; 2.17.8). His *villancico* entitled "Entréme donde no supe" is also filled with references to the divine secrets and the difficulty of comprehending them:

54. On Saint Bernard, see the *Oeuvres mystiques*, sermons 55 (p. 578) and 57 (p. 59) in particular. On Eckhart, see *Meister Eckhart: A Modern Translation*, trans. Raymond Bernard Blakney; and *Meister Eckhart: An Introduction to the Study of His Works with an Anthology of His Sermons*, ed. James Clark. For Tauler, see *The Sermons and Conferences of John Tauler*, trans. Walter Elliott. For Ruysbroeck's complete works see *Oeuvres de Ruysbroeck l'admirable*, trans. the Benedictines of Saint-Paul de Wisques.

55. *Meditaciones sobre los Cantares* (4.1, p. 348), in *Obras completas*, eds. Efrén de la Madre de Dios and Otger Steggink.

De paz y de piedad
era la sciencia perfecta,
en profunda soledad
entendida (vía recta);
era cosa tan secreta
que me quedé balbuciendo. (vv. 11–16)

(Of peace and piety was the *perfect science* made. In profound solitude it taught a straight path. Such secret knowledge did I find that I was left stammering, transcending all human knowledge.)

Related to San Juan's expressions of reverence and amazement about secret knowledge is his awe expressed in terms of sight. He writes that "una de las cosas más principales por que desea el alma *ser desatada y verse con Cristo* es por verle allá cara a cara y entender allí de raíz las profundas vías misterios eternos" (one of the principal reasons for which the soul wishes to be freed and *to see himself with Christ* is to be able to see Him there face to face and to understand completely the profound methods and eternal mysteries; can. 37, 1). Especially notable is the phrase "Mátame tu vista y hermosura" from his "Canciones" (Reveal your presence and let the vision of you and your beauty slay me; can. 11). San Juan relates this to the difficulty of Moses on Mount Sinai and the statement by God that "es tanta la hermosura de mi cara y el deleite de la vista de mi ser, que no la podrá sufrir tu alma en esa suerte de vida tan flaca" (such is the beauty of My face and the joy of the vision of My Being, that your soul will not be able to bear it in this feeble state of life; can. 11, 5, from Exodus 33:12–13). The blinding appearance of God's beauty or the beautiful spiritual state of man is a favorite theme that Cabala expresses in terms of garments of light. Moses was unable to see God with earthly eyes because of the garment of light in which God was clothed. In the Merkavah tradition, God's radiant appearance is thought to have induced mystical experiences.[56]

We have already seen that Luis de León refers to his friend Salinas as a mystic wearing a garment of light when the friar writes

---

56. Scholem, *Jewish Gnosticism, Merkabah Mysticism, and Talmudic Tradition*, pp. 57–60. For discussion of God's Wisdom (*Hokhmah* and the Logos) as a radiant garment in Midrashim, see Altmann, *Studies in Religious Philosophy and Mysticism*, pp. 129–39. San Juan's treatment of the power and beauty of God's appearance and, consequently, of the need for man to see Him through a veil or to view Him while wearing a special garment is similar to a verse in Luis de León's poem to Felipe Ruiz, "¿Cuándo será que pueda?" Fray Luis speaks of his longing to contemplate "la verdad pura, sin velo" (truth pure and unveiled; v. 5). See the discussion of this line in Ángel Custodio Vega, *Poesías de Fray Luis de León; Edición crítica*, p. 284, n. 5.

"viste de hermosura." Perhaps San Juan, like Fray Luis, was aware of the idea of a beautiful, blinding garment of light since it was a rather well-known concept of Cabala.

San Juan uses a similar concept to describe the beauties of God's Creation in "Canciones." He writes of Nature as being a reflection of the divine garment imagery: "vestidos los dejó de hermosura" (He left them dressed in beauty; can. 5). For San Juan, the created world is a wondrous manifestation of God's glory. Especially in the "Canciones," his view of the world is similar to the Cabalistic interpretation of the world as an earthly paradise corresponding to God's dwelling place in the upper world. San Juan marvels at Creation:

¡Oh bosques y espesuras
plantadas por la mano del Amado!
¡oh prado de verduras
de flores esmaltado! (can. 4)

(Oh woods and thickets planted by the hand of the Beloved! Oh meadow of greenness enamelled with flowers!)

In his treatment of the nature motifs from Canticles, San Juan shows an appreciation of Earth's beauty in a manner that some have considered unusual for the ascetic friar. The vivid descriptions of "los ríos sonorosos, / el silbo de los ayres amorosos" (the sonorous rivers, the whisper of the amorous breezes; can. 13), of "flores y esmeraldas / en las frescas mañanas escogidas" (flowers and emeralds gathered in the cool mornings; can. 21), and of numerous other examples in his "Canciones" reveal the saint's profound understanding of the spiritual relationship to Nature in the Song of Songs and in the mystical experience.

In the "Canciones" San Juan is not a mystical writer who disparages the material world as the antithesis of the spiritual. Contrary to those who have attempted to interpret San Juan's poetry as a Neoplatonic rejection of earthly existence, the friar's verses continue to demonstrate his spiritual perspective on Nature.[57] The warm biblical imagery and the Oriental—perhaps Cabalistic—sensuality is too strong to reduce the poem to a Neoplatonic interpretation. It is not to be forgotten that Cabala itself probably originated as a Gnostic system like Neoplatonism, but Cabala developed traditions that found sanctity in earthly life. Since all operations in the upper world are paralleled by events in the lower

57. See, for example, Eugene Maio, St. John of the Cross: The Imagery of Eros.

world, earthly life is closely tied to the spiritual world. Thus the Garden-of-Eden imagery in Canticles or in San Juan's "Canciones" can express the earthly experience that comes closest to the heavenly: the mystical union.

The Dark Night and the Flame

Imagery of dark and light has long been associated with varied mystical traditions;[58] indeed, symbols of dark and light have been considered archetypal religious concerns.[59] For Christian mystics of the Middle Ages, Pseudo-Dionysius's description of the soul's passage through darkness in order to reach the divine light was influential.[60] His work was also a major part of the Renaissance quest for a pansophic synthesis, as we have shown in our survey of Renaissance Christian Cabala.

Recognizing that San Juan was certainly aware of references to light and dark as used in Scripture, the Church, and earlier mystical works, scholars have studied the distinguishing aspects of his treatment of the tradition. They have particularly focused on his concept of the *noche oscura* (dark night), calling it an expression of original intuition that has conveyed a deeper and more cosmic meaning than other Christian references to the mystic's night.[61] San Juan's *noche oscura* is not the usual mystic's night of sin or grief.[62] As Bernard Gicovate has said, "What surprises and seduces in Saint John is his glorying in the distress of the night and his desire for darkness, which he considers a welcome necessity and consequently a preparatory joy."[63] The surprising and seductive quality of the night as light or the joyful anticipation of light is what appears to be so original and intriguing in San Juan's *noche oscura*. His concept of the mystical night separates the friar from other Christian mystics of the West and seems to ally him with Oriental mystical traditions. The indications of similarity between San Juan's treatment of night and light and those of Cabalistic and Sufi mystics raise questions of sources. This chapter will examine the

58. Evelyn Underhill, *Mysticism*, p. 229, et passim.

59. Mircea Eliade, "Le symbolisme des ténèbres dans les religions archaïques," p. 25; Lucien-Marie de St. Joseph, "Expérience mystique et expression symbolique chez Saint Jean de la Croix," pp. 42–43; María Jesús Fernández Leborans, *Campo semántico y connotación*, pp. 114–19, 121–25.

60. Morel, *Le sens de l'existence*, 3:166–67.

61. Baruzi, *Saint Jean de la Croix*, pp. 321, 345.

62. Colin Thompson, *The Poet and the Mystic*, p. 97.

63. *San Juan de la Cruz*, p. 81.

Cabalistic parallels found in the friar's night/light imagery and will suggest possible solutions to the problem of influences.

The night imagery in the Carmelite friar's *Subida del Monte Carmelo* and in the poem and commentary entitled *Noche oscura* is explained by San Juan with an abundance of Old Testament references. Metaphors of dark and light are much less common in the New Testament than in the Old.[64] In general, the Old Testament is said to provide a wider use of darkness as a manifestation of God's transcendence.[65] It is the ancient biblical sense of darkness, which also served as a basis for Cabala's night imagery. As in San Juan's *noche oscura*, the biblical references to night in Cabala become points of departure for a mystical interpretation. In Cabala, the biblical passages on night serve as the object of mystical meditation as well as authoritative support for the mystical activity. For the Cabalist and for San Juan, the night becomes a very positive element. As we saw in Fray Luis's "Noche serena" poem, the Cabalistic night is a sacred time for prayer and unity with God, just as it is the time when God unites with His *Shekhinah*. In San Juan's hands, the sacred sense of night is deeper and closer to the religious Cabalistic sense than Fray Luis's treatment. We have cited examples from the *Zohar* that described that religious sense of night in Cabala. Those also apply to San Juan, but there are other Zoharic references that contribute to our understanding of the friar's *noche oscura* as it relates to his penchant for subtle recollections of the Old Testament.

San Juan's poem "En una noche oscura" conveys the sense of secrecy and difficulty the mystic experiences in his lonely journey through metaphorical darkness before reaching the mystical union. The friar writes of the sacred and secret flight: "*salí* sin ser notada" (*I went out* unnoticed; can. 1) and "a escuras y segura / por la *secreta escala*" (in darkness and secure by the *secret stair*; can. 2). Guided by and aflame with divine love, the mystic traveler continues: "sin otra *luz* y *guía* / sino la que e el corazón arcía" (with no other *light* or *guide* except that which was burning in my heart; can. 3). Ultimately the goal, the mystical love union, is achieved:

> ¡Oh noche que guiaste!
> ¡oh noche amable más que la alborada!
> ¡oh noche que juntaste
> Amado con amada,
> amada en el Amado transformada! (can. 5)

64. Morel, *Le sens de l'existence*, 3:173.
65. Lucien-Marie de St. Joseph, "Expérience mystique," pp. 44–45.

(Oh night which guided me! Oh night more friendly than the dawn! Oh night that joined lover with Beloved, the lover being transformed into the Beloved!)

The three stanzas following the fifth canción convey the ecstasy of the love union and bring the poem to its conclusion. One of the most striking aspects of those final stanzas is the sense of joyful tranquillity conveyed by the friar's choice of biblical imagery. The mood, tempo, and visual quality of the Song of Songs is quite perceptible in the verses that speak of "mi pecho florido" (my flowery breast) and of "el ventalle de cedros aire daba" (the waving motion of the cedars fanned a breeze; can. 6), of "el aire del almena / cuando yo sus cabellos esparcía" (the breeze from the parapet, when I spread out his locks; can. 7), and of the love union "entre las azucenas olvidado" (leaving my cares forgotten among the lilies; can. 8). These final strophes of "En una noche oscura" have been rightly called "a Catholic Song of Songs."[66]

Similar to San Juan's approach, a combination of biblical references and a sensual treatment of the mystical night journey is also found in Spanish Cabala. For the Cabalist, the mystical process could commence by meditating on the Zoharic elaboration of a biblical passage. Thus, the account in Exodus of the Jews' flight from Egypt, their desert wanderings, and the long struggle to reach the Promised Land could take on new meaning as an allegorical prototype of the mystical journey. There is a resemblance between the erotico-mystical sense of night in the Zoharic commentary on Exodus and San Juan's nocturnal flight in "En una noche oscura." Frequently the *Zohar* offers rabbinical and mystical commentary on Exodus, although—in typical Zoharic style—the meaning of the elaboration on the Bible may seem puzzling. For example, the *Zohar* says that sensual language must be used in order "to indicate the union which took place on that night between Masculine and Feminine aspects in the Divine attributes, and also the same union which will take place in the future Redemption: 'As in the days of the coming out of Egypt will I show unto him marvellous things' (Micah vii, 15)" (3.38a–b).

The *Zohar* associates the account in Exodus of the long struggle to reunite the Chosen People in the Promised Land with the divine quest to achieve sexual reunion within the Godhead. The individual Cabalist could express his own longing for union through the difficult journey of the mystical night in the terms that the *Zohar*

66. Leo Spitzer, *A Method of Interpreting Literature*, p. 21.

applied to all of Israel. The Zoharic interpretation of night of Israel's exodus from Egypt describes a time of tribulation, but one also filled with joyful anticipation of redemption and restoration. We must recall that Israel's exile in Egypt is mystically expressed as the exile of the *Shekhinah* from the Godhead. Thus, the Israelites' return to the Promised Land is seen as an earthly manifestation of God's reunion with His *Shekhinah*; the restoration of the male and female aspects of the divine *sefirot* is paralleled by the happy reunion of the Chosen People with their land. On a more personal level, the individual mystic would also aspire to a reunion: through piety and prayerful meditation the Cabalist could hope to achieve the same sense of spiritual unity that had been expressed in sexual terms for the Godhead.

Beyond the mystical interpretation of Exodus, other elements of San Juan's dark night of light present stronger indications of Zoharic similarities. The *noche oscura* and the *llama* (flame) are dependent images in San Juan's poetry, just as the dark night and the anticipatory joy of the light of union are interrelated in his lengthy mystical commentaries. This interdependence of dark and light in San Juan is quite similar to Zoharic Cabala, which carries the same sensual emphasis we find in San Juan's poetry. The *Zohar* states:

> "And God divided the Light from the Darkness," means He prevented dissension between them. Said R. Isaac: "Up to this point the Male principle was represented by Light and the Female by Darkness; subsequently they were joined together and made one. The difference by means of which Light is distinguished from Darkness is one of degree only; both are one in kind, as there is no Light without Darkness and no Darkness without Light; but though one, they are different in colour." (1.32a)

The *Zohar*, like San Juan's poetry and commentaries, conveys a positive sense of the relationship between light and dark. In both, darkness is joyful because it is an essential ingredient of union. On the divine level the images of dark and light are an expression of the tension and ultimate unity among the sacred attributes. For the individual mystic, the anxiety of the night is joyful because of the promise of light, i.e., because of the anticipated union.

An essential aspect of San Juan's treatment of night and light is his use of flame imagery. His "¡Oh llama de amor viva!" surpasses other Christian mystical applications of light symbolism. There is nothing to compare with the drama and intense passion expressed in the poem that begins:

¡Oh llama de amor viva,
que tiernamente hieres
de mi alma en el más profundo centro!
pues ya no eres esquiva,
acaba ya, si quieres;
rompe la tela deste dulce encuentro.
   ¡Oh cauterio suave
¡Oh regalada llaga!
¡Oh mano blanda! ¡Oh toque delicado!
que a vida eterna sabe
y toda deuda paga;
matando, muerte en vida la has trocado.

(Oh living flame of love, how tenderly you wound the deepest center of my soul! Since you no longer avoid me, finish now, if you will; break through the fabric of this sweet encounter.
   Oh gentle cautery! Oh delicate wound! Oh tender hand! Oh gentle touch which tastes of eternal life and pays all debts! By killing you have changed death into life.)

The frankly erotic elements of "¡Oh llama de amor viva!" have been analyzed by Willis Barnstone.[67] He is correct in that the purely physical level of San Juan's imagery should be recognized. However, he does not satisfactorily explain how or why a very unworldly friar would have included such a detailed description of the sexual act in a deeply religious poem. The Christian mystical tradition would not have provided examples of mystico-erotic love of the sort found in the poem. A logical source available for a Spanish mystic, particularly one nurtured in converso society like San Juan, was the *Zohar*. It could have been the *Zohar* known at the popular level—one possibly intermingled with folk elements of Sufi mysticism—or the *Zohar* known through Christian Cabalistic sources. We have already seen in this chapter that symbolism of Zoharic Cabala is saturated with the sacred essence of the sensual. The *Zohar*'s profound reverence for divine sexuality and its concomitant respect for the sacred meaning in human marital relations could have produced the particular combination of the erotic and mystical found in San Juan's poem.

San Juan's flame imagery shows other significant parallels with Spanish Cabala. As the friar expressed in "¡Oh llama de amor viva!" the flame is a purifying *cauterio suave* to be endured yet enjoyed by the mystic, just as the *noche oscura* is considered to be an experience of joyful distress. In the *Zohar*, we also find the same

---

67. See his "Mystico-Erotic Love in 'O Living Flame of Love.'"

sort of flame imagery associated with the nocturnal setting of mystical unity. We read that "by the term 'night' is meant the Community of Israel, which comes to purge man of the evil thought, and so 'on its fire-wood' points to the 'fiery stream,' the place where the unstable (spirits) have to pass through the burning fire and be deprived of their power. When that happens, the Community of Israel, being the embodiment of the Holy Spirit, ascends on high" (4.239b). In this context, we must remember that the individual Cabalist could think of himself as mystical Israel undergoing a process of purification in the dark night. Again the resemblance between the Zoharic tradition and San Juan's night flame is perceptible.

Perhaps the most intriguing parallel between San Juan's flame imagery and Cabalistic symbolism is his depiction of the flame as a lamp. In his prose commentary, *Llama de amor vida*, San Juan explains how darkness is the means by which the soul will become a resplendent lamp made in God's image. He writes that

> de manera que, según esto, la sombra que hace al alma la lámpara de la hermosura de Dios será otra hermosura al talle y propiedad de aquella hermosura de Dios, y la sombra que hace la fortaleza será otra fortaleza al talle de la de Dios, y la sombra que le hace la sabiduría de Dios será otra sabiduría de Dios al talle de la de Dios, y así de las demás lámparas. (*Llama* 3. 14)

> (In this way the shadow cast upon the soul by the lamp of the beauty of God will be another beauty of the nature and proportions of that beauty of God; and the shadow cast by strength will be another strength of the proportions of the strength of God; and the shadow cast by the wisdom of God will be another wisdom of God, and so with the rest of the lamps.)

San Juan's treatment of the beautiful lamp of God's wisdom and beauty is similar to the Cabalistic belief in the corresponding essences of God and man. There are Cabalistic correspondences between the divine emanations or attributes of the *sefirot* that the mystic hopes to contemplate and the parallel human virtues that he imitates during his mystic quest. While on his mystic path (*devekut*), the aspirant may hope to contemplate the divine emanation *Hokhmah*, known as the Primordial Lamp of the Hidden God from which all Creation flowed. All the other divine attributes of the *sefirot* are also called "lamps" in the *Zohar*.[68] For Cabalists, the

---

68. The Aramaic term *bozina*—"lamp"—is also used to mean "spark" and "light" in the *Zohar*. From the High Lamp or High Spark of the Hidden God emanate all the other *sefirot*—sparks, lamps. See Matt, *Zohar: The Book of Enlightment*, pp. 296–97.

sacred symbolic lamps of the *sefirot* become clearer through mystic meditation.[69] Similarly, San Juan speaks of other imitable divine attributes perceived by the soul, referring to them as lamps: "Cada uno de estos atributos es una lámpara que luce al alma y da calor de amor" (each one of these attributes is a lamp which gives light to the soul and gives it also the heat of love; *Llama*, 3.2). He then provides specific examples of the attributes as lamps: "el resplandor que le da esta lámpara de Dios en cuanto es bondad y ni más ni menos, le es lámpara de justicia, y de fortaleza, y de misericordia, y de todos los demás atributos que al alma juntamente se le representan en Dios" (the splendor given to the soul by this lamp of God inasmuch as He is goodness sheds upon the soul the light and heat of the love of God inasmuch as He is good; and thus He is to it a lamp of goodness. And in the same way he is to it a lamp of justice, and of fortitude, and of mercy, and of all the other attributes that together are represented to the soul in God; *Llama*, 3.3). In Cabala, similar attributes are *Hesed* (Love and Greatness), *Gevurah* (Power and Judgment), and *Tif'eret* (Compassion and Beauty).[70]

In speaking of the mystical lamps as divine attributes, it is useful to note some of the similarities shared by San Juan's work, Cabala, and Sufi mysticism. Luce López Baralt has noted the close resemblance between San Juan's lamps of divine attributes and those described by the eleventh-century mystic Nuri of Baghdad.[71] Miguel Asín Palacios pointed out that in the fourteenth century, Ibn-Abbad of Ronda wrote of the "lights of attributes."[72] It should be noted, however, that San Juan relates the divine lamps to the Judaic sense of prophecy and its implications for mystical contemplation of the prophets' messages. We read, for example, that "estas lámparas vio Moisés en el monte Sinaí" (Moses saw these lamps on Mount Sinai; *Llama*, 3.4) and that "el Esposo de los Cantares . . . dijo que las lámparas de amor eran lámparas de fuego" (the Bridegroom of Canticles . . . said that the lamps of love were lamps of fire and flames; *Llama*, 3.5).

The references to *velos* (veils), *cortinas* (curtains), or a *tela* (fabric) are another point of comparison between San Juan and Cabala. In San Juan's "¡Oh llama de amor viva!," the mystic poet beseeches the flame: "acaba ya, siguieres; / rompe la tela deste dulce en-

69. Scholem, *Major Trends*, p. 207, and *Kabbalah*, p. 370.

70. Matt, *Zohar: The Book of Enlightment*, p. 35 (diagram of the *sefirot*).

71. "Simbología mística musulmana en San Juan de la Cruz y Santa Teresa de Jesús," p. 45. See also her recent monograph *San Juan de la Cruz y el Islam*, pp. 249–63, for additional discussion of the lamps.

72. "Sadilies y alumbrados," *Al-Andalus* 13 (1948): 264; cited in López Baralt, "Simbología," p. 45.

cuentro" (finish now, if you will; break through the fabric of this sweet encounter; vv. 5–6). In his prose commentary on the poem, the friar writes that the soul removes "algunos de los muchos velos y cortinas que ella tiene antepuestos para poder ver como El es" (some of the many veils and curtains which are in front of it, so that she may see what He is like; *Llama*, 4.7). He also speaks of his soul's longing "para ver las grandezas de riquezas y hermosura divina que estaban detrás de la catarata" (to see the great riches and divine beauty that were behind the cataract; *Llama*, 3.72). In this context, the *catarata* is also considered to be a curtain or veil.[73] The friar's entreaty to slash the curtain or veil recalls the Cabalistic image of the veil surrounding the Holy One in His Palace. Only the most worthy mystic can break through the curtain of light and perceive the divine glory—the *Kavod*.[74] For the Cabalist, the veil or curtain is a heavenly counterpart of the curtains surrounding the Tabernacle on earth (*Zohar*, 4.213a). The *Zohar* even includes mystical speculation on the dimensions of the curtain (4.233a). Thus for both San Juan and Cabala the veil is a mystical symbol of the barrier separating man from God. For the Christian and the Cabalist alike the goal is to penetrate that barrier and approach the Divine.

An additional point of comparison between possible Cabalistic and Sufi influences in San Juan's work concerns the concepts *apretura* (constriction, distress) and *anchura* (extension, freedom). As in Cabala, the two elements are associated with references to night and light. *Apretura* refers to the state of anguish or constriction experienced during the mystical night. *Anchura* is the opposing feeling of sweet comfort and extension accompanying the anticipation of or actual perception of the mystical light.[75] In Cabala, a similar sense of constriction versus extension is found in the *Zohar*'s description of the Hidden God's progressive self-manifestation by means of the emanations of the *sefirot*: we read that "A blinding spark flashed within the Concealed of Concealed from the mystery of the Infinite . . . . Deep within the spark gushed a flow

73. In defining *catarata*, Sebastián de Covarrubias (*Tesoro de la lengua castellana o española* [Madrid: Luis Sánchez, 1611], p. 211), refers to the "telillas blancas que se hazen en los ojos." The similar appearances of *tela*, *velo*, and *catarata* could explain San Juan's use of the terms in the same contexts.

74. Leonard Orr, "Delineating the Tradition: Merkabah and Zoharic Mysticism," p. 24.

75. See Asín Palacios, "Sadilies y alumbrados," *Al-Andalus* 11 (1946): 1–21; "Un precursor hispano-musulmán de San Juan de la Cruz," pp. 23–26; and *Huellas del Islam*, pp. 248–51, 259–62. See also López Baralt, *San Juan de la Cruz y el Islam*, pp. 244–46; and "Simbología," pp. 32–34.

. . . . The flow broke through and did not break through its aura."[76]
When the Zoharic mystic attempts to approach the Hidden God, he
enters through the structures of the *sefirot* present within his own
soul and then through the parallel gradations within the divine
sefirot. The *Zohar* says that "*neshamah* of a human being is unknowable . . . . Thus she is known and unknown . . . . The Blessed
Holy One too is known and unknown for He is *Neshamah* of
neshamah . . . completely hidden away; but through these gates,
openings for *neshamah*, the Blessed Holy One beomes known . . . .
There is opening within opening."[77] In his translation of these
Zoharic passages, Daniel Matt explains that "the *sefirot* are openings for the human *neshamah* to approach the Hidden God, and
openings for *Neshamah* [*Ein Sof*, the Infinite] of *neshamah* [the
human soul of divine origin] to manifest. The *sefirot* are revealed
one by one as the mystic journeys within and beyond."[78] The terms
"breaking through" and "openings" or "known" and "unknown"
seem to have some similarity to Sufi and Carmelite references to
openings and closures encountered on the mystic's journey through
the dark night in pursuit of the divine light.

The Question of Sources

Scholars continue to search for the sources, other than scriptural
ones, that may have influenced San Juan's mystical imagery. A
viewpoint that has been in vogue for some time is that espoused by
Dámaso Alonso and supported by Emilio Orozco.[79] They have
attempted to show that San Juan was influenced by Spanish literature: profane folk traditions, popular "a lo divino" variations,
culto or Italianate love poetry, and religious variations of poetry in
the style of Garcilaso. Colin Thompson has pointed out the short-
comings of the Alonso theory with reference to the *Cántico espiritual*.[80] His close examination shows no direct links between San
Juan's poetry and the "divino" (divinified) version of Garcilaso.
Thompson also finds flaws in the popular poetry theory, pointing
out that traditional Spanish poetry was open to Judaic influences
from Canticles or even Muslim erotico-mystical literature.

76. Matt, *Zohar: The Book of Enlightment*, pp. 47, 208. For this citation of the
Zohar we have used Matt's translation rather than that of Sperling and Simon. Matt
adds explanatory notes not available in the earlier translation.
77. Matt translation, in ibid., pp. 66–67.
78. Ibid., p. 222.
79. Alonso, *La poesía de San Juan de la Cruz*; Orozco, *Poesía y mística*.
80. *The Poet and the Mystic*, pp. 70–80 in particular.

The case for an Islamic influence on San Juan de la Cruz was advanced by Miguel Asín Palacios.[81] Critics have replied that the Muslim elements similar to San Juan's work are very general and could just as easily have been derived from Christian sources.[82] They also point out that there is no evidence of specific works to which San Juan might have had access. Ariel Bension has suggested the *Zohar* as a possible source for Muslim imagery as well as some images used by Ramón Lull, Santa Teresa, and San Juan.[83] He does not, however, provide any significant textual comparisons to demonstrate the influence of the *Zohar* on Muslim or Christian mystics.

Nevertheless, the possibility of intermingled Cabalistic and Sufi influences on the Carmelite mystics does warrant further exploration. In recent studies, Luce López Baralt has expanded Asín Palacios's investigation of the Sufi tradition in North Africa and al-Andalus to include older Persian and Syrian sources. In the case of San Juan, she points to descriptions of wine or mystical intoxication, the solitary bird, and the white lily as elements similar to Sufi mystical symbolism.[84] Other aspects she discusses, however, also show remarkable similarity to Cabalistic elements of San Juan's imagery that we have discussed in this study: the significance of night, light, flame, lamps, veils, and concepts of *apretura* and *anchura*.

Ultimately, we must be concerned with the problem of sources—Cabalistic as well as Sufi. How were the Carmelite mystics exposed to non-Christian mystical traditions in sixteenth-century Spain? The situation is particularly problematic in the case of Sufi influences. For instance, it has been shown that elements of San Juan's and Santa Teresa's mystical symbolism can be seen to have more in common with early Persian-language Sufism than with the later Arabic-speaking Sufis who could have been known more easily to Arab mystics in Spain.[85] More importantly, attempts to uncover evidence of Sufi mystic traditions in sixteenth-century *morisco* culture have not been successful. Extant *morisco* manuscripts from the period reveal only a vague understanding of Islamic mysticism and—significantly—a weak command of Arabic.[86] However,

81. *Huellas del Islam*, pp. 237–304.

82. Nieto, *Mystic, Rebel, Saint*, pp. 25–27; Helmut Hatzfeld, *Estudios literarios sobre la mística española*, pp. 37–38; and Hatzfeld, "Los elementos constitutivos de la poesía mística," p. 43.

83. *The "Zohar" in Moslem and Christian Spain*.

84. In addition to López Baralt's "Simbología," see also her "Para la génesis del pájaro solitario de San Juan de la Cruz."

85. López Baralt, "Simbología," p. 22, n. 2.

86. López Baralt, *San Juan de la Cruz y el Islam*, pp. 314–20.

López Baralt concludes that we are still faced with the curious situation—particularly in San Juan's case. The Carmelite friar sometimes shows more in common with remote Islamic mystics than with the more contemporary Christian intermediaries.[87]

The question of Cabalistic influences on the Carmelites is not so problematic as the matter of finding possible Sufi sources. Our study has shown that from the eleventh century onward, Spanish Christians borrowed elements of Judaic Cabala and applied them to suit their needs. During the sixteenth century, the Christian Cabalistic studies from Italy and northern Europe enabled Spanish Christian humanists such as Luis de León to integrate new Cabalistic emphases with the Christian Cabala in the Spanish apologetic tradition. Instruction in Hebrew at Spanish universities made access to Judaic Cabalistic materials possible for the educated. In terms of popular culture, the evidence is clear that Jewish New Christians maintained varied Judaic customs well into the seventeenth century. Popularized elements of Cabala, particularly Zoharic Cabala, were possibly retained in the converso population and in the converso-influenced society as a whole. And we cannot ignore the possible intermingling of Sufi and Cabalistic elements at the popular level. The interdependence of Cabala and Sufism may offer solutions to questions of influences in the works of San Juan and Santa Teresa, although the investigation of such questions in the folk culture will continue to present problems. Future study in Hebrew sources on Spanish Cabala may discover new clues about the interrelationship of the Judaic and Islamic mystical traditions.[88]

Perhaps the answers to many questions about non-Christian influences on the works of the two saints will be found through research on the interaction of Cabala and Sufi mysticism in Spain. For the present study, however, the evidence of Cabalistic elements in the works of the two Carmelites is substantial. The availability of Christian Cabalistic material in Spain and the persistence of Cabala in converso culture made Cabalistic influences possible. The two traditions reinforced each other and were supported, in addition, by the Judaic heritage of Christianity. San Juan's works in particular show a preoccupation with establishing the Old Testament heritage of Christianity and the Old Testament roots of his own mystical experience. The elements of Cabala found in the works of both San Juan and Santa Teresa are another link to the Judaic

87. Ibid., pp. 368, 395–401.
88. A recent study that may contribute to the investigation of the relations between Sufism and Cabala is Ronald Kiener, "Ibn al-Arabi and the Qabballah."

heritage of all Christians—Old and New. That was the apologetic essence of Cabala as it was used by Christian Cabalists such as Egidio da Viterbo and Fray Luis de León.

In Spain attempts to bridge the Jewish and Christian traditions seemed to persist well beyond the era of polemics and disputes. Apologetics may have become an unconsciously integrated aspect of the culture—an aspect we can see reflected in three of Spain's best-known religious writers: San Juan de la Cruz, Santa Teresa de Jesús, and Fray Luis de León.

7

conclusion: the christian cabala of spiritual renewal and apologetics in literature

The question "Did Spain participate in the cultural ferment of the Renaissance along with the other major European nations?" usually receives the rejoinder "Yes, but in its own way." We can provide a similar response to the issue of Spanish involvement in Renaissance Christian Cabala. It was a matter of applying the new trappings of Renaissance culture to the solid and more popular Spanish framework. In addition, the Spanish Christian Cabalists differed from each other in the degree to which they relied on the old Spanish groundwork or on the new European building blocks.

Of the three writers in our study, Luis de León is the Spanish Christian Cabalist who most frequently applies the European Renaissance approach to Christian Cabala. In several aspects, he resembles the former general of his order, Egidio da Viterbo. Like the cardinal, Fray Luis was at home with the great Latin and Greek poets and philosophers. Both Augustinians saw Neoplatonism—and perhaps other elements of the *prisca theologia*—as a confirmation of Christianity. For both, Hebraic and Cabalistic studies were the link between the literary and the religio-philosophical aspects of their interest in antique culture. Like Egidio da Viterbo and his successor, Girolamo Seripando, Luis de León used Cabala as a spiritual bridge between the past and the future of mankind. Christian Cabala provided support for their views on reform within the Church and on the restoration of world peace and harmony. In the early sixteenth century, Egidio had looked to Carlos V for leadership in providing a new world order, and later Fray Luis would see Spain as the likely moral and political force to fulfill that role.

Luis de León's particular combination of interests in the revival of ancient culture, in Christian renewal, and in world harmony was also similar to Francesco Giorgi's. Neither Fray Luis nor the Franciscan Giorgi was as accomplished or informed on Cabala as Egidio. Nevertheless, like Giorgi, Fray Luis skillfully and subtly incorporated Cabalistic material into his works. The similarities of their techniques are most apparent in their Christocentric works: *De los nombres de Cristo* and *De harmonia mundi*.

Among Fray Luis's Castilian works, his use of Christian Cabala is most explicit in *Nombres*, which illustrates most clearly the three major aspects of Christian Cabala: the importance of sacred language; the significance of letters; and the power of divine words and names. In *Nombres* we find the Christian Cabalistic concern for the Tetragrammaton in the manner of Reuchlin's *De Verbo Mirifico*. The ternary structure, cultivated dialogue, and exquisite setting of *Nombres* are the sort favored by other humanistically trained Renaissance authors. But Luis de León's elegant dialogue reveals a more popular and traditional Spanish concern. He chose to write in Castilian and, therefore, to reach a wider public than his Latin prose might have. In using Cabala to glorify Christ and His Church in *Nombres*, he emphasized the apologetic core of Christian Cabalism. In so doing, he not only conformed with other European Christian Cabalists, but he also participated in a Spanish tradition. Like his converso predecessors Ramón Martín, Alfonso de Zamora, and others, he used Cabala to reveal the truth of Christianity. But as a sixteenth-century Christian humanist, he took advantage of the development of contemporary European Christian Cabalism.

In *Nombres*—and especially in Fray Luis's Castilian poetry—we see a more subtle and more symbolic application of Christian Cabala. When he refers to the mystical ascent through the spheres or to astronomical imagery, the influence of Renaissance Neoplatonism seems obvious. However, the Cabalistic congruities of his Neoplatonism are also apparent and relevant. In the syncretic tradition of Renaissance humanism, Luis de León made use of Cabala along with Neoplatonism and associated theological traditions. The Cabalistic side of the friar's imagery is especially apparent in his references to light and his mystical tendencies, and Cabala is linked to nationalism in one intensely religious and patriotic poem.

When Luis de León reveals his particularly Spanish side, he comes closest to the sort of Christian Cabala found in the works of Santa Teresa or San Juan de la Cruz. Spanish Cabala had survived the Expulsion, and it coexisted with other elements of the Judaic heritage among conversos and the converso-influenced society as a whole. The travels of Agrippa and Agostino Ricci in Spain attest the availability of information on Cabala in its practical guise as well as the mystical. Beyond the erudite knowledge of Cabala that attracted the two Christian Cabalists, a simpler Cabala survived in Spain.

Although Santa Teresa may have learned of Cabalistic imagery from her mystic masters, who indeed could have described to her the symbols used by Christian Cabalists, it is also quite possible that she became familiar with such symbols in the converso society from which she sprang. The acculturation of New Christians was a slow, ongoing transition during which elements of the old values and symbol systems lingered to enrich the new. The presence of Cabalistic images in the *Moradas*—the centerpiece of Teresian mystical writings—does not render the work any less Christian. The Carmelite mother was simply using artistic means at her disposal that she felt would be most convincing and appealing to her nuns. She even may have used metaphors such as those of the silkworm or the *palmito* because they were familiar and agreeable images for her daughters. If Santa Teresa acquired her use of such images at the folk level, she may or may not have been aware of their Cabalistic origin. The very fact that she used them illustrates the continued appeal of Cabalistic imagery and its power as a tool of Christian apologetics in a converso-influenced society.

The Cabalism of San Juan de la Cruz can be seen to stand between two poles of Spanish Christian Cabala. If Santa Teresa represents the more popular and traditional end of the spectrum and Fray Luis the more educated and Renaissance-oriented, then San Juan de la Cruz holds the middle ground. Having pursued a program of study at Salamanca, he was capable of reading the Renaissance Christian Cabalists in Latin or communicating with those who had. Although he could not study the Hebrew texts accessible to Fray Luis, San Juan had a deep and abiding love for Scripture. In the manner of a Christian apologist, he relied heavily on the Old Testament to express his devotion and to describe his mystical experience to others longing to develop their spiritual awareness. Cabala's tradition of scriptural interpretation provided images and emphases to aid San Juan's pedagogical intent. Like Santa Teresa and Fray Luis, the Carmelite friar used Christian Cabala in an instructional and apologetic setting.

The Christian Cabalistic influence on San Juan's mystical writings is most apparent when one compares his imagery with that of earlier Christian mystics. His predecessors' works alone cannot account for the intensity of his Dark Night symbolism or of his passionate imagery of the unitive stage. Cabala's emphasis on divine sexuality and the sanctity of the sensual help to make San

Juan's imagery more comprehensible. If we look at the friar and Santa Teresa as Christian Cabalists, their sincere devotional works can be seen to participate in an old tradition of Spanish Judaic Cabala: the promotion of the spiritual aspects of religion above more narrowly rationalistic theology.

The Christian Cabala of Fray Luis, Santa Teresa, and San Juan was necessarily more cautious than that of earlier Renaissance Christian Cabalists or even some of their European contemporaries. The restrictions of the Spanish Index—earlier and more stringent than the Papal—and the threat of the Inquisition made more forthright Cabalistic references dangerous. Our three authors were certainly not given to using Cabala in the magical context of Pico, Agrippa, and others. Nevertheless, their writings reveal their cognizance of the religious beliefs of the society in which they lived and a possible awareness of the links between Cabala and both traditional and Renaissance magic.

The three Spanish writers on whom this study has focused were all reform-minded. Fray Luis was a member of an Augustinian house reformed under the guidelines of the Christian Cabalists Egidio da Viterbo and Girolamo Seripando. The Spanish Augustinians were participating in a renewal of spiritual values similar to the two Carmelites' restoration of their order's primitive rule and their return to sincere devotional concerns. With all three writers, Christian Cabalistic symbolism is put into the service of Christian spiritual renewal and reform within the Church. In a sense, their use of Cabala is a very Christian and sixteenth-century version of the reformation of Judaic spirituality a century or more earlier in Spain, when Cabala provided the focus for the victory of pietistic Judaism over the rationalistic. In both cases, a deep-felt and popular pietistic movement was underway.

The role of Christian Cabala must be taken into account in studying the spiritual and reform developments in Spain before and during the Counter-Reformation. Perhaps Christian Cabala is a factor as significant as Erasmism in the spiritual revival and the growth of more personalized religion in Spain. Bataillon has recognized the strength of indigenous movements for Church reform and spiritual renewal even before the availability of Erasmian works in Spain.[1] Although he suggested that Erasmism was perhaps more influential in Spain than elsewhere in Europe,[2] he con-

---

1. *Erasmo y España*, trans. Antonio Alatorre, pp. xiii-xiv, 1–278.

2. Bataillon notes the ironic fact that Erasmus's works were most available in translation—and therefore open to a wider public—in the land that would later have the most severe censorship of texts. See ibid., p. 314.

ceded that the Erasmism as understood by Spaniards was a Spanish adaptation of the humanist's original program.[3]

Thus some of the spiritual developments scholars ascribe to Erasmus's popularity in Spain are attributable to an independent native spiritual growth that later coincided with and reinforced the adapted Erasmian current. As our study and others have shown, Christian Cabala was an element of the Spanish spiritual development from the fourteenth through the sixteenth century. Spain—the country Erasmus had disparaged as a land of Jews[4]—made very Christian use of its Judaic heritage. Through Cabala and other Hebraic studies, Fray Luis, San Juan, and even Santa Teresa reinforced Christianity in a manner comprehensible to a converso society. While Erasmus had been negative toward the revival of Hebraic studies for fear that the symbolic, mystical, and ritualistic elements of religion would be emphasized,[5] our Spanish writers found the Hebraic and Cabalistic approach a natural one. For Fray Luis, Santa Teresa, and San Juan, mysticism was the late flowering of a native tendency; and the imagery of Cabala was a source enriching the expression of their spiritual growth.

Beyond their mutual interests in authentic spirituality and reform, our three writers shared their society's continuing concern for establishing and maintaining a community of believers. Fray Luis, Santa Teresa, and San Juan were heirs to a legacy of peaceful coexistence and interaction, which had ultimately terminated in

3. The "Hispanified Erasmus" was principally a result of the efforts of his Spanish translator, Alonso Ruiz de Virués. This Burgos priest not only wrote extensive introductions to Erasmian works, but he also inserted extraneous Erasmian material and elaborated profusely on themes of interest to Spaniards. See ibid., pp. 294–309.

4. Ibid., pp. 77–78.

5. See Werner L. Gundersheimer, "Erasmus, Humanism, and the Christian Cabala." Gundersheimer writes that in Erasmus's statements there is "a deep-seated distrust . . . of mystical exuberance. . . . Erasmus did not like the mystic's particular kind of confidence that man could ascend to an immediate contemplation of God, or to some beatific vision" (p. 50). Gundersheimer quotes a letter to Wolfgang Koepfel in which Erasmus first comments in writing on Cabala: "I should wish that you had a greater propensity toward Greek than to those Hebrew matters, though I do not censure them. I see that nation filled with the most frigid fables, casting forth nothing but various smokes: Talmud, Cabala, Tetragrammaton, 'Gates of Light,' inane names. I would prefer that Christ be infected by Scotus than by such dirges. Italy has many Jews, Spain scarcely any Christians. I am afraid that by this opportunity the head of the plague formerly stifled may rise up. And would that the church of the Christians did not give so much preference to the Old Testament" (p. 40). Charles Zika writes that Erasmus generally lacked sympathy for the exuberance of Neoplatonic scholars and their interests in the more exotic aspects of the *prisca theologia*. He concludes that "it is these tendencies in the Kabbalistic speculations of scholars such as Reuchlin, this sacerdotal and ritualistic religiosity, which Erasmus must have feared in the revival of Hebrew studies." See "Reuchlin and Erasmus," pp. 240–41.

confrontation among the three rival religio-cultural groups. By the time of the Renaissance, the religious polemics had lost their supposed raison d'être, but they endured nevertheless. Spanish Catholicism demanded more from the conversos than the mere appearance of corporate belief or the external manifestation of common religious behavior. A century after the Expulsion, Spanish religious literature continued to show concern for the doubtful Jew and his descendant, the phantom disbeliever. Just as the statutes of purity of blood kept alive the memory of an era of religious confrontation, the continuing apologetic tendency recalled the old polemical debates and treatises. In the writings of Fray Luis, Santa Teresa, San Juan, and their contemporaries, the old apologetic approach took on a new tone and new forms. Now that all Spaniards were to be counted among the faithful—at least theoretically—the formal treatise in Latin or Hebrew was no longer the only framework for apologetic content. As the old polemics faded they were to be replaced by a more sublimated and subdued apologetic.

Those who followed our three writers may have considered the application of subtle apologetics as the maintenance of customary spiritual topoi rather than as a reaction to any currently existing religio-social conditions. Whatever the authors' motivations, the apologetic element remained discernible in their works. Sometimes the remnants of the apologetic tradition appear to be direct imitations of Luis de León's Christian Cabalistic elements in *De los nombres de Cristo*. Francisco de Quevedo y Villegas, for example, utilized Cabala and the Talmud in his translation, *Lágrimas de Hieremías castellanas*.[6] He declared that the purpose of his work was to employ original Hebrew sources and the Vulgate while defending Catholic orthodoxy. In pursuit of that goal, he expressed his admiration for Luis de León's *Nombres* and the manner in which the friar had explained the Christian significance of the Tetragrammaton. Just as Fray Luis had demonstrated his reverence for the Hebrew language, Quevedo stated his belief that Castilian was the language that most resembled Hebrew. Perhaps most indicative of his admiration for the friar's work and of the persistence of the apologetic tradition is Quevedo's wish that "Otra vez, si Dios me da ocio, trataré rigurosamente de los nombres de Dios."[7]

In Lope de Vega's *auto sacramental* called *El nombre de Jesús*, there are again reminiscences of the classic Christian apologetic

6. See Michèle Gendreau's *Héritage et création: recherches sur l'humanisme de Quevedo*, pp. 57–63.
7. Ibid., p. 59.

proof used by Luis de León, his Spanish predecessors, and his Christian Cabalistic contemporaries. Like Fray Luis, Lope identifies the name *Jesús* with the Tetragrammaton—in this case represented by the name *Jehová*. In the concluding lines of the *auto* we read: "Y los hombres os adoran, / Gran Jehová, Jesús divino" (Mankind adores you, Great Jehovah, Divine Jesus).[8] Moreover, as we have seen in *Nombres*, Lope reminds his audience that the *Verbo* is the Christian equivalent of the Hebrew or Aramaic *Dabar* (p. 154). Within the structure of Lope's *auto*, the Cabalistic commonplaces *Dabar* and *Jehová*—along with the generally apologetic tone of the work—are directed toward the *Dudoso*. The allegorical figure can be considered not only as the doubting Jew, but—within the broader contemporary setting—as the phantom disbeliever in Spanish society. If the *Dudoso* is the doubting seventeenth-century descendant of Spanish conversos, then his antitype in Lope's *auto* is Saint Paul, the quintessential convert to Christianity. The new convert expresses his devotion to the name *Jesus*: "Pablo soy, que fue primero / perseguidor deste nombre, / y ya le adora y respeto" (I am Paul, who formerly persecuted this name which I now adore and respect; p. 167). It is Lope's San Pablo who conveys the central theme of the *auto* to the *Dudoso*: Christ is indeed the Divine Messiah.

El nombre de Jesús is probably not an isolated instance of Christian Cabala in Lope's works,[9] and it is certainly not the only *auto sacramental* with apologetic overtones.[10] The same tendency can be perceived in some of the precursors of the Corpus Christi *autos* as well as in the fully mature and consummate *autos sacramentales* of Pedro Calderón de la Barca. The early passion plays of Juan del Encina have also been examined for their somewhat apologetic context.[11] Encina seems to have used the figure of Christ the loving Shepherd as the symbol of conciliation in which all Christians— New and Old alike—could unite in establishing a peaceful and harmonious society. A similar use of typological figures continues in the development of the *autos sacramentales*. In that genre,

8. See p. 170 of *Obras de Lope de Vega: autos y coloquios*, ed. Marcelino Menéndez y Pelayo, vol. 157. The additional references to the Lopean *auto* are also from this edition. The translations are my own.

9. In his forthcoming edition of Lope's *Los pastores de Belén* (to be published in Madrid by Castalia), Antonio Carreño will point out Cabalistic elements of the play.

10. See my "The Bible, *Conversos*, and Apologetics: Another Look at Spain's *Auto Sacramental*" in the selected *Proceedings of the Fourth Annual Golden Age Drama Symposium*, University of Texas at El Paso, 7–9 March 1984, pp. 139–54.

11. On Encina's apologetics, see Ana María Rambaldo, "El cancionero de Juan del Encina dentro de su ámbito histórico y literario"; and Yvonne Yarbro-Bejarano, "Juan del Encina y Lucas Fernández: Conflicting Attitudes towards the Passion."

however, the emphasis on salvation history and biblical types is more clearly defined. The audience is frequently reminded that the Old Testament is fulfilled and continued by the New, that Christ is the prophesied Messiah, and that the prophets or other biblical features are Christian prefigurations. Allegorical figures such as Judaísmo and Sinagoga are contrasted with Cristiandad and Iglesia. Frequently the message heard—as witnessed by the words of Judaísmo in the conclusion of Calderón's *Los misterios de la misa*—is that "cuando nace el error, nace ya perdonado el error."[12] Just as Golden Age *comedias* offer evidence of Spanish society's continuing preoccupation with Judaic or converso elements in the culture,[13] so too the *autos* seem to demonstrate the society's need to forever convert the converted.

Perhaps it is not curious that Spain—alone among the Catholic nations of Europe—perfected the religious dramatic known as the *auto sacramental* precisely when similar dramatic forms were on the decline elsewhere.[14] To Spaniards for whom the reading of

12. See Pedro Calderón de la Barca, *Autos sacramentales*, in *Obras Completas*, ed. Ángel Valbuena Prat, 2d ed. (Madrid: Aguilar, 1967), 2:314. Other examples rich in typology used apologetically in Calderón's *autos* are to be found in *La iglesia sitiada* and *El arca de Dios cautiva*.

13. On the treatment of Jews and conversos in the *comedia* see David Gitlitz, "The Jew in the *Comedia* of the Golden Age," Ph.D. diss., Harvard University, 1968; Gitlitz, "The New Christian Dilemma in Two Plays of Lope de Vega," *Bulletin of the Comediantes* 34 (1982): 62–81; Roberta Zimmerman Lavine, "The Jew and the Converso in the Dramatic Works of Lope de Vega," Ph.D. diss., Catholic University of America, 1983; Joseph Silverman, "Los 'hidalgos cansados' de Lope de Vega," in *Homenaje a William J. Fichter*, ed. D. Kossoff and J. Amor y Vázquez (Madrid: Castalia, 1971), pp. 693–711; Silverman, "Spanish Jews: Early References and Later Affects," in *Américo Castro and the Meaning of Spanish Civilization*, ed. José Rubia Barcia (Berkeley: University of California Press, 1976), pp. 144–47; Carroll B. Johnson, "The Classical Theater and Its Reflection of Life," in *Américo Castro*, pp. 211–18; Edward Glaser, "Referencias antisemíticas en la literatura de la Edad de Oro," *Nueva Revista de Filología Hispánica* 8 (1954): 39–62; Américo Castro, *La realidad histórica de España*, 3d ed. (México: Porrúa, 1966); and Castro, *De la edad conflictiva* (Madrid: Taurus, 1963).

14. Outside Spain, popular religious theater—the mystery, morality, and miracle plays—declined steadily in the sixteenth century. The Protestants, who had initially used the theater as a polemical tool, eventually rejected all theatrical representations as immoral. The biblical works in vogue in the Catholic countries and in the more Protestant nations were mainly concerned with the Bible as the stuff from which fine tragedies could be made. For information on European attitudes toward biblical theater in the sixteenth and seventeenth centuries, see Murray Roston, *Biblical Drama in England* (Evanston: Northwestern University Press, 1968); G. D. Jonker, *Le protestantisme et le théâtre de langue française au XVIe siècle* (Groninque, Batavia: J. B. Wolters, 1939); Geoffrey Brereton, *French Tragic Drama in the Sixteenth and Seventeenth Centuries* (London: Methuen, 1973); Madeleine Lazard, *Le théâtre en France au XVIe siècle* (Paris: Presses Universitaires de France, 1980); and Ernest Hatch Wilkins, *A History of Italian Literature*, 2d ed. (Cambridge: Harvard University Press, 1974).

Scripture was forbidden, the *autos* were sources of biblical information, but they were also lessons in traditional Spanish religious
acculturation. The *autos* served, as did the works of Luis de León,
Santa Teresa, and San Juan, to further Spanish Catholicism's continuing process of assimilation. At times the polemical attitudes
were more apparent than the gentle and persuasive tones of the
apologetics exemplified by our three authors. Nevertheless, the
tendency can be seen to persist in Spanish religious works written
after the era of Fray Luis and the Carmelites. The question for
continued investigation remains: to what extent did elements of
Christian Cabala linger—however subtly—in the imagery and content of the sublimated apologetic tendency? Further study of other
Spanish works of the Golden Age may reveal the influence of our
three authors' different Christian Cabalistic approaches and may
indicate new directions for exploration. Just as the works of Fray
Luis de León, Santa Teresa de Jesús, and San Juan de la Cruz were a
more literary and integrated form of the earlier polemical treatises,
so too the works of their successors may reveal other, more subdued elements of the Spanish apologetic tradition in the Christian
Cabalistic mode.

bibliogRaphy of woRks consulted

Primary Sources

Agrippa von Nettesheim, Henry Cornelius. *The Philosophy of Natural Magic*. Edited by L. W. Laurence. Chicago: Laurence, Scott & Co., 1913.

————. *Three Books of Occult Philosophy*. Translated by J[ohn] F[rench]. London: R. W. for Gregory Moule, 1651.

Bernard of Clairvaux, Saint. *Oeuvres mystiques*. Translated by Albert Béguin. Paris: Editions du Seuil, 1953.

Blumenthal, David R., ed. "Pirkei Heikhalot." In *Understanding Jewish Mysticism*. New York: KTAV, 1978, pp. 56–91.

Bonaventure, Saint. *Mystical Opuscula*. Vol. 1 of *The Works of Bonaventure*. Translated by José de Vinck. Patterson, N.J.: St. Anthony Guild Press, 1960.

Ciruelo, Pedro. *A Treatise Reproving All Superstitions and Forms of Witchcraft, Very Necessary and Useful for All Good Christians Zealous for Their Salvation*. Translated and edited by Eugene Maio and D'Orsay Pearson. London: Associated University Presses; Rutherford, N.J.: Fairleigh Dickinson University Press, 1977.

Dionysius the Areopagite. *On the Divine Names and the Mystical Theology*. Translated by C. E. Rolt. New York: Macmillan, 1920.

Ebreo, Leone. *The Philosophy of Love*. Translated by F. Friedberg-Seeley and Jean H. Barnes. London: Soncino Press, 1937.

Eckhart, Meister. *Meister Eckhart: An Introduction to the Study of His Works with an Anthology of His Sermons*. Edited by James Clark. London: Thomas Nelson, 1957.

————. *Meister Eckhart: A Modern Translation*. Translated by Raymond Bernard Blakney. New York/London: Harper, 1941.

Egidio da Viterbo, Cardinal. *Scechina et libellus de litteris ebraicis*. 2 vols. Edited by François Secret. Rome: Centro Internazionale di Studi Umanistici, 1959.

Galatino, Pietro. *Opus toti christianae, reipublicae maxime utile de arcanis catholicae veritatis, contra obstinatissimam iudaeorum nostrae tempestatis perfidiam: ex Talmud, aliisque hebraicis libris nuper excerptum: & quadruplici linguarum genere eleganter congestum.* [Ortona, H. Suncinum, 1518.]

Giorgi, Francesco. *De harmonia mundi*. Paris: Andreas Berthelin, 1545.

Gottfarstein, Josepf, trans. *Le Bahir: le livre de la clarté*. Paris: Verdier, 1983.

Juan de la Cruz, San. *Vida y obras de San Juan de la Cruz*. Eds. Crisógono de Jesús, Matías del Niño Jesús, and Luciano Ruano. 8th ed. Madrid: Biblioteca de Autores Cristianos, 1974.

Ludolphe of Saxony. *Vida de nuestro adorable Redentor Jesucristo*. 3 vols. Madrid: Celestino Álvarez & Joaquín Sierra, 1847–1849.

Luis de León. *Exposición del Libro de Job*. Autograph manuscript, 1581. Library of the University of Salamanca. MS 219.

———. *Fray Luis de León: obras completas castellanas*. Edited by Félix García. 3d ed. Madrid: Biblioteca de Autores Cristianos, 1951.

———. *Fray Luis de León: poesías*. Edited by Ángel Custodio Vega. Barcelona: Planeta, 1970.

———. *De los nombres de Cristo*. Salamanca: Juan Fernández, 1583 (1584).

———. *De los nombres de Cristo*. Salamanca: Herederos de Mathías Gast, 1585 (1586).

———. *De los nombres de Cristo*. Salamanca: Guillelmo Foquel, 1587.

———. *De los nombres de Cristo*. Barcelona: Hierónymo Genovés, 1587.

———. *De los nombres de Cristo*. Barcelona: Juan Pablo Mareschal, 1587.

———. *De los nombres de Cristo*. Salamanca: Juan Fernández, 1595.

———. *De los nombres de Cristo*. Edited by Cristóbal Cuevas García. Madrid: Cátedra, 1977.

———. *La poesía de Fray Luis de León*. Edited by Oreste Macrí; translated by Francisco del Pino Calzacorta. Madrid: Anaya, 1970.

Martín, Ramón. *Pugio fidei adversus mauros et judaeos cum observationibus Josephi de Voisin, et introductione Jo. Benedicti Carpozovi*. Lipsiae et Francofurti, 1687.

Meltzer, David, ed. *The Secret Garden: An Anthology in the Kabbalah*. New York: Seabury, 1976.

Moses of León. *The Wisdom of the Kabbalah (As Represented by Chapters Taken from the Book "Zohar")*. Edited by Dagobert D. Runes. New York: Philosophical Library, 1957.

———. *The Zohar*. Edited and translated by Harry Sperling and Maurice Simon. 5 vols. London: Soncino, 1949.

———. *Zohar: The Book of Enlightenment*. Edited and translated by Daniel Chanan Matt. New York: Paulist Press, 1983.

———. *Zohar: The Book of Splendor*. Edited by Gershom Scholem. New York: Schocken, 1963.

Osuna, Francisco de. *Tercera parte del libro llamado Abecedario espiritual*. Vol. 1 of *Escritores místicos españoles*. No. 16 of NBAE. Madrid: Bailly/Bailliére, 1911, pp. 319–587.

———. *The Third Spiritual Alphabet*. Translated and edited by a Benedictine of Stanbrook. London: Burnes, Oates, & Washbourne, 1931.

Pérez de Moya, Juan. *Philosophia secreta*. Clásicos olvidados 6. 2 vols. Madrid: NBAE, 1928.

Quevedo y Villegas, Francisco de. *Sueños y discursos de verdades descubridoras de abusos vicios y engaños en todos los oficios y estados del mundo*. Edited by Felipe Maldonado. Madrid: Clásicos Castalia, 1972.

Reuchlin, Johannes. *De arte cabalistica: id est, de divinae revelationis, ad saluti feram Dei, et formarum separatarum contemplationem traditae, symbolica receptione.* Edited by Johannes Pistorius. In *Ars Cabalistica.* Basel, 1587; facsimile rpt. Unveranderter Nachdruck/Frankfurt: Minerva GMBH, 1970.

———. *De arte cabalistica.* French translation by François Secret, in his *La kabbale.* Paris: Aubier Montagne, 1973.

———. *De Verbo Mirifico. In laudeum disertissimi atque trium linguarum peritissimi viri Ioannis Reuchlin.* Edited by Johannes Pistorius. In *Ars Cabalistica.*

Ricci, Agostino. *De motu octavae sphaerae, opus mathematica, atque philosophia plenum. Ubi tam antiquorum, quam iuniorum errores, luce clarius demonstrantur: inquo & quam plurima Platonicorum, & antiquae magiae, (quam Cabalam Hebrei dicunt) dogmata videre licet intellectu suavissima.* Imprimebat Lutetiae Simon Colinaeus, 1521.

Ricci, Paolo. *Compendium quo mirifico acumine . . . apostolicam veritatem: Ratione: Prophetice: Talmudistice: Cabalistice: plane confirmat.* Impressum papie y magistruz Jacob de Burgofrancho. 1507.

———. *Pavli Ricii doctissimi ac sapientissimi viri ex iudaiaca familia: De coelesti agricultura.* Edited by Johannes Pistorius. In *Ars Cabalistica.* Basel, 1587; facsimile rpt. Unveranderter Nachdruck/Frankfurt: Minerva GMBH, 1970.

Rothenberg, Jerome, Harris Lenowitz, and Charles Doria, eds. *A Big Jewish Book.* Garden City, N.Y.: Anchor/Doubleday, 1978.

Ruysbroeck, Master. *Oeuvres de Ruysbroeck l'admirable.* Translated by the Benedictines of Saint-Paul de Wisques. 6 vols. Paris: Vromant, 1928–1937.

Stenring, Knut, trans. and ed. *The Book of Formation or Sepher Yetzirah.* London: Rider, 1923.

Tauler, John. *The Sermons and Conferences of John Tauler.* Translated by Walter Elliott. Washington, D.C.: Apostolic Mission House, 1910.

Teresa de Jesús, Santa. *Santa Teresa de Jesús: obras completas.* Eds. Efrén de la Madre de Dios and Otger Steggink. 6th ed. Madrid: Biblioteca de Autores Cristianos, 1979.

Vetus Testamentum, multiplici lingua nunc primo impressum. Et imprimis Pentateuchus hebraico greco atque chaldaico idiomate. Adiuncta unicuique sua latina interpretatione. In Academia Complutensi. Industria Arnaldi Guillelmi de Brocario. 1517.

Zamora, Alfonso de. *El manuscrito apologético de Alfonso de Zamora (Séfer Hokmat Elohim).* Edited by Federico Pérez Castro. Madrid: CSIC, 1950.

Secondary Sources

Allendy, René. *Le symbolisme des nombres.* Paris: Bibliothèque Chacornac, 1921.

Alonso Cortés, Narciso. "Pleitos de los Cepeda." *Boletín de la Real Academia Española* 25 (1946): 85–110.

Alonso, Dámaso. "Ante la selva (con Fray Luis)." In *Poesía española*, pp. 109–98. 1950; rpt. Madrid: Gredos, 1971.

———. "El misterio técnico de la poesía de San Juan de la Cruz." In *Poesía española*, pp. 217–305.

———. *La poesía de San Juan de la Cruz; Desde esta ladera.* 4th ed. Madrid: Aguilar, 1966.

Altmann, Alexander. *Studies in Religious Philosophy and Mysticism.* Ithaca: Cornell University Press, 1969.

Álvarez, Guzmán. "En el texto de *Las Moradas.*" In *Santa Teresa y la literatura mística hispánica.* Actas del I Congreso Internacional sobre Santa Teresa y la Mística Hispánica, edited by Manuel Criado de Val. Madrid: EDI-6, 1984.

Álvarez Turienzo, Saturnino. "La ley y vida en el pensamiento moral de Fray Luis de León." *Religión y Cultura* 22 (1976): 507–47.

———. "Clave epistemológica para leer a Fray Luis de León." Fray Luis de León, Actas de la I Academia literaria renacentista, Salamanca 10–12 diciembre 1979. Salamanca: University de Salamanca, 1981, pp. 23–45.

Amador de los Ríos, José. "De las artes mágicas y de adivinación en el suelo ibérico." *Revista de España* 18 (1871): 1–26, 321–48.

Anastasio del Santo Rosario. "L'eremitismo della Regola Carmelitana." *Ephermerides Carmeliticae* 2 (1948): 245–62.

Andrés Martín, Melquíades. *Los recogidos; nueva visión de la mística española (1500–1700).* Madrid: Fundación Universitaria Española, 1975.

———. "Tradición conversa y alumbramiento (1480–1487); Una veta de los alumbrados de 1525." In *Stvdia Hieronymiana*, 1:381–98. Madrid: Rivadeneyra, 1973.

"Aragón, Enrique de [Marqués de Villena]." In *Enciclopedia universal ilustrada.* Barcelona: Hijos de Espasa [Espasa-Calpe], n.d.

Asensio, Eugenio. "El erasmismo y corrientes espirituales afines." *Revista de Filología Española* 36 (1952): 31–90.

Asín Palacios, Miguel. "Un precursor hispano-musulmán de San Juan de la Cruz." *Al-Andalus* 1 (1933): 7–79.

———. "Un precursor hispano-musulmán de San Juan de la Cruz." In *Huellas del Islam*, pp. 235–304. Madrid: Espasa-Calpe, 1941.

———. "Sadalíes y alumbrados." *Al-Andalus* 9–16 (1944–1951).

———. "El símil de los castillos y moradas del alma en la mística islámica y en Santa Teresa." *Al-Andalus* 11 (1946): 263–74.

Aubier, Dominique. *Don Quichotte, prophète d'Israël.* Paris: Robert Laffont, 1966.

Azcona, Tarsicio de. "Dictamen en defensa de los judíos conversos de la orden de San Jerónimo a principios del siglo XVI." In *Stvdia Hieronymiana*, vol. 2. Madrid: Rivadeneyra, 1973.

Bacher, William. "Judaeo-Christian Polemics in the Zohar." *Jewish Quarterly Review* 3 (1891): 776.

Baer, Yitzhak. *A History of the Jews in Christian Spain.* Translated by Louis Schoffman. 2 vols. Philadelphia: Jewish Publication Society of America, 1961.

Barnstone, Willis. "Mystico-Erotic Love in 'O Living Flame of Love.' " *Revista Hispánica Moderna* 37 (1972–1973): 253–61.

Baruzi, Jean. *Saint Jean de la Croix et le problème de l'expérience mystique.* Paris: Librairie de Félix Alcan, 1924.

Bataillon, Marcel. "Charles-Quint Bon Pasteur selon Fray Cipriano de Huerga." *Bulletin Hispanique* 50 (1948): 398–406.

———. *Erasmo y España.* 2d ed. Translated by Antonio Alatorre. México: Fondo de Cultura Económica, 1966.

Batallori, Miguel. "Los jesuitas y la combinatoria lulliana." In *Umanesimo e esoterismo,* edited by Enrico Castelli. Atti del V Convegno Internazionale di Studi Umanistici. Padua: CEDAM, 1960.

Beaudoire, Théophile. *Genèse de la cryptographie apostolique et de l'architecture rituelle du premier au seizième siècle.* Paris: n.p., 1902.

Becerra Hiraldo, José María. "Fray Luis de León y Honorio de Atún." *Arbor,* 94, no. 367–68 (1976), 91–96.

———. "La personalidad de Fray Luis a través de sus obras latinas." *Religión y Cultura* 23 (1977): 395–419.

Beinart, Haim. "The Converso Community in Fifteenth-Century Spain." In *The Sephardi Heritage,* edited by R. D. Barnett, 1:425–56. London: Valentine & Mitchell, 1971.

———. "The *Converso* Community in Sixteenth and Seventeenth-Century Spain." In *The Sephardi Heritage,* 1:457–78.

———. "The Judaizing Movement in the Order of San Jerónimo in Castile." *Scripta Hierosolymitana* 7 (1961): 167–92.

Bell, Aubrey. *Luis de León; A Study of the Spanish Renaissance.* Oxford: Clarendon Press, 1925.

———. "Luis de León and the Inquisition." *Revista de Historia* 2 (1914): 202–11.

———. "Notes on Luis de León's Lyrics." *Modern Language Review* 21 (1926): 168–77.

A Benedictine of Stanbrook Abbey. *Mediaeval Mystic Tradition and Saint John of the Cross.* London: Burns & Oates, 1954.

Bensimon, Marc. "Modes of Perception of Reality in the Renaissance." In *The Darker Vision of the Renaissance,* edited by Robert S. Kinsman, pp. 221–92. Berkeley: University of California Press, 1974.

Bension, Ariel. *The "Zohar" in Moslem and Christian Spain.* London: Routledge, 1932.

Berger, David. *Judaism on Trial.* London/Toronto: Associated University Presses, 1982.

Biale, David. *Gershom Scholem: Kabbalah and Counter-History.* Cambridge: Harvard University Press, 1979.

Blanco, Mayling. "San Juan de la Cruz's Water Imagery in 'Aunque es de noche.'" *Romance Notes* 15 (1973): 346–48.

Blau, Joseph Leon. *The Christian Interpretation of the Cabala.* New York: Columbia University Press, 1944.

———. "The Diffusion of the Christian Interpretation of the Cabala in English Literature." *The Review of Religion* 6 (1941–1942): 146–68.

Bloom, Harold. *Kabbalah and Criticism.* New York: Seabury, 1975.

Blumenthal, David R. *Understanding Jewish Mysticism.* 2 vols. New York: KTAV, 1978, 1982.

Bolle, Kees W. "Structures of Renaissance Mysticism." In *The Darker Vision of the Renaissance,* edited by Robert S. Kinsman, pp. 119–45. Berkeley: University of California Press, 1974.

Bonner, Anthony. "Llull's Influence: The History of Lullism." In *Selected Works of Ramon Llull,* edited and translated by Anthony Bonner, 1:71–89. Princeton: Princeton University Press, 1985.

Bousset, Wilhelm. *Kyrios Christos: A History of the Belief in Christ from the Beginning of Christianity to Irenaeous.* Translated by John E. Steely. Nashville: Abingdon Press, 1970.

Bouwsma, William J. *Concordia Mundi: The Career and Thought of Guillaume Postel.* Cambridge: Harvard University Press, 1957.

Braunstein, Baruch. *The Chuetas of Majorca: Conversos and the Inquisition of Majorca.* 1936. New York: KTAV, 1972.

Brenan, Gerald. *Saint John of the Cross.* London: Cambridge University Press, 1973.

Burke, John G. "Hermeticism as a Renaissance World View." In *The Darker Vision of the Renaissance,* edited by Robert S. Kinsman, pp. 95–118. Berkeley: University of California Press, 1974.

Bustos, Eugenio de. "Observaciones semiológicas y semánticas en torno a Fray Luis." Fray Luis de León, Actas de la I Academia Literaria Renacentista, Salamanca 10–12 diciembre 1979. Salamanca, 1981, pp. 101–45.

Butler, Christopher. *Number Symbolism.* New York: Barnes and Noble, 1970.

Camón Aznar, José. *Arte y pensamiento en San Juan de la Cruz.* Madrid: Biblioteca de Autores Cristianos, 1972.

Cantera Burgos, Francisco. "¿Santa Teresa de Jesús de ascendencia judía?" *Sefarad* 13 (1953): 402–4.

———. "El Cancionero de Baena: judíos y conversos en él." *Sefarad* 27 (1967): 71–111.

Cantera Burgos, Francisco, and José María Millás Vallicrosa. *Las inscripciones hebraicas de España.* Madrid: CSIC, 1956.

Caro Baroja, Julio. *Inquisición, brujería, y criptojudaísmo.* 2d ed. Barcelona: Ariel, 1972.

———. *Los judíos en la España moderna y contemporánea.* Vol. 1. Madrid: Arión, 1961.

———. "La magia en Castilla durante los siglos XVI y XVII." In

Algunos mitos españoles y otros ensayos. 2d ed. Madrid: Editora Nacional, 1944, pp. 185–303.

Carpentier, J. A., and Come Carpentier. "La experiencia y la escatología mística de Santa Teresa y sus paralelos en el Islam medieval de los sufis." In *Santa Teresa y la literatura mística hispánica.* Actas del I Congreso Internacional sobre Santa Teresa y la Mística Hispánica, edited by Manuel Criado de Val, pp. 159–87. Madrid: EDI-6, 1984.

Carreras y Artau, Joaquín. "Arnaldo de Vilanova, apologista antijudaico." *Sefarad* 7 (1947): 49–61.

———. "Raimundo Lulio y la Cábala." *Las Ciencias* 22 (1957): 146–64.

Cassirer, Ernst. *The Platonic Renaissance in England.* Translated by James P. Pettegrove. Edinburgh/London: Thomas Nelson, 1953.

Castro, Américo. *La realidad histórica de España.* 2d ed. México: Porrúa, 1954.

———. *Santa Teresa y otros ensayos.* Madrid: Historia Nueva, 1929.

Chorpenning, Joseph F. "The Literary Method of the *Castillo Interior.*" *Journal of Hispanic Philology* 3 (1979): 121–33.

———. "The Monastery, Paradise, and the Castle: Literary Images and Spiritual Development in St. Teresa of Ávila." *Bulletin of Hispanic Studies* 62 (1985): 245–57.

Cilleruelo, Lope. "La mística de la imagen en Fray Luis de León." *Religión y Cultura* 22 (1976): 435–64.

Cirac Estopañán, Sebastián. *Los procesos de hechicerías en la Inquisición de Castilla la Nueva: Tribunales de Toledo y Cuenca.* Madrid: Consejo Superior de Investigaciones Científicas, 1942.

Clissold, Stephen. "St. Teresa and the Visionary Nuns." *History Today* 25 (1975): 561–67.

Cohn, Norman. *The Pursuit of the Millennium.* Rev. and expanded ed. New York/Oxford: Oxford University Press, 1970.

Colunga, Alberto. "San Juan de la Cruz, intérprete de la Santa Escritura." *Ciencia Tomista* 63 (1942): 257–76.

Comas, Antonio. "Espirituales, letrados y confesores en Santa Teresa de Jesús." In *Homenaje a Jaime Vicens Vives,* edited by J. Maluguer de Motes, pp. 85–99. Barcelona: University of Barcelona, 1967.

Conger, George Perrigo. *Theories of Macrocosms and Microcosms in the History of Philosophy.* New York: Columbia University Press, 1922.

Constant, Alphonse Louis (Eliphas Levi). *The Mysteries of the Qabalah or The Occult Agreement of the Two Testaments.* Vol. 2 of *Studies in Hermetic Tradition.* New York: Samuel Weiser, 1974.

Copenhaver, Brian P. "Lefèvre d'Etaples, Symphorien Champier, and the Secret Names of God." *Journal of the Warburg and Courtauld Institutes* 40 (1977): 189–211.

Corré, Alan. *Understanding the Talmud.* New York: KTAV, 1975.

Coster, Adolphe. "Bibliographie de Luis de León." *Revue Hispanique* 59 (1923): 1–104.

———. *Luis de León* (Extraits de la *Revue Hispanique,* 53–54). New York/Tours: E. Arrault, 1921–1922.

Cotarelo y Mori, Emilio. *Don Enrique de Villena*. Madrid: Sucesores de Rivadeneyra, 1896.

Cristiani, Monseigneur. *Saint Jean de la Croix; Prince de la mystique*. Paris: Editions France-Empire, 1960.

Crovetto, P. L. "Fray Luis e il Rinascimento spagnolo." *Alla Bottega* 7 (1969): 41–45.

Crowley, Aleister. *Seven, Seven, Seven: Vel Prolegomena Symbolica ad Systemam Sceptico-Mysticae Viae Explicandae, Fundamentum Hieroglyphicum Santissimorum Scientiae Summae*. New York: Gordon, 1974.

Cuán Pérez, Enrique. "Fray Luis de León y el sentido de la imagen del puerto." *Religión y Cultura* 23 (1977): 439–65.

———. "Oda de Fray Luis de León a Francisco Salinas: una expresión de unidad y amor." *Religión y Cultura* 24 (1978): 701–12.

Curtius, Ernst Robert. *European Literature and the Latin Middle Ages*. Translated by Willard R. Trask. 1953; corr. ed., Princeton: Princeton University Press, 1967.

———. "Nomina Christi." In *Mélanges Joseph de Ghellinek*, 2:1029–32. Gembloux: Editions J. Duculot, 1951.

Dagens, Jean. "Hermétisme et Cabale en France de Lefèvre d'Etaples à Boussuet." *Revue de littérature comparée* 35 (1961): 5–16.

Daniélou, Jean. *Les symboles chrétiens primitifs*. Paris: Editions du Seuil, 1961.

———. *The Theology of Jewish Christianity*. Edited and translated by John A. Baker. Vol. 1 of *A History of Early Christian Doctrine*. London: Darton, Longman & Todd, 1964.

Darst, David H. "El discurso sobre la magia en *La cueva de Salamanca* de Ruiz de Alarcón." *Duquesne Hispanic Review* 9 (1970): 31–44.

———. "Teorías de la magia en Ruiz de Alarcón: análisis e interpretación." *Hispanófila*, número especial (1974), 71–80.

Davies, Steven L., Jeffrey A. Goldstein, and Zalman M. Schachter. "Anglicization of Jewish Kabbalah." *Studia Mystica*, 3, no. 3 (1980), 34–47.

De Armas, Frederick. "The Hunter and the Twins; Astrological Imagery in *La estrella de Sevilla*." *Bulletin of the Comediantes* 32 (1980): 11–20.

———. "El planeta más impío: Basilio's Role in *La vida es sueño*." *Modern Language Review* 81 (1986).

———. "The Saturn Factor: Examples of Astrological Imagery in Lope de Vega's Works." In *Studies in Honor of Everett Hesse*, edited by José Antonio Maravall and William C. McCrary, pp. 63–80. Lincoln, Neb.: Society of Spanish and Spanish American Studies, 1981.

Dhorme, P. E. "L'emploi métaphorique des noms de parties du corps en hébreu et en akkadien." *Revue Biblique* 29–32 (1920–1923): 464–506; 374–79, 517–540; 215–33, 489–517; and 185–212, respectively.

Díaz Infante Núñez, Josefina. *La poesía de San Juan de la Cruz; influencias y coincidencias*. México: Universidad Nacional Autónoma de México, 1957.

Dicken, E. W. Trueman. *The Crucible of Love: A Study of the Mysticism of*

Saint Teresa and Saint John of the Cross. London: Darton, Longman & Todd; New York: Sheed & Ward, 1963.

———. "The Imagery of the Interior Castle and Its Implications." *Ephemerides Carmeliticae* 21 (1970): 190–218.

Domínguez Ortiz, Antonio. *Los conversos de origen judío después de la Expulsión*. Madrid: Consejo Superior de Investigaciones Científicas, 1955.

———. *Los judeo-conversos en España y América*. Madrid: ISTMO, 1971.

Durán, Manuel. "Américo Castro, Luis de León, and Inner Tensions of Spain's Golden Age." In *Collected Studies in Honor of Américo Castro's Eightieth Year*, edited by Marcel P. Hornik, pp. 83–90. Oxford: Lincombe Lodge Research Library, 1965.

———. *Luis de León*. New York: Twayne, 1971.

Duvivier, Roger. "L'Histoire des écrits de saint Jean de la Croix." *Les lettres romanes* 27 (1973): 323–80; 31 (1977): 343–52.

Edwards, John. "The Conversos: A Theological Approach." *Bulletin of Hispanic Studies* 57 (1985): 39–49.

Efrén de la Madre de Dios and Otger Steggink. *Tiempo y vida de Santa Teresa*. Madrid: Biblioteca de Autores Cristianos, 1968.

Eguiagaray, Francisco. *Los intelectuales españoles de Carlos V*. Madrid: Instituto de Estudios Políticos, 1965.

Eliade, Mircea. "Le symbolisme des ténèbres dans les religions archaïques." In *Polarité du symbole*, edited by Mircea Eliade, pp. 15–28. Bruges: Études Carmelitaines chez Desclée de Brouwer, 1960.

Elisée de la Nativité. "Les carmes imitateurs d'Elie." *Études Carmélitaines* 35 (1956): 82–116.

Espantoso-Foley, A. *The Occult Art and Doctrines in the Theater of Alarcón*. Geneva, 1972.

Estébanez Estébanez, Cayetano. "Naturaleza, literatura, e ideas en la obra de Fray Luis de León." *Revista de Ideas Estéticas* 31 (1973): 107–24.

Etchegoyen, Gaston. *L'amour divin; essai sur les sources de Sainte Thérèse*. Bordeaux/Paris: Firet, 1923.

Evans, Robert James Weston. *Rudolf II and His World: A Study in Intellectual History (1576–1612)*. Oxford: Clarendon Press, 1973.

Ferguson, Wallace. *The Renaissance in Historical Thought*. Boston: Houghton-Mifflin, 1948.

Fernández, Ángel Raimundo. "Génesis y estructura de Las Moradas del *Castillo interior*." Actas del Congreso Internacional Teresiano, Salamanca, 4–7 Octubre 1982, 2:609–36. Salamanca: University de Salamanca, University Pontificia de Salamanca, Ministerio de Cultura, 1983.

Fernández Leborans, María Jesús. *Campo semántico y connotación*. Madrid: Cupsa, 1977.

———. *Luz y oscuridad en la mística española*. Madrid: Cupsa, 1978.

Fita, Fidel. "Pico de la Mirándola y la Inquisición española; breve inédito de Inocencio VIII." *Boletín de la Real Academia de la Historia* 16 (1890): 314–16.

Fitzmaurice-Kelly, James. *Fray Luis de León; A Biographical Fragment.* Oxford: Oxford University Press, 1921.

Fraker, Charles F. *Studies on the "Cancionero de Baena."* University of North Carolina Studies in Romance Languages and Literature 61. Chapel Hill: University of North Carolina Press, 1966.

Franck, Adolphe. *The Kabbalah.* Translated by I. Sossnitz. New York: Bell, 1940.

François de Sainte Marie, ed. and trans. *Les plus vieux textes du Carmel.* 2d ed. Paris: Editions du Seuil, 1945.

French, Peter J. *John Dee: The World of an Elizabethan Magus.* London: Routledge & Kegan Paul, 1972.

Friedman, Jerome. *The Most Ancient Testimony (Sixteenth-Century Hebraica in the Age of Renaissance Nostalgia).* Athens: Ohio University Press, 1983.

García de la Concha, Víctor. *El arte literario de Santa Teresa.* Barcelona: Ariel, 1978.

———. "Mística, estética y arte literario en Teresa de Jesús." Actas del Congreso Internacional Teresiano, Salamanca, 4–7 Octubre, 1982. Salamanca, Ministerio de Cultura, 1983, 2:459–78.

García Lorca, Francisco. *De Fray Luis a San Juan: la escondida senda.* Madrid: Castalia, 1972.

Garin, Eugenio. *Medioevo e Rinascimento: studi e richerche.* Bari: G. Laterza, 1954.

Gerli, E. Michael. "*El castillo interior* y el *Arte de la memoria.*" *Bulletin Hispanique* 86 (1984): 154–63.

Gendreau, Michèle. *Héritage et création: recherches sur l'humanisme de Quevedo.* Diss., University of Paris, 1975. Lille: Atelier Reproduction des Thèses, University of Lille, 1977.

Getino, Luis G. Alonso. *Vida y procesos del maestro Fray Luis de León.* Salamanca: Calatrava, 1907.

Gicovate, Bernard. *San Juan de la Cruz.* New York: Twayne, 1971.

Giles, Mary E. "Poetic Expressiveness and Mystical Consciousness: A Reading of Saint John's 'Dark Night of the Soul.'" *Studia Mystica*, 2, no. 3 (1979), 3–15.

Gilman, Stephen. *The Spain of Fernando de Rojas: The Intellectual and Social Landscape of "La Celestina."* Princeton: Princeton University Press, 1972.

Gitlitz, David. "Fray Luis' Psalm Translations: From Hebrew or Latin?" *Romance Notes* 24 (1983): 142–47.

Goiten, S. D. "A Jewish Addict to Sufism." *Jewish Quarterly Review* 44 (1953–1954): 37–47.

Gómez-Menor Fuentes, José. *El linaje familiar de Santa Teresa y de San Juan de la Cruz: sus parientes toledanos.* Toledo: Gráficas Cervantes, 1970.

González Novalín, José Luis. "Teresa de Jesús y el Luteranismo en España." *Actas del Congreso Internacional Teresiano, Salamanca, 4–7 Octubre 1982*, 1:351–87. Salamanca: University de Salamanca, University Pontificia de Salamanca, Ministerio de Cultura, 1983.

Goode, Helen. *La prosa retórica de Fray Luis de León en "De los nombres de Cristo."* Madrid: Gredos, 1969.

Graef, Hilda. *The Story of Mysticism.* Garden City, N.Y.: Doubleday, 1965.

Graf, Pablo. *Luis Vives como apologeta.* Translated by José María Millás Vallicrosa. Madrid: Consejo Superior de Investigaciones Científicas, 1943.

Green, Deirdre. "Saint Teresa of Avila and Heikhalot Mysticism." *Sciences Religieuses/Studies in Religion* 13 (1984): 279–87.

Green, Otis H. *Spain and the Western Tradition.* 4 vols. Madison: University of Wisconsin Press, 1963.

Grendler, Paul F. *The Roman Inquisition and the Venetian Press, 1540–1605.* Princeton: Princeton University Press, 1977.

Groult, Pierre. *Los místicos de los países bajos y la literatura espiritual española del siglo XVI.* Translated by Rodrigo A. Molina. Madrid: Fundación Universitaria Española, 1976.

Gruenwald, Ithamar. *Apocalyptic and Merkabah Mysticism.* Leiden/Köln: E. J. Brill, 1980.

———. "Jewish Merkavah Mysticism and Gnosticism." In *Studies in Jewish Mysticism.* Proceedings of Regional Conferences Held at the University of California, Los Angeles, and McGill University in April 1978, edited by Joseph Dan and Frank Talmage, pp. 41–55. Cambridge, Mass.: Association for Jewish Studies, 1982.

Guillén, Jorge. "Lenguaje insuficiente: San Juan de la Cruz o lo inefable místico." In *Lenguaje y poesía*, pp. 95–142. Madrid: Revista de Occidente, 1962.

Gullón, Agnes Moncy. "Santa Teresa y sus demonios." *Papeles de Son Armadans* 107 (1965): 149–66.

Gundersheimer, Werner L. "Erasmus, Humanism, and the Christian Cabala." *Journal of the Warburg and Courtauld Institutes* 26 (1963): 38–52.

Gutiérrez, David. "Fray Luis de León, autor místico." *Religión y Cultura* 22 (1976): 409–33.

———. "Fray Luis de León y la exégesis rabínica." *Augustinianum* 1 (1961): 533–50.

Gutiérrez, Marcelino. *Fray Luis de León y la filosofía española del siglo XVI.* Madrid: Gregorio del Amo, 1885.

———. *El misticismo ortodoxo (en sus relaciones con la filosofía).* Valladolid: Luis N. de Gaviria, 1886.

Guy, Alain. "Le bien comun selon Fray Luis de León." *Religión y Cultura* 22 (1976): 549–61.

———. *El pensamiento filosófico de Fray Luis de León.* Translated by Ricardo María Ibáñez. Madrid: Rialp, 1960.

————. *La pensée de Fray Luis de León*. Paris: Vrin, 1943.

Habib Arkin, Alexander. "La influencia de la exégesis hebrea en los comentarios biblicos de Fray Luis de León." *Sefarad* 24 (1964): 276–87.

————. *La influencia de la exégesis hebrea en los comentarios bíblicos de Fray Luis de León*. Madrid: Consejo Superior de Investigaciones Científicas, 1966.

————. "La presencia rabínica en la explicación que hizo Fray Luis de León del salmo 42." In *Studies in Honor of M[air] J[osé] Benardete; Essays in Hispanic and Sephardic Culture*, edited by Izaak Langnas and Barton Sholod, pp. 83–88. New York: Las Américas, 1965.

Hahn, Ferdinand. *The Titles of Jesus in Christology*. Translated by Harold Knight and George Ogg. New York: World Publishing, 1969.

Halperin, David J. *The Merkabah in Rabbinic Literature*. American Oriental Series, vol. 62. New Haven, Conn.: American Oriental Society, 1980.

Hardy, Richard P. "The Hidden God and Juan de la Cruz." *Ephemerides Carmeliticae* 27 (1976): 241–62.

Hatzfeld, Helmut. "Los elementos constitutivos de la poesía mística: San Juan de la Cruz." *Nueva Revista de Filología Hispánica* 17 (1963–1964): 40–59.

————. *Estudios literarios sobre la mística española*. 2d ed. Madrid: Gredos, 1968.

————. *Santa Teresa de Ávila*. New York: Twayne, 1969.

Hausherr, Irénée. *The Name of Jesus*. Translated by Charles Cummings. Kalamazoo: Cistercian Publications, 1978.

Henningsen, Gustav. *The Witches' Advocate: Basque Witchcraft and the Spanish Inquisition, 1609–1614*. Reno: University of Nevada Press, 1980.

Hoffman, Edward. *The Way of Splendor: Jewish Mysticism and Modern Psychology*. Boulder/London: Shambhala, 1981.

Hoornaert, Rodolphe. "Le progrès de la pensée de Sainte Thérèse entre la *Vie* et le *Chateau*." *Revue des Sciences Philosophiques* 13 (1924): 20–43.

Hopper, V. F. *Medieval Number Symbolism*. New York: Columbia University Press, 1938.

Hornedo, Rafael María. "Sobre la exposición de Santa Teresa y su tiempo." *Razón y fe* 879 (1971): 413–24.

Hornik, Henry. "More on the Hermetica and French Renaissance Literature." *Studi Francesi* 18 (1974): 1–12.

Huerta, Alberto. "La composición de lugar y la oda al apartamiento." *Religión y Cultura* 23 (1977): 421–37.

————. "Katharsis en la 'Oda a Salinas.'" *Religión y Cultura* 25 (1979): 669–78.

————. "El lugar de los astros en Fray Luis de León." *Religión y Cultura* 25 (1979): 477–92.

————. "Música de ser: trascendente e inminente." *Religión y Cultura* 22 (1976): 581–94.

Huffman, William. "Robert Fludd: The End of an Era." Ph.D. diss., University of Missouri-Columbia, 1977.

Huizinga, J[ohan]. *The Waning of the Middle Ages: A Study of the Forms of Life, Thought, and Art in France and the Netherlands in the Dawn of the Renaissance.* Translated by F. Hopman. 1924; rpt. Garden City, N.Y.: Doubleday-Anchor, 1954.

Hurtado Torres, Antonio. *La astrología en la literatura del Siglo de Oro, índice bibliográfico.* Alicante: Instituto de Estudios Alicantinos, 1984.

Idel, Moshe. "The Ladder of Ascension—The Reverberations of a Medieval Motif in the Renaissance." In *Studies in Medieval Jewish History and Literature,* edited by Isadore Twersky, 2:83–94. Cambridge: Harvard University Press, 1984.

Izquierdo Hernández, Manuel. "Enfermedades y muerte." In *Santa Teresa de Jesús,* pp. 55–131. Madrid: Iberoamericanas, 1963.

Izquierdo Luque, María Magdalena. "Metáforas y símbolos." In *Santa Teresa de Jesús,* pp. 9–53. Madrid: Iberoamericanas, 1963.

Jacobs, Louis, ed. *Jewish Mystical Testimonies.* New York: Schocken, 1977.

Jedin, Hubert. *Papal Legate at the Council of Trent: Cardinal Seripando.* Translated by Frederic Clement Eckhoff. St. Louis: Herder, 1947.

Jiménez Salas, María. *Santa Teresa de Jesús: bibliografía fundamental.* Madrid: Consejo Superior de Investigaciones Científicas, 1962.

Johnson, Aubrey Rodway. *The One and the Many in the Israelite Conception of God.* Cardiff: University of Wales Press, 1942.

Jones, J. A. "Arias Montano and Pedro de Valencia: Three Further Documents." *Bibliothèque d'Humanisme et Renaissance* 38 (1976): 351–55.

Junco, Alfonso. "Ámbito de Teresa de Jesús: lo humano en lo divino." *Ábside* 35 (1971): 127–43.

Kallenberg, Pascal. "Le culte liturgique d'Elie dans l'Ordre du Carmel." *Études Carmélitaines* 35 (1956): 134–50.

Kamen, Henry. *Inquisition and Society in Spain in the Sixteenth and Seventeenth Centuries.* Bloomington: Indiana University Press, 1985.

Keniston, Hayward. *Life and Works of Garcilaso.* New York: Hispanic Society of America, 1922.

Kenton, Warren (Z'ev ben Shimon Halevi). *Kabbalah and Exodus.* Boulder: Shambhala, 1980.

———. *A Kabbalistic Universe.* New York: Samuel Weiser, 1977.

———. *The Way of Kabbalah.* London: Rider, 1976.

Kiener, Ronald. "Ibn al-Arabi and the Qabbalah: A Study of Thirteenth-Century Iberian Mysticism." *Studies in Mystical Literature* 2 (1982): 26–52.

Kimpel, Benjamin. *The Symbols of Religious Faith: A Preface to an Understanding of the Nature of Religion.* New York: The Philosophical Library, 1954.

Kirsopp, Wallace. "The Family of Love in France." *Journal of Religious History* (Sydney) 3 (1964–1965): 103–18.

Klibansky, Raymond, Erwin Panofsky, and Fritz Saxl. *Saturn and Melancholy*. London: Thomas Nelson, 1964.

Knight, Gareth. *A Practical Guide to Qabalistic Symbolism*. 2 vols. 1915; rpt. New York: Semuel Weiser, 1978.

Köhler, Eugen. "Fray Luis de León et la théorie du nom." *Bulletin Hispanique* 50 (1948): 421–28.

Kottman, Karl A. *Law and Apocalypse: The Moral Thought of Luis de León*. The Hague: Martinus Nijhoff, 1972.

Krynen, Jean. "De la teología humanística a la mística de las luces." *Religión y Cultura* 22 (1976): 465–83.

Kubler, George. *Building the Escorial*. Princeton: Princeton University Press, 1982.

Lapesa, Rafael. "Las odas de Fray Luis de León a Felipe Ruiz." In *Studia Philologica; homenaje ofrecido a Dámaso Alonso*, 2:301–18. Madrid: Gredos, 1961.

Leocadio Garasa, Delfín. "Ángeles y demonios en el teatro de Lope de Vega." *Boletín de la Academia Argentina de Letras* 25 (1960): 233–67.

Lida de Malkiel, María Rosa. *La tradición clásica en España*. Barcelona: Ariel, 1975.

Llamas, José. "Documental inédito de exégesis rabínica en antiguas universidades españolas." *Sefarad* 6 (1946): 289–311.

Llamas Martínez, Enrique. *Santa Teresa de Jesús y la Inquisición española*. Madrid: Consejo Superior de Investigaciones Científicas, 1972.

Loeb, Isidore. "Polémistes chrétiens et juives en France et Espagne." *Revue des Études Juives* 18 (1889): 52–62.

López Baralt, Luce. "Huellas del Islam en San Juan de la Cruz." *Vuelta*, 4, no. 45 (1980), 5–11.

———. "Los lenguajes infinitos de San Juan de la Cruz e Ibn Arabi de Murcia." Actas del Sexto Congreso Internacional de Hispanistas, pp. 473–77. Toronto, 1980.

———. "De Nuri de Bagdad a Santa Teresa de Jesús: el símbolo de los siete castillos e moradas concéntricas del alma." *Vuelta* 80 (1983): 18–22.

———. "Para la génesis del pájaro solitario de San Juan de la Cruz." *Romance Philology* 37 (1984): 409–24.

———. "San Juan de la Cruz: una concepción del lenguaje poético." *Bulletin of Hispanic Studies* 55 (1978): 19–32.

———. *San Juan de la Cruz y el Islam*. México: Colegio de México; Río Piedras: University of Puerto Rico, 1985.

———. "Santa Teresa de Jesús y el Oriente: el símbolo de los siete castillos del alma." *Sin Nombre* 13 (1983): 25–44.

———. "El símbolo de los siete castillos concéntricos del alma en Santa Teresa y en el Islam." In *Huellas del Islam en la literatura española: de Juan Ruiz a Juan Goytisolo*. Madrid: Hiperión, 1986.

———. "Simbología mística musulmana en San Juan de la Cruz y Santa Teresa de Jesús." *Nueva Revista de Filología Hispánica* 30 (1981 [but appeared in 1983]): 21–91.

López de Toro, José. "Fray Luis de León y Benito Arias Montano." *Archivo Agustiniano* 50 (1956): 5–28.

López Martínez, Nicolás. *Los judaizantes castellanos y la Inquisición en tiempo de Isabel la Católica*. Burgos: Publicaciones del Seminario Metropolitano de Burgos, 1954.

Lowinsky, Edward Elias. *Secret Chromatic Art in the Netherlands Motet*. New York: Russell & Russell, 1967.

Luby, Barry J. "The Names of Christ in Fray Luis de León's *De los nombres de Cristo*." *Names* 18 (1970): 20–28.

Lucien-Marie de St. Joseph. "Expérience mystique et expression symbolique chez Saint Jean de la Croix." In *Polarité du symbole*, edited by Mircea Eliade, pp. 29–51. Bruges: Desclée de Brouwer, 1960.

Luis de San José. *Concordancias de las obras y escritos de Santa Teresa de Jesús*. Burgos: El Monte Carmelo, 1965.

Lumsden-Kouvel, Audrey. "Problems in Garcilaso's *Egloga II*." *Hispanic Review* 15 (1947): 225–71.

Maccoby, Hyam, ed. and trans. *Judaism on Trial: Jewish-Christian Disputations in the Middle Ages*. London and Toronto: Associated Presses, 1982.

Macedo, Helder. *Do significado oculto da "Menina e Moça."* Lisbon: Moraes, 1977.

McMahon, John J. *The Divine Union in the "Subida del Monte Carmelo" and the "Noche oscura" of Saint John of the Cross*. Washington, D.C.: Catholic University of America Press, 1941.

Macrí, Oreste, ed. *La poesía de Fray Luis de León*. Translated by Francisco del Pino Calzacorta. Madrid: Anaya, 1970.

Maio, Eugene. *Saint John of the Cross; The Imagery of Eros*. Madrid: Playor, 1973.

Marcos del Río, Francisco. "La doctrina mística de Fray Luis de León." *Religión y Cultura* 2–4 (1928): 531–43, 205–20, 223–36, respectively.

Marlay, Peter. "On Structure and Symbol in the Cántico Espiritual." In *Homenaje a Casalduero*, pp. 363–69. Madrid: Gredos, 1972.

Márquez, Antonio. *Los alumbrados: orígenes y filosofía*. Madrid: Taurus, 1972.

Márquez Villanueva, Francisco. "The *Converso* Problem: An Assessment." In *Collected Studies in Honor of Américo Castro's Eightieth Year*, edited by Marcel P. Hornik, pp. 317–33. Oxford: Lincombe Research Library, 1965.

———. "Santa Teresa y el linaje." In *Espiritualidad y literatura en el siglo XVI*, pp. 141–205. Madrid/Barcelona: Alfaguara, 1968.

———. "El símil del *Castillo interior*: sentido y génesis." Actas del Congreso Internacional Teresiano, Salamanca, 4–7 Octubre 1982, 2:495–522. Salamanca: University of Salamanca, University Pontificia de Salamanca, Ministerio de Cultura, 1983.

Martin, Francis X. "The Problem of Giles of Viterbo: A Historiographical Survey." *Augustiniana* 9–10 (1959–1960): 357–79; 43–60, respectively.

Martín de Jesús María. "El concepto del alma en las *Moradas* de Santa Teresa." *Revista de Espiritualidad* 1 (1942): 206–15.

Martino, Alberto. "Il commento della Regola nel Carmelo antico." *Ephemerides Carmeliticae* 2 (1948): 99–122.

Massa, Eugenio. "Egidio da Viterbo e la metodologia del sapere nel cinquecento." In *Pensée humaniste et tradition chrétienne (aux XVe et XVIe siècles)*, edited by H. Bédarida, pp. 185–239. Paris: Centre National de la Recherche Scientifique, 1950.

Masters, G. Mallory. *The Rabelasian Dialectic (and the Platonic-Hermetic Tradition)*. Albany: State University of New York Press, 1969.

Matt, Daniel Chanan. Introduction to *The Book of Mirrors: Sefer Mar'ot ha-Zove'ot by R. David ben Yehudah he-Hasid*. Edited by Daniel Chanan Matt. Brown Judaic Studies Series. Chico, Calif.: Scholars Press, 1982.

———, ed. and trans. *Zohar: The Book of Enlightenment*. New York: Paulist Press, 1983.

Menéndez y Pelayo, Marcelino. *Historia de los heterodoxos*. Vols. 35–42 of *Edición nacional de las obras completas*. Madrid: Consejo Superior de Investigaciones Científicas, 1947.

———. *Historia de las ideas estéticas en España*. 3d ed. Vol. 3. Madrid: Tello, 1920.

———. "Las obras latinas de Fr. Luis de León." *Religión y Cultura* 2 (1928): 460–65.

Millás Vallicrosa, José María. "Algunas relaciones entre la doctrina luliana y la Cábala." *Sefarad* 15 (1958): 241–53.

———. *La poesía hebraica postbíblica*. Barcelona: José Janés, 1953.

———. *La poesía sagrada hebraico-española*. 2d ed. Madrid/Barcelona: Consejo Superior de Investigaciones Científicas, 1948.

———. "Probable influencia de la poesía sagrada hebraico-española en la poesía de Fr. Luis de León." *Sefarad* 15 (1955): 261–85.

———, ed. and trans. *El "Liber predicationis contra judeos" de Ramón Lull*. Madrid/Barcelona: Consejo Superior de Investigaciones Científicas, 1957.

———. *Literatura hebraico-española*. Barcelona: Nueva Collección Labor, 1967.

———. *Selomo ibn Gabirol como poeta y filósofo*. Madrid/Barcelona: Consejo Superior de Investigaciones Científicas, 1948.

Moore, Kenneth. *Those of the Street: The Catholic-Jews of Mallorca*. Notre Dame/London: Notre Dame University Press, 1976.

Morales Oliver, Luis. "Arias Montano y la Orden de San Jerónimo." In *Stvdia Hieronymiana*, 2:381–403. Madrid: Rivadeneyra, 1973.

Morel, Georges. *Le sens de l'existence selon Saint Jean de la Croix*. 3 vols. Paris: Aubier, 1960–1961.

Muñoz Iglesias, Salvador. *Fray Luis de León, teólogo*. Madrid: Consejo Superior de Investigaciones Científicas, 1950.

Musaph-Andriesse, R. C. *From Torah to Kabbalah: Introduction to the Writings of Judaism*. Oxford: Oxford University Press, 1982.

Myer, Isaac. *Qabbalah: The Philosophical Writings of Avicebron.* 1888; rpt. New York: Samuel Weiser, 1970.

Nauert, Charles G. *Agrippa and the Crisis of Renaissance Thought.* Urbana: University of Illinois Press, 1965.

Nazario de Santa Teresa. *La mística de occidente; San Juan de la Cruz, filósofo contemporáneo.* Trujillo, República Dominicana: Montalvo, 1956.

Netanyahu, Benzion. *The Marranos of Spain.* New York: American Academy for Jewish Research, 1966.

Newman, Louis Israel. *Jewish Influence on Christian Reform Movements.* New York: Columbia University Press, 1925.

Nieto, José. "The Franciscan *Alumbrados* and the Prophetic-Apocalyptic Tradition." *Sixteenth Century Journal* 8 (1977): 3–17.

———. *Mystic, Rebel, Saint: A Study of Saint John of the Cross.* Geneva: Droz, 1979.

Noreña, Carlos G. "Fray Luis de León and the Concern with Language." In *Studies in Spanish Renaissance Thought*, pp. 150–209. The Hague: Martinus Nijhoff, 1975.

Nowotny, Karl Anton. "The Construction of Certain Seals and Characters in the Work of Agrippa of Nettesheim." *Journal of the Warburg and Courtauld Institutes* 12 (1949): 46–57.

Oelman, Timothy. "Tres poetas marranos." *Nueva Revista de Filología Hispánica* 30 (1981): 184–206.

Oeschlin, Louis. *L'intuition mystique de Sainte Thérèse.* Paris: Presses Universitaires de France, 1946.

Oesterley, W. O. E., and G. H. Box. *A Short Survey of the Literature of Rabbinical and Mediaeval Judaism.* 1920; rpt. New York: Burt Franklin, 1973.

Olabarrieta, Sister Miriam Thérèse. *The Influence of Ramón Lull on the Style of Early Spanish Mystics and Santa Teresa.* Washington, D.C.: Catholic University of America Press, 1963.

O'Malley, John W. *Giles of Viterbo on Church and Reform.* Leiden: E. J. Brill, 1968.

Orozco, Emilio. *Poesía y mística: introducción a la lírica de San Juan de la Cruz.* Madrid: Guadarrama, 1959.

Orr, Leonard. "Delineating the Tradition: Merkabah and Zoharic Mysticism." *Studia Mystica* 2 (1979): 20–31.

Paquier, Jules. "Un essai de théologie platonicienne á la Renaissance: le commentaire de Gilles de Viterbe sur le premier livre des Sentences." *Recherches de Science Religieuse* 13 (1923): 293–312, 419–36.

Parrinder, Geoffrey. *Mysticism in the World's Religions.* London: Sheldon Press, 1976.

Patrides, C. A., ed. *The Cambridge Platonists.* 1969; rpt. Cambridge: Cambridge University Press, 1980.

Pavia, Mario N. *Drama of the "Siglo de Oro": A Study of Magic, Witchcraft and Other Occult Beliefs.* New York: Hispanic Society of the United States, 1959.

Peers, E. Allison. *Spirit of Flame; A Study of Saint John of the Cross.* New York: Morehouse-Gorham, 1944.

——. *Studies of the Spanish Mystics.* 3 vols. 2d ed. New York: Macmillan, 1951; London: SPCK, 1960.

——, trans. *The Complete Works of St. John of the Cross.* London: Burns Oates, 1943.

——, trans. *The Complete Works of St. Teresa of Jesus.* New York: Sheed & Ward, 1946.

Pélisson, Nicole. "Les noms divins dans l'oeuvre de Sainte Thérèse de Jesus." In *Études sur Sainte Thérèse*, edited by Robert Ricard, pp. 57–199. Paris: Centre de Recherches Hispaniques, 1968.

Pellé-Douël, Yvonne. *San Juan de la Cruz y la noche mística.* Translated by Luis Hernández Alfonso. Madrid: Aguilar, 1963.

Pérez Castro, Federico. "España y los judíos españoles." *The Sephardi Heritage*, edited by R. D. Barnett, 1:275–322. London: Valentine & Mitchell, 1971.

——, ed. *El manuscrito apologético de Alfonso de Zamora: Séfer Hokmat Elohim.* Madrid: Consejo Superior de Investigaciones Científicas, 1950.

Piccus, Jules. "Fray Luis de León y la figura del tetragrámaton en *De los nombres de Cristo.*" *Hispania* 55 (1972): 848–56.

Picerno, Richard A. "Temas espirituales en la 'Vida retirada' y puntos de contacto entre esta obra y el 'Cántico espiritual.'" *Duquesne Hispanic Review* 9 (1970): 1–11.

Pietro della Madre di Dio. "Le fonti bibliche della Regola Carmelitana." *Ephermerides Carmeliticae* 2 (1948): 65–97.

——. "La sacra scrittura nelle opere di S. Teresa." *Rivista di vita spirituale* 18 (1964): 41–102.

Piñera, Humberto. *El pensamiento español de los siglos XVI y XVII.* New York: Las Américas, 1970.

Pinta Llorente, Miguel de la. "Autores y problemas literarios en torno a Fray Luis de León." *Revista de Literatura* 6 (1954): 31–68.

——. *Estudios y polémicas sobre Fray Luis de León.* Madrid: Consejo Superior de Investigaciones Científicas, 1956.

——. "Fray Luis de León y los hebraistas de Salamanca." *Archivo Agustiniano* 45 (1952): 147–69, 334–37.

——. *La Inquisición española y los problemas de la cultura y de la intolerancia.* Madrid: Ediciones de Cultura Hispánica, 1953.

Pope, Marvin H., trans. and ed. *Song of Songs.* In *The Anchor Bible.* Garden City, N.Y.: Doubleday, 1977.

Popkin, Richard. *The History of Scepticism from Erasmus to Descartes.* Assen: Van Gorcum, 1960.

Quintana Fernández, Guillermo. "Las bases filosóficas de la teología de Fray Luis de León." *Revista de la Universidad de Madrid* 12 (1963): 746–47.

Rambaldo, Ana María. "El cancionero de Juan del Encina dentro de su ámbito histórico y literario." Ph.D. diss., New York University, 1971.

Rappoport, Angelo S., and Raphael Patai. *Myth and Legend of Ancient Israel*. 3 vols. New York: KTAV, 1966.

Reeves, Marjorie. *The Influence of Prophecy in the Later Middle Ages: A Study of Joachimism*. Oxford: Clarendon Press, 1969.

Rekers, Bernard. *Benito Arias Montano (1527–1598)*. London: The Warburg Institute/University of London, 1972.

Repges, Walter. "Para la historia de *Los nombres de Cristo*: de la patrística a Fray Luis de León." *Thesaurus* 20 (1965): 325–46.

Revilla, Mariano. "Fray Luis de León y los estudios bíblicos en el siglo XVI." *Revista Española de Estudios Bíbliocos* 3 (1928): 27–81.

Ricard, Robert. "Quelques remarques sur les *Moradas* de Sainte Thérèse." *Bulletin Hispanique* 47 (1945): 187–98.

———. "Saint Jean de la Croix et la 'bûche enflammée.' Contribution à l'étude d'un thème symbolique." *Les lettres romanes* 33 (1970): 73–85.

———. "Le symbolisme du *Chateau interior* chez Sainte Thérèse." *Bulletin Hispanique* 67 (1965): 25–41.

———. "Le symbolisme du *Chateau interior* chez Sainte Thérèse." In *Études sur Sainte Thérèse*, edited by Robert Ricard, pp. 21–38. Paris: Centre de Recherches Hispaniques, 1968.

Rico, Francisco. *El pequeño mundo del hombre: varia fortuna de una idea en las letras españolas*. Madrid: Castalia, 1970.

Rivera de Ventosa, Enrique. "El primado de Cristo en Duns Escoto y Fray Luis de León." *Religión y Cultura* 22 (1976): 485–502.

Rivers, Elias, ed. and trans. *Renaissance and Baroque Poetry of Spain*. New York: Scribner's, 1966.

Robb, Nesca A. *Neoplatonism of the Italian Renaissance*. 1935; rpt. New York: Octagon Books, 1968.

Roberts, Gemma. "Trasfondo cristiano en la oda 'Morada del cielo' de Fray Luis de León." *Explicación de Textos Literarios* 4 (1975): 61–68.

Rose, Constance, and Timothy Oelman, eds. *Loa sacramental de los siete planetas*, by Enríquez Gómez. Exeter: Exeter Hispanic Monographs, 1987.

Rossi, Paolo. "Le origini della pansofia e il lullismo del secolo XVII." In *Umanesimo e esoterismo*, edited by Enrico Castelli, pp. 199–216. Atti del V Convegno Internazionale di Studi Umanestici. Padua: CEDAM, 1960.

Roth, Cecil. *A History of the Marranos*. 1932; rpt. New York: Schocken, 1974.

———. *The Jews in the Renaissance*. Philadelphia: Jewish Publication Society of America, 1959.

Roussel, Bernard. "Histoire de l'Eglise et histoire de l'exégèse au XVIe siècle." *Bibliothèque de Humanisme et Renaissance* 37 (1975): 181–92.

Rousselot, Paul. *Los místicos españoles*. Barcelona: Biblioteca de Escritores Contemporáneos, 1907.

Ruiz, Javier. "Los alquimistas de Felipe II." *Historia 16* 2 (1977): 49–55.

Ruiz Jurado, Manuel. "Un caso de profetismo reformista en la compañía de Jesús: Gandía, 1547–1549." *Archivum Historicum Societatis Iesu*, n.v. (1974), 217–66.

Sabat de Rivers, Georgina. "Sor Juana y su 'Sueño': antecedentes científicos en la poesía española del Siglo de Oro." *Cuadernos Hispanoamericanos*, no. 310 (1976), 186–204.

Sabourin, Leopold. *The Names and Titles of Jesus*. Translated by Maurice Carroll. New York: Macmillan, 1967.

Sagrado Corazón, Enrique del. "Santa Teresa de Jesús ante la Inquisición española." *Ephemerides Carmeliticae* 13 (1962): 518–65.

———. "Santa Teresa de Jesús ante la Inquisición española: estudio introductivo." *Revista de Espiritualidad* 24 (1965): 307–42.

Sainz Rodríguez, Pedro. "Critiques et biographes de Fray Luis León." *La Table Ronde* 144 (1959): 73–82.

———. *Espiritualidad española*. Madrid: Rialp, 1961.

Sajón de Cuello, Raquel. "La tradición esotérica del Septenario y las siete *Moradas*." In *Santa Teresa y la literatura mística hispánica*. Actas del I Congreso Internacional sobre Santa Teresa y la Mística Hispánica, edited by Manuel Criado de Val, pp. 375–90. Madrid: EDI-6, 1984.

Sala-Molins, Louis. *La philosophie de l'amour chez Raymond Lulle*. Paris: Mouton, 1974.

Salinas, Pedro. "The Escape from Reality: Fray Luis de León and San Juan de la Cruz." In *Reality and the Poet in Spanish Poetry*, translated by Edith Fishtine Helman, pp. 95–128. Baltimore: Johns Hopkins University Press, 1966.

Sánchez Cantón, F. J. *La librería de Juan de Herrera*. Madrid: Consejo Superior de Investigaciones Científicas, 1941.

Sánchez Moguel, Antonio. *El lenguaje de Santa Teresa de Jesús*. Madrid: Imprenta Clásica Española, 1915.

Sánchez Pérez, Aquilino. *La literatura emblemática española (Siglos XVI y XVII)*. Madrid: Sociedad General Española de Librería, 1977.

Saulnier, V. L. *Maurice Scève*. 2 vols. Paris: Librairie C. Klincksieck, 1948.

Saurat, Denis. *Literature and Occult Tradition*. Translated by Dorothy Bolton. London: O. Bell, 1930.

Schaya, Leo. *The Universal Meaning of Kabbalah*. Translated by Nancy Pearson. Baltimore: Penguin, 1973.

Scholem, Gershom. *Jewish Gnosticism, Merkabah Mysticism, and Talmudic Tradition*. 2d ed. New York: Jewish Theological Seminary, 1965.

———. *Kabbalah*. 1974; rpt. New York: New American Library, 1978.

———. *Major Trends in Jewish Mysticism*. Translated by George Lichtheim. New York: Schocken, 1961.

———. "The Meaning of the Torah in Jewish Mysticism." *Diogenes* 14–15 (1956): 36–47; 65–94, respectively.

———. *On the Kabbalah and Its Symbolism*. Translated by Ralph Manheim. New York: Schocken, 1965.

Schuster, Edward J. "Alonso de Orozco and Fray Luis de León: *De los nombres de Cristo*." *Hispanic Review* 24 (1956): 261–70.

————. "Fray Luis de León and the Linguistic Approach to Epistemology." *Kentucky Foreign Language Quarterly* 6 (1959): 195–200.

Secret, François. "Aegidiana Hebraica." *Revue des Études Juives* 121 (1962): 409–16.

————. "L'astrologie et les kabbalistes chrétiens à la Renaissance." *La Tour Saint-Jacques* 4 (1956): 45–56.

————. "Les débuts du kabbalisme chrétien en Espagne et son histoire à la Renaissance." *Sefarad* 17 (1957): 36–48.

————. "Les dominicains et la kabbale chrétienne à la Renaissance." *Archivum Fratrum Praedicatorum* 27 (1957): 319–36.

————. "Egidio da Viterbo et quelques-uns de ses contemporains." *Augustiniana* 16 (1966): 371–85.

————. "L'*Ensis Pauli* de Paulus de Heredia." *Sefarad* 26 (1966): 79–102, 252–71.

————. "L'interpretazione della Kabbala nel Rinascimento." *Convivium*, n.s. 24 (1956): 541–52.

————. "Les jésuites et le kabbalisme chrétien à la Renaissance." *Bibliothèque d'Humanisme et Renaissance* 20 (1958): 542–55.

————. *Les kabbalistes chrétiens de la Renaissance*. Paris: Dunod, 1964.

————. "Notes pour une histoire du *Pugio Fidei* à la Renaissance." *Sefarad* 20 (1960): 401–7.

————. Notes sur Guillaume Postel." *Bibliothéque d'Humanisme et Renaissance* 21 (1959): 453–67.

————. "Notes sur les hébraïsants chrétiens de la Renaissance." *Sefarad* 22 (1962): 107–27.

————. "Notes sur Paulus Ricius et la kabbale chrétienne en Italie." *Rinascimento* 11 (1960): 169–92.

————. "Pedro Ciruelo: critique de la kabbale et de son usage par les chrétiens." *Sefarad* 19 (1959): 48–77.

————. "Le symbolisme de la kabbale chrétienne dans la *Scechina* de Egidio da Viterbo." In *Umanesimo e simbolismo*, edited by Enrico Castelli, pp. 131–54. Atti del IV Congreso Internazionale di Studi Umanistici. Padua: CEDAM, 1958.

————. *Le "Zohar" chez les kabbalistes chrétiens de la Renaissance*. Paris: Mouton, 1964.

Septimus, Bernard. "Piety and Power in Thirteenth-Century Catalonia." In *Studies in Medieval Jewish History and Literature*, edited by Isadore Twersky, 1:197–230. Cambridge: Harvard University Press, 1979.

Serís, Homero. "Nueva genealogía de Santa Teresa." *Nueva Revista de Filología Hispánica* 10 (1956): 365–84.

Serouya, Henri. *La kabbale*. Paris: Presses Universitaires de France, 1964.

Serrano Plaja, Arturo. "El 'ansia de armonía' o 'son eterno' en Juan de Herrera y Fray Luis de León; Y de El Escorial al cubismo." *Cuadernos Hispanoamericanos*, 53, no. 157 (1963), 29–40.

————. "Dos notas a San Juan de la Cruz; Más 'caza' y una copla flamenca que es una 'profanización.'" *Cuadernos Hispanoamericanos*, 81, no. 242 (1970), 406–18.

————. "Una noche toledana: del castillo interior al castillo fugitivo; Santa Teresa, Kafka, y el Greco." *Papeles de Son Armandans* 35 (1964): 263–302.

Seznec, Jean. *The Survival of the Pagan Gods*. Translated by Barbara Sessions. New York: Pantheon, 1953.

Shiloah, Amnon. "The Symbolism of Music in the Kabbalistic Tradition." *World of Music* 20 (1978): 56–65.

Sicroff, Albert. "Clandestine Judaism in the Hieronymite Monastery of Nuestra Señora de Guadalupe." In *Studies in Honor of M[air] J[osé] Benardete*, edited by Izaak Abram Langnas and Barton Sholod, pp. 89–125. New York: Las Américas, 1965.

————. *Les controverses des statuts de "Pureté de sang" en Espagne du XVe au XVIIe siècle*. Paris: Didier, 1960.

Spitz, Lewis W. *The Religious Renaissance of the German Humanists*. Cambridge: Harvard University Press, 1963.

Spitzer, Leo. *Classical and Christian Ideas of World Harmony*. Baltimore: Johns Hopkins University Press, 1963.

————. "Three Poems on Ecstasy: John Donne, Saint John of the Cross, Richard Wagner." In *A Method of Interpreting Literature*, pp. 1–63. Northampton, Mass.: Smith College, 1949.

Stackhouse, Kenneth A. "Verisimilitude, Magic and the Supernatural in the *Novelas* of María de Zayas y Sotomayor." *Hispanófila* 62 (1978): 65–76.

Stamm, James R. "Las *Moradas del castillo interior*: ¿Alegoría literaria o manera de decir?" In *Santa Teresa y la literatura mística hispánica*. Actas del I Congreso Internacional sobre Santa Teresa y la Mística Hispánica. Edited by Manuel Criado de Val. Madrid: EDI-6, 1984.

Suarès, Carlo. *The Song of Songs: The Canonical Song of Solomon Deciphered According to the Original Code of the Qabala*. Berkeley: Shambhala, 1972.

Sugranyes de Franch, Ramon. *Raymond Lull, docteur des missions*. Schoneck-Beckenreid, Switzerland: Nouvelle Revue de Science Missionaire, 1954.

Swietlicki, Catherine. "The Bible, *Conversos*, and Apologetics: Another Look at Spain's *Auto Sacramental*." In [Selected] *Proceedings of the Fourth Annual Golden Age Drama Symposium*. University of Texas at El Paso, 7–9 March 1984 (published 1986), pp. 139–54.

Taylor, René. "Architecture and Magic: Considerations on the Idea of the Escorial." In *Essays in the History of Architecture Presented to Rudolf Wittkower*, edited by Douglas Fraser, Howard Hibbard, and Milton Lewine, pp. 81–109. London: Phaidon Press, 1967.

Taylor, Vincent. *The Names of Jesus*. London: Macmillan, 1953.

Thomas, Keith. *Religion and the Decline of Magic*. London: Weidenfeld & Nicolson, 1971.

Thompson, Colin P. *The Poet and the Mystic: A Study of the "Cántico Espiritual" of San Juan de la Cruz*. Oxford: Oxford University Press, 1977.

Thorndike, Lynn. *A History of Magic and Experimental Science.* Vols. 4, 7. New York: Columbia University Press, 1958.

Ticknor, George. *History of Spanish Literature.* Vol. 2. Boston: Houghton-Mifflin, 1863.

Underhill, Evelyn. *Mysticism: A Study in the Nature and Development of Man's Spiritual Consciousness.* 2d ed. 1930; rpt. London: Methuen, 1962.

Urbano, Fray Luis. *Las analogías predilectas de Santa Teresa de Jesús.* Madrid: n.p., 1924.

Vajda, Georges. *Introduction à la pensée juive du moyen âge.* Paris: Vrin, 1947.

———. "La philosophie juive en Espagne." In *The Sephardi Heritage,* edited by R. D. Barnett, 1:81–111. London: Valentine & Mitchell, 1971.

———. *Recherches sur la philosophie et la kabbale dans la pensée juive.* Paris: Mouton, 1962.

Vallejo, Gustavo. *Fray Luis de León: su ambiente, su doctrina espiritual, huellas de Santa Teresa.* Rome: Colegio Internacional de Santa Teresa, 1959.

Vasoli, Cesare. "Intorno a Francesco Giorgio Veneto e all' 'armonia del mondo.'" In *Profezia e ragione: Studi sulla cultura del Cinquecento e del Seicento,* pp. 129–403. Naples: Morano Editore, 1974.

Vásquez Fernández, Antonio. "Las Moradas del Castillo interior como proceso de individuación." Actas del Congreso Internacional Teresiano, Salamanca, 4–7 Octubre 1982, 2:1075–1121. Salamanca: University de Salamanca, University Pontificia de Salamanca, Ministerio de Cultura, 1983.

Vega, Ángel Custodio. *Cumbres místicas: Fray Luis de León y San Juan de la Cruz.* Madrid: Aguilar, 1963.

———. *Poesías de Fray Luis de León; edición crítica.* Madrid: Saeta, 1955.

Vendrell, Francisca. "La obra de polémica anti-judaica de Fray Bernardo Oliver." *Sefarad* 5 (1945): 303–36.

Vermes, Geza. *Jesus the Jew. A Historian's Reading of the Gospels.* New York: Macmillan, 1973.

Vilnet, Jean. *Bible et mystique chez Saint Jean de la Croix.* Bruges: Desclée de Brouwer, 1949.

Vossler, Karl. *Fray Luis de León.* Translated by Carlos Clavería. Buenos Aires: Espasa-Calpe, 1946.

Vulliaud, Paul. *La kabbale juive: histoire et doctrine.* 2 vols. 1923; rpt. Paris: Aujourd'hui, 1976.

Walker, Daniel Pickering. *The Ancient Theology: Studies in Christian Platonism from the Fifteenth to the Eighteenth Century.* London: Duckworth; Ithaca, N.Y.: Cornell University Press, 1972.

———. *Spiritual and Demonic Magic from Ficino to Campanella.* 1958; rpt. London/Notre Dame: University of Notre Dame Press, 1975.

Walsh, William Thomas. *Santa Teresa de Ávila.* 3d ed. Madrid: Espasa-Calpe, 1960.

Watkin, Edward Ingram. *The Philosophy of Mysticism*. New York: Harcourt, Brace & Howe, 1920.

Waxman, Samuel M. "Chapters on Magic in Spanish Literature." *Revue Hispanique* 38 (1916): 325–463.

Welsh, Robert J. *Introduction to the Spiritual Doctrine of Fray Luis de León, O.S.A.* Washington: Augustinian Press, 1951.

Wilson, Dudley. *French Renaissance Scientific Poetry*. London: Athlone Press, 1974.

Wirszubski, Chaim. "Giovanni Pico's Companion to Kabbalistic Symbolism." In *Studies in Mysticism and Religion Presented to G. G. Scholem*, pp. 353–62. Jerusalem: Hebrew University Press, 1967.

Wittkower, Rudolf. *Allegory and the Migration of Symbols*. Boulder: Westview Press; London: Thames & Hudson, 1977.

———. "Architectural Principles in the Age of Humanism." *Studies of the Warburg Institute* 19 (1949): 89–137.

Woodward, L. J. "Fray Luis de León's 'Oda a Francisco Salinas.'" *Bulletin of Hispanic Studies* 39 (1962): 69–77.

Yarbro-Bejarano, Yvonne. "Juan del Encina and Lucas Fernández: Conflicting Attitudes towards the Passion." *Bulletin of the Comediantes* 36 (1984): 5–19.

Yates, Frances. *The Art of Memory*. Chicago: University of Chicago Press, 1966.

———. "The Art of Ramón Lull." *Journal of the Warburg and Courtauld Institutes* 17 (1954): 115–73.

———. *Astrea*. London/Boston: Routledge & Kegan Paul, 1975.

———. *The French Academies of the Sixteenth Century*. London: University of London/Warburg Institute, 1947.

———. *Giordano Bruno and the Hermetic Tradition*. 1964; rpt. Chicago: Midway, 1979.

———. *The Occult Philosophy in the Elizabethan Age*. London/Boston: Routledge & Kegan Paul, 1979.

———. *The Rosicrucian Enlightenment*. 1972; rpt. Boulder: Shambhala, 1978.

Yerushalmi, Yosef Hayim. *From Spanish Court to Italian Ghetto. Isaac Cardoso: A Study in Seventeenth-Century Marranism and Jewish Apologetics*. New York/London: Columbia University Press, 1971.

Zaehner, R. C. *Concordant Discord*. Oxford: Clarendon Press, 1970.

———. *Mysticism, Sacred and Profane*. Oxford: Clarendon Press, 1957.

Zambelli, Paola. "Cornelio Agrippa, Erasmo e la teologia umanistica." *Rinascimento* 20 (1969): 1–59.

———. "Magic and Radical Reformation in Agrippa of Nettesheim." *Journal of the Warburg and Courtauld Institutes* 36 (1976): 69–103.

———. "Umanesimo magico-astrologico e reggrupamenti secreti nei platonici della preriforma." In *Umanesimo e esoterismo*, edited by Enrico Castelli, pp. 141–74. Atti del V Convegno Internazionale di Studi Umanistici. Padua: CEDAM, 1960.

Zarco Cuevas, Julián. *Bibliografía de Fray Luis de León*. Málaga: Revista Española de Estudios Filosóficos, 1928–1929.

Zika, Charles. "Reuchlin's *De Verbo Mirifico* and the Magic Debate of the Late Fifteenth Century." *Journal of the Warburg and Courtauld Institutes* 39 (1976): 104–38.

———. "Reuchlin and Erasmus: Humanism and the Occult Philosophy." *Journal of Religious History* (Sydney) 9 (1977): 223–46.